Palmetto Pioneers

From Harmony to Hostility

By Cindy Roe Littlejohn

Palmetto Pioneers: From Harmony to Hostility Copyright, 2024

by Cindy Roe Littlejohn

All Rights Reserved

All rights reserved. No part of this book may be reproduced in any form or by any electronic or mechanical means including information storage and retrieval systems, without permission in writing from the author. The only exception is by a reviewer, who may quote about excerpts in a review.

Cover designed by Hannah McDonald
Cover Art by Susan Rissman

First Printing in 2024
Amazon Publishing

ISBN 979-8-9899691-0-4

Dedication

Though Granddaddy died when I was only fourteen, I have fond memories. I remember fishing with him several times on Lake Miccosukee in a small leaky boat. I was a talker, and he was a silent man.

I don't remember much, but I remember his admonishment. "Cindy, hush! You're scaring the fish away." I remember those quiet moments when we were close. They didn't last long.

This story is dedicated to my grandfather Lester Hamrick, son of Jesse and Augusta Lightsey Hamrick and grandson of George and Laura Andrews, both of whom are introduced in this book. He never knew his grandmother Laura. She died long before he was born.

Table of Contents

Dedication 4
Preface 7
   Acknowledgments 9
   How to Read this Book 12

Chapter 1 16
   An Undesirable Reputation, 1844-1849 16
Chapter 2 41
   With Peace Comes Enough and to Spare, 1850 41
Chapter 3 65
   Before Its Time, 1852 65
Chapter 4 89
   The High Sheriff - A Thankless Job, 1855 89
Chapter 5 115
   To Take One's Leave, 1858-1859 115
Chapter 6 144
   Happy, Healthy, & Prosperous, 1860 144
Chapter 7 168
   Every Set of Three is Complete, 1860 168
Chapter 8 189
   Imminent Enmity, Fall, 1860 189
Chapter 9 218
   Mr. Andrews Goes to Tallahassee, 1861 218
Chapter 10 261
   Seizing Forts and Raising Militias, ... 261
   February to August, 1861 261

Chapter 11 300
    Defending Florida's Coasts, ... 300
    August to December, 1861 300

Appendix 1 357
    Fort Brooke (Tampa Town) 357
Appendix 2 359
    1850 Census, Growth of the Town and County .. 359
Appendix 3 364
    Who is Buried at the 364
    Old Elizabeth Church Cemetery? 364
Appendix 4 366
    1860 Census, Growth of the Town and County .. 366
Appendix 5 369
    Henry Walker's Death Notices 369
    Media 376
    Life in Antebellum Florida 380
    The War Between the States: 1861 to 1862 385

Bibliograhy

Preface

Florida, to many, seems new and historically deficient. But this is untrue! Florida has a rich history dating to before the Spanish arrived. My home county, Jefferson, is home to the Aucilla Research Institute, whose archaeological and anthropological work uncovers daily evidence of some of the earliest humans in the nation and the remains of prehistoric animals.

The Spanish explorers explored this area long before British colonies were established in the New England region to the north. Their journals describe a thriving native population with its villages and agriculture. The oldest city in the country, St. Augustine, is in Florida.

After the French and Indian War and the First Treaty of Paris in 1763, Spain gave up Florida, and east and west Florida became the 14th and 15th colonies of England and were loyalist during the American Revolutionary War. This British period only lasted until 1784, when in return for Spain's help during the American Revolution, Florida was granted to Spain by the Peace of Paris in 1783.

Because of the wars at home (the Napoleonic invasions), Spain struggled to retain Florida.

Because of the newly-formed United States of America, Florida's modern story began in 1821, over two hundred years ago. This date marks the signing of the Adams-Onis Treaty, and it opened Florida's boundaries for settlement in 1822. This series of books is a story of Florida, beginning in 1829.

I have always been interested in who made me who I am because I am an extension of who made my parents, of who made my grandparents, and so forth. The main character in this series is my third-great-grandmother. These are her stories. She is a part of my mother's paternal lineage.

This story is a continuation of an earlier story. Like Book 1, *Palmetto Pioneers: The Emigrants*, the people, places, and events actually existed. If you read the first book, you met Mary Adeline Walker and later her husband William Henry Andrews. You watched seven-year-old Mary make the long wagon trip from South Carolina to frontier Florida. You watched her family leave most of what they had behind to carve their homestead out of the Florida wilderness. What it was like to settle the Florida territory in 1829? There is a realization that the then-current residents, the Indians, believed the land was still their home, and the family is caught up in an Indian War.

Despite the hardships, Mary grew into a young twenty-three-year-old married woman. In this second book, you will follow her family and Florida into their prosperous years and then into the first year of the Civil War, which southerners call the War Between the States.

It is important that you read the section entitled "How to Read this Book." It explains how the book was written and how to follow the narrator's explanations of what we know is true and what we believe is true. Mostly, these people communicated orally, and the family has many stories to share, but there were also many documents, newspapers, diaries, and journals used to fill in the back story.

This is a story of Florida within the overall history of America.

#

Acknowledgments

My thank yous are the same as my first book, except for the following.

A special thank you to Frankie Smith Rosie, who is a distant Walker cousin. She read the first book and offered valuable information I did not know. For example, in the first book I questioned whether the Walker families might have built a fort for protection during the Second Seminole Indian War.

She shared her memories of their evening walks on her grandparents' farm with her Grandmother Elizabeth "Lizzie" Walker Stanley. Aunt Lizzie described a family fort near the Fort Pond. When Frankie was a young girl, one could still see scattered logs, tree trunks, where the fort once stood by the pond. The family named the pond Fort Pond. The land initially belonged to Mary's Uncle James Walker.

Also a special thank you to Bruce Warren, another Walker cousin, who allowed me and Linda Demott (you guessed it, a Walker cousin) an opportunity to walk around the pond one winter day. It was a wonderful experience. As far as any of us know, the Walkers were never attacked.

The Fort Pond, Personal Photo

Auley Rowell from Perry, Taylor County, Florida, next door

to Jefferson County, read the first book and shared information he discovered many years ago. His Jefferson County ancestor is William Rowell, who is in the book and who married Peniopy McSwain Hamrick, my 3rd-great-grandmother from another lineage who moved to the county after statehood.

While working on the Rowell genealogy for his family, he and his son made a trip to visit the late Mrs. Ethel Hartsfield Lewis who was born in Jefferson County in 1898 and attended Elizabeth Baptist Church since she was a child.

Mrs. Lewis told Auley that the first Elizabeth Baptist church building burned. Before this information, none of us in Jefferson County remembered what happened to the first church. We only knew that the site of the current church is not where the first church was located. She also told him that all its records burned too. Many thanks to Auley for sharing this information. It will be important to this book, especially since he also shared the approximate date it burned.

Many people read drafts and offered important feedback. Dr. James Sledge, now 99-years-old, again read it for family content. Dee Counts, too, read it for local history content. Thank you both so much!

A new content reader was author and Civil War historian Clint Johnson, who has written eight nonfiction books on the war. Johnson, born in Fish Branch, Florida, in Desoto County, now lives in the North Carolina mountains, but he and I worked in the 1970s for a lobbyist and association manager named Bill Owens in Tallahassee. Thank you, Clint.

Again, my friend and watercolor artist Susan Rissman painted the artwork for the cover, and my niece Hannah McDonald did its graphic design. Thank you both so much!

A special thanks to my sweetheart husband who listened to every single word of this manuscript numerous times. I am so blessed for his support and encouragement. And I'm also blessed with two great daughters Jamie Harper Sheehan and Tracy Harper Kistler, both of whom are always quick to come to my aid, especially if I need technical advice.

#

How to Read this Book

Note: This is a regurgitation of the first book's instructions, except what is highlighted. There are instructions on how to read letters sent to and from home and there is a QR code that leads to an Ancestry tree.

This book, written in a genre called creative nonfiction, may be classified in a sub-genre called family history writing. It uses elements of creative writing to present a factual, true story. *Palmetto Pioneers* uses literary techniques usually reserved for writing fiction. I used dialog, scene-setting, and narrative arcs. It is rooted in facts. No part of the story is made up or fabricated unless the author signals otherwise.

To write this story, I used primary and secondary sources. The subject was extensively researched, and a bibliography follows at the end of the book. It is divided into time periods, such as "Life in Antebellum Florida" and "The War Between the States."

Because this book takes place almost two hundred years ago, the dialog is almost always "composed." Dialog only in quotation marks is simply created dialog, dialog I made up word for word. They are from my imagination—what I think a character would have said in that situation. I wanted to give the characters more life, and the character's personalities reflect their descendants. One can hear my mother's voice in Mary's mother's.

True dialog, not created or actual word-for-word quotes, is

set in quotations marks and is also italicized. Mary's father was quoted in a newspaper article when he described his wife in her obituary. When characters read aloud from a newspaper, the dialog is set in quotation marks and italicized.

I created homes and businesses using written examples and photos from that era. Diaries and journals were used, as were local newspapers. For example, was there a photo of the inside of Palmer's store? No, but I recreated its interior using other period photos and newspaper ads to describe what Palmer probably stocked in his store.

I added scenes that reflect the realities of living in Florida or the south. I added them for interest and to give the reader a feeling of what it was like to grow up in territorial Florida. Some of these scenes are stories from my life. I grew up in the Florida county where most of this story takes place. I also gleaned scenes from diaries, journals, and family lore.

I added letters sent home from those who traveled away for the war. These letters are what I thought they would have said to each other, using actual letters as a guide, from others who wrote during the Civil War. We have no letters from any of the Walkers or Andrews. The letters in this book are in italics with no quotation marks.

Following this part of my family's story, I discovered their place in Florida's history; and this became a secondary purpose of this book. Hopefully, others will learn more about our state's history through the eyes of Mary and her family and can help us all appreciate who we are and where we come from.

There is no genealogical tree in this book. The tree I created and used is online at Ancestry.com. It is a public tree, so anyone can take a look. The link below will take you to Mary Adeline Walker in the tree. A tree search (upper right-hand screen) will let you search for any other family members mentioned in the book, though there are many people in this tree.

It is entitled the Lightsey, Andrews, Walker tree. If you are a Lightsey, Andrews, or Walker and your ancestors have been in this state for a few generations, your ancestors may be in this tree. There are over 5,500 people in it.

You can view the tree at https://www.ancestry.com/family-tree/person/tree/23894133/person/1441730272/facts or you can use your cell phone to take a picture of this QR code below. While it is trying to focus, notice what appears in your screen. When you see a web address, click on it. It will take you directly to the tree. You will have to register yourself to log in, and Ancestry will try to get you to join; but you don't have to join to see this tree. It is free to take a look.

Cindy Roe Littlejohn

Chapter 1
An Undesirable Reputation, 1844-1849

In the fall of 1844, the town's mayor stood midway up the courthouse steps amongst a sea of men from both Georgia and Florida. "I've got good news," he bellowed. "By passing the hat, we've collected five hundred dollars." There was much rumbling from the crowd below. At thirty-four and taller than most, William Andrews stood at the back of the mob. Added the mayor, "We have collected it from over 175 of you."

Jefferson County's people built their courthouse in the center of Monticello. Its two main streets intersected there. Horses, wagons, and buggies had to circle the building when moving through town. The courthouse faced north. The buildings and stores of planed wood were mostly built due north facing one another, but an inn faced the southeast side of the courthouse. A school sat at the western boundary of the town, also facing the courthouse.

Florida's general assembly had established the county and its county seat only sixteen years before in 1827. The county reached from the Gulf of Mexico to the Georgia line eight miles north of Monticello in Middle Florida. This area was known as Middle Florida because South Florida did not exist for the newcomers. Middle Florida was located between East and West Florida and would become North Florida when South Florida was settled.

Monticello's Courthouse during William's Life

Later, in front of the fireplace after their five kids were in bed, William told his twenty-three-year-old wife Mary, "Something has to be done about those thugs." He had removed his jacket, and she watched him as he stared into the fire, its light reflecting on his white shirt with its high upstanding collar. She liked his new sideburns, though his sandy hair softened the look. Only married for two years, she admired the way he dressed and carried himself.

She was William's second wife. His first had died almost two years before she married him, leaving William alone with his three motherless children, ages six, four, and three—a boy and two girls, in that order. William was eleven years older than she, but Mary was the oldest of her ten siblings and had had to grow up quickly with the family's migration to Florida from South Carolina when she was only seven. She helped her mother raise the rest of the children through an Indian war and all the other problems that came with living on a frontier—*the extreme limit of settled land, beyond which lies wilderness.* Her parents Jesse and Elizabeth Walker initially lived on land not yet provided by their government. For the first dozen years, they were squatters.

But Florida's sparsely populated wilderness became a refuge for people to misbehave. A gang of outlaws, headed by Stephen Yeomans, a county man, operated for months throughout South Georgia and Middle Florida, stealing livestock, slaves, and anything else they could tote off. Some who tried to fight back lost their lives.

The gang disguised themselves as Indians, but people noticed several blue-eyed men amongst them. William added, "The crowd indicted Yeomans himself in absentia. He's a fugitive with a bounty on his head of five hundred dollars to anyone who can deliver him to our sheriff."

Initially, though, the bounty was for naught. The gang pillaged unimpeded throughout the rest of the year. Later during the holidays, William said, "When it simmers this long, the outcome is never good. A confrontation is coming, and I'm afraid it won't be pretty." The two of them were again in front of their fireplace after the children were down for the evening. Its light flickered its amber luminescence on their faces. He took a sip of whiskey, its contents casting a yellow glow upon his hand.

Before New Year's Day of 1845, three South Georgia men captured Yeomans. Word spread. Rumors were rampant. Yeoman's gang plotted to free him either while he was being transported to the jail or as soon as a posse brought him back to town. Everyone worried the rickety old Monticello jail could not hold him long. So the Florida men planned to meet the three South Georgia men and their prisoner at the Florida-Georgia line for the exchange in "No-Man's Land." An assembly of ninety men rode north from Monticello, a ride of eight miles.

"No Man's Land" was the name for the area of land located along the state line. It received its name because of an ongoing dispute between the two states about where exactly the state line stood. The dispute was finally decided by the US Supreme Court in the 1870s. Because both Florida and Georgia claimed it, it belonged to neither and was not subject to either's laws.

In "No Man's Land," the exchange of the prisoner took place; and subsequently, the men chose a committee on the spot to serve as a jury. Yeomans's impromptu trial was out of the jurisdiction of either state.

One man was voted chair. "I need one of you men of the cloth to swear in the witnesses." Earlier, Yeomans confessed, naming fourteen men as his accomplices. Several were Jefferson County citizens.

The trial lasted all day. "Guilty!" said the juror's foreman.

The crowd of men hesitated. Said one tall gaunt man, "His gang knows how poor our jail is. They'll be waiting on us by the time we get back. They'll probably set fire to our town to break him out."

Added another, "Even if they don't show up, our jail will never hold him, anyway. We've just wasted our time if we take him to Monticello."

"It's a long way back, and there are many places where an ambush is certain." It was as if they were trying to convince themselves that what they were going to do had to be done.

Another vote followed. The chair spoke. "I need a show of

hands. Who votes to take him back? And who votes to hang him here?" On a vote of sixty-seven to twenty-three, they voted to hang him in "No Man's Land" on the following day. A guard of twenty-five men watched him during the night, as they expected his gang to free him at any moment.

Early the next morning, Yeomans asked for a prayer on his behalf. Since there were four ministers in the group, one stepped forward to pray. All the men removed their hats.

At noon, January 2nd, they hung Yeoman.

The press in cities such as Savannah called it a lynching, a subsequence of mob rule. A month later with the lynching of a man of color, a leader of another gang in "No Man's Land," Jefferson County gained a poor reputation.

In early February, William was in the warmth of Mary's kitchen early on a Saturday morning. The two of them enjoyed the quiet of their household, which wasn't quite awake. He watched her as she moved about the kitchen. Her dark wavy brown hair cascaded down her back. She had not pulled it up yet.

William sighed as he went back to his several day's old copy of the Tallahassee newspaper. "Mary, we are not looking too good to people outside of Jefferson County. The lynchings have to stop." He hesitated and added, "City people cannot understand what it is like to live on the frontier, and our newspapers are painting a sad picture of us." He continued to read to himself.

Mary's kitchen was detached from their four-room house. Kitchens were detached because of the heat and the fire hazard. William and Mary's home was east of the Bellamy Plantation and sat in a yard free of grass and shrubs. Mary and the older kids kept it free of debris in case of fire.

More bad news followed but from Texas several months later. "Mary, Mary," William said as he walked through the house. He found her in the kitchen nursing James with a shawl over her shoulder. Seven-year-old Ellen kept watch over the toddler Sarah. On the stove was a big pot of boiling soup. The fragrance of boiling ham and vegetables filled the air. The oldest, John Slicer, who was nine, spent most of his days in school but kept the family in firewood. It had been an unusually cold winter.

William said, "Washington annexed Texas. Now it's a part of the nation. The Mexicans won't like it a bit, and everyone thinks we are headed for war." He sat down at the table. "Hey, would you like to take a carriage ride Saturday to Monticello to see the new jail?"

"Yes, I would. I need a trip to Palmer's." The ride (an all-day trip) would originate at their home in Elizabeth, eight miles east of Monticello. There had been many discussions about the county's need for a jail. After the Yeomans fiasco, the county built a compact brick jail on Pearl Street near the northeast corner of North Cherry, today near the Mexican restaurant (Rancho Grande). William would get to know the new jail quite well soon.

Many Americans moved to Texas, but most of them wanted to remain American. Subsequently, the Federals annexed Texas despite the Mexicans' warning. The Mexicans felt annexation was an act of war, but days passed into weeks and the nation heard nothing more. Except for breaking off diplomatic relations, Mexico remained quiet; and being so far away,

Jefferson County soon forgot the problem—but not for long.

Later, there was a boundary dispute in which the Mexicans argued the traditional boundary was the Nueces River farther north, not the Rio Grande. When General Zachary Taylor occupied Point Isabel at the mouth of the Rio Grande River in April, the Mexican government subsequently invaded Texas. The United States considered Texas an American state while Mexico considered it a rebellious Mexican province.

Each night around the fireplace, William read weekly updates about the Texas controversy. This continued until one night in mid-May of 1846 when William came in from town talking nonstop and pacing. "Well, we're at war with Mexico. It's official! Congress declared war."

Mary noticed the excitement in his eyes. She had seen it before in her dad's and uncle's. She thought to herself, "I'll never understand why men get so excited about war."

In the spring of 1846, Governor Moseley, who was from Jefferson County, appointed William as Jefferson County's auctioneer for all public sales at auction. He, B. H. Russell, and John Stevens signed his bonding papers, still found in the courthouse.

Mary's mornings were always early, but now he frequently had to leave before dawn. The two of them would be up and him long gone before the children stirred. His job was to collect and pay into the treasury of the state two percent of the gross sales made at the auction.

It was unlawful for him to charge and receive over four percent above the tax accrued to the territory, provided the amount of property sold did not exceed one thousand dollars.

Above a thousand, he could only collect two percent. He kept track and reported quarterly to the state treasurer. The appointment added to Mary and William's income. Properties sold included everything from probate to confiscations made during arrests and prosecution.

One night he came in with more war news: "Our state might be new and sparsely populated, but Washington City asked us to provide a battalion of five companies for Texas. The word is the governor appointed five commanders to recruit volunteers from our militiamen. Governor Moseley's boy himself signed up."

She said, "I'm glad our sons are too young to go." She was also glad William was gainfully employed and less likely to want to go.

In April, William picked up a letter from the post office in Monticello. He immediately opened it because it was from Washington where he had spent most of his childhood. Standing on the boardwalk outside, he learned his sibling Julia Ann had died of smallpox. She was forty-seven. Most likely her son John F. Pic sent the letter, being the oldest of her children.

Later, while lying in bed, William said, "Poor Julia Ann. She was so strong and such a kind-hearted person; but she had a hard life. Her husband John crossed over almost a dozen years ago and left her pregnant with a house full of children. Their home was near the Navy Yard. It saddens me to no end. Sweet, charitable Julia Ann spent time isolated in her final hours."

Mary let him talk. He only needed someone to listen. Smallpox patients were isolated, their family forbidden to visit. Most did not survive.

Later, she said, "William, don't you think it's time to go home for a visit? I think it would do you good."

The next morning in Mary's kitchen, she and her mother Elizabeth, who was visiting, talked about Julia Ann. Elizabeth said, "We must remember the Good Lord taketh and giveth. Uncle David has a newborn son, just as Julia Ann departs." The sage comment took Mary aback as she rolled out dough for the biscuits.

"Is that a new dress?" asked her mother.

"Yes, I just made it last week. William brought home the fabric. He thought my everyday dress was looking worn. Do you like the pattern?" She twirled in the brown and beige plaid frock with its low and sloping shoulders. The skirt was a little fuller than most everyone else's.

"Mary, you've got the Wilson waistline. We just don't get as thick through our middle as other women." It was true. William had mentioned it just last week in her kitchen. He told her he was surprised after she had had two children.

Mary changed back to their earlier conversation. "David was beside himself throughout Caroline's entire pregnancy. He was so worried Caroline might succumb like his Sarah. Mama, birthing is risky business." A silence fell between the mother and daughter.

David and Caroline named their firstborn son Stephen Jesse Walker. They lived in the cabin formerly owned by Mary's grandfather Joel Walker, most likely back of the Elizabeth church, the evidence of which was a warranty deed dated 1841. David's siblings, including Mary's father, relinquished their title to the property for $50.

All signed their names except for Jane and Littleberry, who

signed with an X, like Mary. It appears the two of them never learned to read or write. No deed was found showing the initial purchase of this property between John Bellamy and Joel Walker, but this later warranty deed shows Joel Walker did claim ownership.

Mary's mother was one of the many Elizabeths living there. Elizabeth wasn't quite a town but had several residences, a church, and a graveyard. The latter two were under a grove of oaks still standing today. William and Mary's house was an easy wagon ride away from the church.

Elizabeth Baptist Church Cemetery, AKA Walker Cemetery, located on Walker Cemetery

That summer William joined a new organization called the Independent Riflemen's Hall, which may have been a local militia unit in Monticello. Meanwhile, only three of the five companies raised in Florida for the Mexican War saw service. Two companies never left Fort Brooke, present-day Tampa, which served as a staging post for Florida's troops in the Mexican War (see Appendix 1). Men from Jefferson County joined the conflict, and some saw service in the war.

In late summer, the Texas war continued. Staying busy with his new appointment, William assessed the state taxes for Jefferson County. He came in late one afternoon and found Mary on the back steps holding one of her favorite laying hens and taking a rest. He had come home to work on his report, which was due at the end of the month, but instead, he sat and chatted with Mary. Though James was only eight months old, she was three months pregnant again. These babies would be only fourteen months apart. He worried about her.

He asked her about her day, but she said, "Any news from Monticello?"

"None except the war in Texas. Our army pushed the Mexicans back across the border, and we took Santa Fe."

Almost sorry she asked, she listened to him talk about the war until she said she needed to get back to the kitchen. He rose and went inside to his desk and his auctioneer's report.

By the next year, in August 1847, William with ten-year-old John went to the courthouse. They walked up the long steps and into the clerk's office. William's spurs jangled as he walked across the wooden floors. "Craven, I need to register my mark and brand." Though by today's standards William would be considered a white-collar worker, he still lived in a saddle, as did all the men of his day. Hitching posts were common in front of all their homes and businesses. Their horses were their cars, their way of getting about.

We know from this filing that William was either in or about to be in the livestock business, something Mary's father had been doing all his life. On the same day, William got good news from Tallahassee.

Later, he told Mary, "It happened. Governor Moseley signed the re-appointment papers for me to be auctioneer again." Florida's general assembly approved his appointment and Richard Harrison, John Stevens, Stephen Ellenwood, and William signed a bond for $2,000. The position was for two years, ending in 1850, and provided a good salary for the growing family.

On September 14, 1847, US troops entered Mexico City. For over a decade, there had been skirmishes. The Alamo fell in 1836. Negotiations for a treaty began, and there is no evidence William or any of the Walker boys went to Texas to fight. Victorious, though, the US gained vast new territory—including New Mexico and California. One of William and Mary's children would one day be buried in the former.

By November, it was unseasonably warm as William got up early and dressed in his dressier black frock coat. In the kitchen, Mary prepared breakfast and a packed lunch. Over breakfast, the two talked about his call for jury duty. He left while it was still dark, headed for Monticello. He was away all day for the trials.

During a break at the courthouse, William and a couple of other men walked down the hill south to see the newly finished Baptist church. Rev. Goodman, who had been a pastor at Elizabeth Baptist and who had married William and Mary, was there along with Bill Scruggs, a trustee. It was a planed wood building with a gabled roof line and two doors, each leading down an aisle inside.

The big talk of the day though was the passing of Prince Murat, Jefferson County's most illustrious citizen, the great-grandnephew of Napoleon Bonaparte. In exile, was the deposed crown prince of Naples but had lived in Jefferson County for quite some time, serving as its judge and as an attorney.

First Baptist Church, Monticello, Keystone Genealogical Library

Meanwhile, at home, Mary entertained visitors. Ann Lightsey and her daughter-in-law Mary Howell Lightsey called. She received them in front of the fireplace, and the three enjoyed their time together working on a quilt Ann brought.

The conversation, as it frequently did, turned to their younger days in South Carolina. Mary was from Colleton District, while Ann and the other Mary were from a district next door, Barnwell. It was common for the South Carolinians to talk about home, as it was for the Virginians and North Carolinians too. It was a common bond. Plus we know from the

1840 census that Ann Lightsey lived near Jesse Walker's family. She was widowed by this date and still living in the Elizabeth area.

The conversation moved to their children. Said Mary, "James has thrush again. He keeps getting it. I don't know what else to do."

Asked Ann, "Have you tried vinegar?"

"Yes," replied Mary, "and sour milk too."

Added the other Mary, "My mama swore by sauerkraut. She said it was the fermentation."

"I'll try it," replied Mary.

The next February in 1848, John Slicer went out to the kitchen to light Mary's kitchen fire and came tearing back into the house. "Get up, get up!" he yelled. Everyone thought this couldn't be good, but it was. "It's snowing!" he shouted as he ran outside.

Snow is relatively rare in Middle Florida, even in this most northern part of the state. William, who was born in Georgetown and raised in Washington, DC, noticed Mary was as fascinated by it as their children.

By mid-March, everything leafed out in bright green. Mary planned her kitchen garden. She wanted to grow green peas this year along with tomatoes, Irish potatoes, and other vegetables. She and her mother both believed vegetables were good for one's soul, if not the body. They heard the people in the cities thought vegetables were bad for you, but her family didn't believe it for a minute.

William had gone early to Monticello for the day. There were auctions there because so many moved from the area. In one case, a man's slaves were sold to pay his debts.

This office of auctioneer was also probably part of the probate court, auctioning properties caught in the probate process. In addition, this means William was close to Judge Thomas J. Chase, who lived on the south side of town on Anderson Lane, today behind the Tri-County Electric Co-op building.

Later, as the day warmed, William rode into Monticello to meet with Judge Chase, who was at home, bedridden. He secured his horse at the judge's fancy metal hitching post.

Palmetto Pioneers

Hitching Post, Historic American Buildings Survey Alex Bush, Photographer, April 17, 1936 HITCHING POSTS ON NORTH SIDE OF HOME - Elmoreland, U.S. Highway 241, Glenville, Russell County, AL, Wikimedia Commons

The judge's open porch wrapped around the eastern front side to the northern end of the family's classic revival home. The judge's missus met him at the front door.

"Good morning, madam," William said as he tipped his hat.

"Come on in, Mr. Andrews; the judge is expecting you."

Removing his hat and wearing his brown coat, he found the judge sitting in the parlor in front of a window overlooking the porch. He had a cup of coffee, and she had another for William. Both men were members of the local Masonic lodge, and William saw the judge looked worried. They quickly got into their discussion, but William knew something was wrong.

At a break from their work, the judge said, "I guess you've heard about Richard Cole."

William hadn't because he had ridden straight to the judge's house, skirting to the east of the downtown area. He shook his head.

"His own slaves killed him last night." It was devastating news. Everyone feared a general uprising.

Later, eighteen-year-old Thomas Holten killed a man in a drunken brawl. They tried him, found him guilty of murder, and hanged him by December. By this date, they held hangings in the enclosed yard at the jail. Before, they had held hangings at a tree in front of the jail.

Of the occurrence, William later said to Mary, "Times are changing. Our county is cracking down on the lawlessness in our midst, and public hangings are frowned upon. Thankfully, our frontier days are behind us."

Later, when William received his latest appointment as

appraiser, Mary wasn't pregnant for the first time in three years. Vollie (Valentine) was almost a year old, and Zech (Zechariah) would not be born until the following January in 1849. Mary probably thought to herself, "Thank goodness! My body needs a break." It would not last long, though. By April she was pregnant again.

During the previous summer, William had registered his livestock mark and brand at the courthouse. If he hadn't become adept at working cattle through his mother's people in Virginia, he most certainly would have in Jefferson County. The rounding of cattle by his wife's people required all hands to help. It is apparent he would have been a part of these operations and would have learned quickly if he didn't have these skills.

He and his brother-in-law Henry had been making improvements on vacant, unsold government land north of Monticello. They probably built a pen there for rounding cattle, which most likely ranged free. His mark and brand were a pole handle in the right ear and a poplar leaf in the left. By late 1848, his son John Slicer was old enough to be a big help.

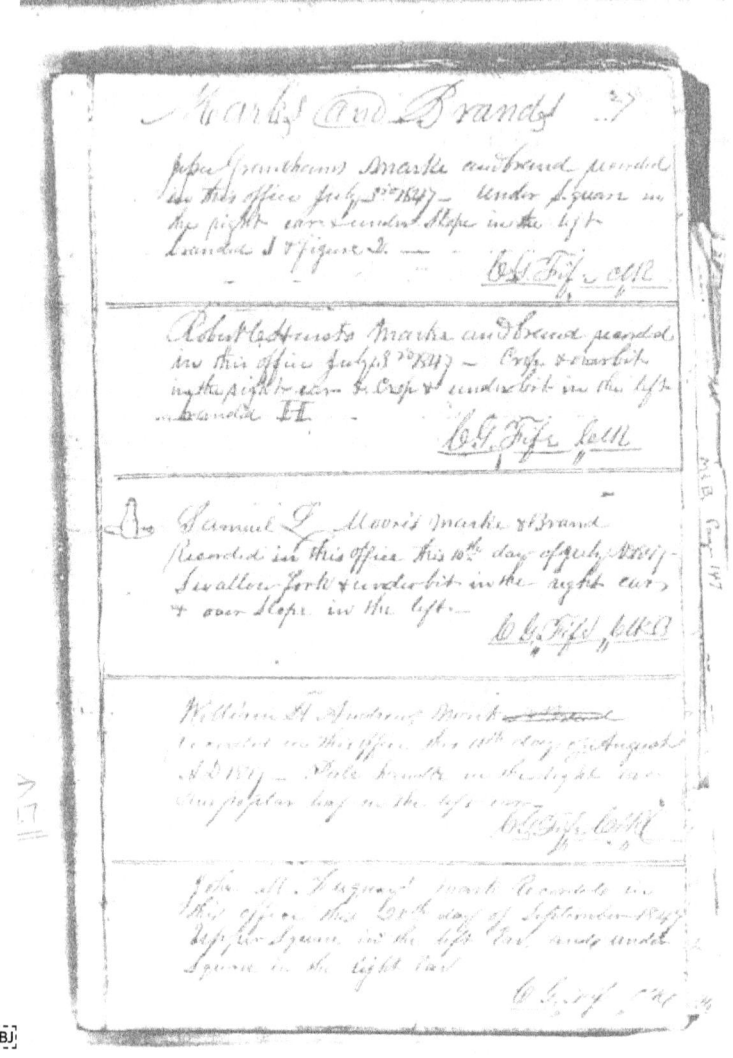

*Registered next to the last, William H. Andrews,
Pole Handle in the Right Ear, Poplar Leaf in the Left Ear*

Strange for today, but in the mid-1800s it was common for people to "squat" on a piece of property and begin improvements, such as the cattle pen mentioned earlier. The government owned most of Florida, so the squatter would wait and later make his move to obtain the land fee simple when the government was ready to sell.

This is how Mary's father and her uncles got their land earlier. People who had made improvements were permitted to enter in preference to other applicants for the land. Probably, her father Jesse and his brothers made improvements and were able to obtain the land over other buyers. William and Henry were trying to do the same. The ones owning the oldest improvements were preferred, as were the first residents.

Current US 19 did not exist, nor probably did a trail or wagon road either. This land was several miles from any main road. The closest was the Old Lake Road which ran west around the north end of Lake Miccosukee. The Walkers probably used this road to enter Monticello in the late 1820s and to travel from Monticello to Tallahassee. The road circled north of the lake.

Mary's brother Henry, though, was a formidable business owner. By 1858, he owned several large tracts of land in the county. In people's minds, he was simply another Walker buying land and adding to all the other Walker lands.

In fact, the earlier generations of Walkers (of Mary's father's age) bought a good bit of land in the 1830s when the federal government was having problems paying its bills and when the Second Seminole Indian War became the costliest Indian war in the nation's history, a title it still holds today. Charles, James, Littleberry, and Mary's father Jesse Walker all succeeded in obtaining Jefferson County land. They owned much of the land on the east side of Salt Road from several miles below Ashville Road down to the Old Jacksonville Road, today's Bassett's Dairy Road.

One can see the patent and deed recordings on the Bureau of Land Management website or in the courthouse today, where they bought eighty acres here as early as 1837 to forty acres there as late as 1843, until they owned significant acreage throughout the area. The buying continued into the 1850s by the next generation, not only with Mary's brother Henry but also with her other brothers J.J. and William. There was also much selling, often between family members. Because of so much land under the Walker families, people thought all Walkers were wealthy; but there were lots of Walker families.

One night in 1849, William came home with sad news. On the porch, he said, "I don't know why it is so hard to get better transportation into and out of this county. Today I heard at Budd's store that the Wacissa and Aucilla Navigation Company has failed in its attempt to utilize the canal (known today as the Slave Canal). They say the limestone ridges across the waterway make further digging useless. They stopped the project, and the prince would have been crushed, but worse, it is so much money lost."

Breastfeeding Zech, Mary sat in her rocking chair by the window, looking through the blooming native azalea in her side yard. She watched the red rooster outside which stood with his dark red tail feathers swirling and curling in the breeze. He was strutting for his hens, who showed no interest. The hens with their heads down scratched and hunted for food.

It was a beautiful day, but she couldn't help thinking William's auctioneer appointment would end soon. He had not mentioned any new employment on the horizon. Also, the livestock farm was not as lucrative as he had hoped. She knew William didn't have the time needed to run as many cattle or raise as many hogs as her father.

She moved through her days, rising to cook breakfast, with Zech wrapped around her, James tugging at her skirts, and four-year-old Sarah not quite old enough to help. Thank goodness for Florida and Ellen.

The girls were nine and eleven respectively, and they helped her keep order in the household, but both girls had schooling to take them away. Earlier, Mary admired how cute they looked in their dresses with their snow-white bloomers peeking from under their skirts. She was actually thankful they were in school, as she didn't want her younger children to be a burden on them. She wanted all her girls to get a wonderful education, and thank goodness she still wasn't pregnant.

She looked down at Zech, who had unlatched and slept peacefully. She fingered his cheek, and he latched again. William had wandered away. Frankly, these moments were a godsend. The rest of the household napped, and she had time to sit for a spell in peace and quiet. The only sound was the creak of her rocking chair on the loose boards. She remembered something her mother told her. She was never as chronically tired as when her children were babies. Mary couldn't remember a time when she wasn't tired.

Still, she worried about Zech. He was puny, the runt of her litter. She decided she might try one of her mother's remedies. She would get William to find her some rusty nails when he came back so she could soak them in vinegar and give Zech the liquid.

Suddenly, she heard someone climbing the front stairs. The front door creaked open, and William greeted a man, whom he ushered into their parlor. William's footsteps came softly, treading to her door.

He peeked in, and she raised her eyebrows, but he closed the door and went back to the parlor. She could hear them discussing something.

Congressman Edward Cabell, a local man, offered William his next position as one of Cabell's seven assistant marshals for Florida in the 1850 federal census.

We know there were seven assistants because of an article dated February 19, 1852 in the *Florida Republican,* the Jacksonville newspaper. It said Congressman Edward Carrington Cabell *"presented the memorials of William H. Andrews, George J. Jennings, Joseph D. Morris, Edward R. Ives, George J. Lehnbaun, Hiram T. Mann and Joel B. Smith, assistant marshals of the State of Florida."*

Cabell will play another important role in William's life, and one wonders if William knew him or someone else in his family before coming to Florida from Washington, DC.

As mentioned earlier in the first book, there were no sources to show where William was educated. He is not in the 1830 census records anywhere. There is uncertainty about what he was doing during this time. However, William had ties to the state of Virginia, as did Edward Cabell.

Congressman Cabell was the grandson of Governor William H. Cabell, former governor of Virginia. His grandfather Governor Cabell had married Agnes Sarah Bell Gamble, sister of Robert and John Gamble, also of Jefferson County, Florida. So we know Edward Cabell had ties to the Gamble family, a grand nephew of Robert and John Gamble.

Governor Cabell's son bought Dulce Domum (Sweet Home) Plantation in Jefferson County. For many years, the locals called it Jumpie Run, but it recently sold and is renamed Tall Tines Plantation. It sits on the southeast side of Monticello. He bought this property in the 1820s but never came to Florida to live. Instead, he sent his oldest son Abram Cabell to manage the lands; and upon Abram's death in 1831, he sent a younger son, Edward, only a few years younger than William.

By the stream of Jumper's Run was where the big house sat, which initially was a house of logs built by Abram Cabell. A short distance from the home and flowing through steep, thickly wooded hills were springs called Cool Springs.

Chief Jumper, a sub chief under the Seminole leader Tiger Tail, lived there in earlier days. Chief Jumper, a great warrior, was probably one of those who vanished like a ghost into the swamps of Jefferson County during the Second Seminole War.

John Jumper, Heneha Mekko (Assistant Chief) born 1820, died 1896; became principal chief of the Seminole Nation from 1849 to 1865 and again from 1882 to 1885. He was a lieutenant colonel for the Confederacy during the Civil War and nephew of Micanopy.
Wikipedia

William was right again. Something always came through. Jobs followed jobs, and Mary knew William kept his ear to the wind and hotly pursued the leads. He was a diligent man and was never afraid of failure. He had a saying: You can't expect your ship to come in if you never launch it.

Mary needn't have worried because two more positions came through later. When William was thirty-eight, Governor Moseley appointed him constable; and by November 1850, after his work on the census, Sheriff James Tucker appointed him deputy sheriff. Her husband was a truly busy man.

#

Chapter 2
With Peace Comes Enough and to Spare, 1850

Gone much of the day, up before daylight and until long after dark, William was glad to get the work. He always told her, "Don't despair, my fair maid Mary; work always comes." And it looked as if he was right. As one job ended, another came along. His ability to write, cipher, and lead men were his skill sets.

By the 1850s, he was doing well. Unlike the closely fitted coats of earlier years, now his coats were full-skirted, as was the fashion of the day, and more loosely tailored with even broader lapels. He was glad because at almost forty he felt middle age coming on with more weight carried around his middle.

He needed a fresh coat for special occasions, one with notched lapels done in velvet, but he still had his earlier tailcoat, which was saved for anything more formal. As he and Mary prospered, people invited them over from time to time.

Today, he wore a plain dark brown coat, a rich sorrel color. Sitting on his bay mare, his harmonizing vest of dark indigo had two front pockets. He kept the vest buttoned and adjusted the back to fit correctly.

On his loose un-tapered light wool trousers, he kept a watch in an extra little pocket near his waist. His silver watch was probably hung by a silver chain.

A few years ago, a cousin called and said her brother received a watch which once belonged to their second-great-grandfather Zachery (Zech) Andrews. The watch sat for years under a glass dome to protect it. Upon receipt, her brother opened it to see if he could find its manufacturer. Inside, the watchmaker etched his name, and her brother found three small pieces of paper.

Upon cleaning and a closer inspection, he could barely read an engraving. As he cleaned it, the inscription became clearer. It read "Wm Andrews." The watch had belonged to William, Zech's father.

On the watch and above his inscribed name is a mysterious hole in the watch case.

Personal Photo

The watch face also lacks its hands.

Personal Photo

Watches from this time period frequently have inserted service papers that show repairs. Of the three papers inside, one read Leesburg, VA, another Georgetown, and the last one was Tallahassee. It appears William had it serviced before he moved from the Washington, DC area around 1835 and later after he lived in Florida. The repair in Tallahassee was by Towles & Myers. In the April 25, 1840 edition of *The Floridian*, Tallahassee's newspaper, Frederick Towles advertised his "watch repairing" service. The ad omitted Myers.

Personal Photo

Personal Photo

A Liverpool, England watchmaker named D. Edmunds

made the watch. It appears he made it before William's birth because D. Edmunds was born in 1787 and died in 1810, one year before William was born. The watch initially belonged to someone else.

Personal Photo

On his trousers with pewter buttons for a fly, William wore suspenders to hold them up, suspenders buttoned twice on each side in the front.

Underneath, he wore ankle-length long drawers made of bleached cotton muslin with a waistband and stirrups to hold the pants' legs down. The drawers were buttoned in the front with a cut V in the back for adjustment. Most southern men liked these because they didn't want the wool next to their skin, especially in the hot, sticky summer.

William needed to see Dr. Waller Taylor, who now lived

west of town down West Washington. At this end of town in 1842, Dr. Taylor built a house which would later become the Dixie Hotel. It was located where the Sledge family lives now. Dr. Sledge is a descendant of Mary's Uncle James Walker.

William roped off his mare in front of the home, and Dr. Taylor greeted him as he approached the house. William paid off his debt to the good doctor, a sign the family was prospering.

The Taylor Home was built in 1842 (probably additions were made, and the home became the Dixie Hotel), Florida Memory Collection, about 1940.

At Elizabeth Baptist, William and Mary sat four pews back from the front, Mary holding little Vollie. Beside her in ascending order were five more heads, from three-year-old James up to twelve-year-old John Slicer, who was almost thirteen. Usually, John Slicer sat with his friends, but the pastor had asked families to stay together because of the sacred harp singing held later. Membership in the church was seventy-four souls, with Reverend H. S. Linton their pastor.

Church at Pioneer Village, Silver Springs State Park, Personal Photo

Mary loved these sings, especially the all-day ones, but a short one was wonderful too. The songs from the old country were of a folk variety from Scotland, England, Wales, and Ireland. Her mother especially enjoyed it, and her parents were down front on the second row.

Sacred harp music was written in four notes and was widely sung prior to the War Between the States. There was even a *Book of Songs* in print and had been since 1844. The four notes were Fa, Sol, La, and Mi.

They sang the notes first to get the notes, then sang the words. The congregation joined in, and someone led by beating time vigorously with long sweeps of his right arm, up and down, right and left. Since there was no piano, this is how they worshiped in song.

At the end of the service, they went out under the shade of the oaks while the men brought out the pews. They placed rows of pews in a triangular shape where the men and children took their places, with the leader in the middle.

They began singing while the women pulled together the dinner bowls and placed them on the long tablecloths spread on the ground. There was a pause when even the children grew quiet.

Joseph Kinsey removed his hat and led them in a few moments of prayer: "We thank you, Lord, for the beauty of this land, for its abundance, for these treasured friends gathered here today, and especially for the feast you've spread before us." Up above, songbirds trilled, and a breeze pushed the moss. It drifted in the wind.

Mary thought about what her mama always said. The pleasures in their lives were not to be measured in hours or days but in moments. Mary thought, "moments like these."

The ladies piled the bowls high with roasted pork, chicken and rice, chicken and dumplings, all kinds of vegetables, cornbread, grits, biscuits, sliced tomatoes, strawberry cake, and much more. When they were ready, everyone knelt down, young and old, to have their Sunday dinner on the grounds.

Later, Mary noticed John Slicer slipping away with one of the girls from the congregation. She looked over at William and noticed he was watching too. She knew there was no need to say anything; he was on it.

After the Sunday dinner, the women joined their families in the sing, which lasted until mid-afternoon.

In the 1850 census, William shows himself on the last page, the third family from the end, listed as inhabitants of the 10th Division. This showed they still lived near Elizabeth. Others on the same page are Drucilla Hartsfield, Frances Cuthbert, and

James Carter, all with surnames of families who lived in the Elizabeth area; but William is the assistant marshal for the census and may have simply waited to list his family at the end of the census itself. Thus there is some uncertainty.

Ten years later, *the Family Friend* in 1860 explained the position of an assistant marshal. It read, *"The duties of this undertaking devolve upon the United States' Marshals, who appoint their own assistants."* In each state, there are one or more judicial districts, each of which is connected to a marshal. Each judicial district is subdivided into subdivisions led by an assistant, a subdivision with under 20,000 in population.

The assistant marshal was qualified by oath and furnished with blanks and instructions. In their work, they had to make two copies of their report—two handwritten copies. William filed the original with the clerk of court of each county, and he forwarded the copies to the marshal.

William's compensation was in proportion to the population enumerated by his enumerators. His pay was two cents for each person enumerated, ten cents for each farm, and for each establishment of productive industry, fifteen cents. He received ten cents for travel, which was figured using the square root of the number of square miles in his division. He also got eight cents per page for the two copies. For more information on Jefferson County and Monticello in 1850, see Appendix 2.

In ten years, since the 1840 census, Jefferson County boomed, having grown another 36% for a total population of 7,718. During the last decade, 2,005 people moved into the county.

In all of Monticello, there were only 190 white people and 139 slaves. Throughout the county, there were 520 dwellings with 520 families. There were no free colored people. Its economy was a planter and plantation culture, with forty-five farms accounting for almost 75% of the cotton produced. In the county were 377 farms in all.

Jefferson County had the smallest white population in the Jackson, Gadsden, Leon, and Madison red hills area, but more than twice as many slaves. Counting its slaves, it was the third most populated county in the state. Counting only the whites, it was the seventh. William and Mary lived in a major slave-holding county.

In Monticello, there were now businesses running east and west on Dogwood Street besides those running north on Jefferson Street and east and west on Washington Street. The courthouse stood in the middle of the four spokes where Jefferson and Washington connected.

Mary, born in South Carolina, is part of an interesting statistic for both Jefferson County and Florida. By 1850, 4,600 native-born South Carolinians lived in Florida out of 47,000 white Floridians, or almost 10% were born in South Carolina. Many lived in Jefferson County.

By this date, almost thirty years after Florida became a territory, many more of the 47,000 were only one generation removed from South Carolina. South Carolina is a grandparent of Florida, as are Georgia, North Carolina, and Virginia.

Jefferson County filled up with Carolinians and Virginians. The latter were more educated, but the former were more plentiful. Virginians were more often elected to office. For the Andrews, theirs was a mixed marriage. William was a Virginian, having grown up on the Virginia side of Washington City, and Mary was a Carolinian. He was more educated, and she could not read nor write.

Because William was the enumerator of the 1850 census, his handwriting and signature are on the last page. Also on the census's last page, he wrote at the top, "Classified." Researchers believe this was because of the earlier Seminole Indian War and the US military fort near Elizabeth and Aucilla. It may have been near Sandy Ford.

As stated, it is uncertain whether he lived in Monticello by 1850. Monticello residents are on the first five pages, and his signature appears at the end of the entire census. The rest, around sixty pages, are not listed as being from any other city or community in the county.

William does not list his occupation, though he lists everyone else on the page as a farmer. The Cuthberts had property on what today is Bassett's Dairy Road. William's family appears to be farther down the road toward Sandy Ford from the Bellamys. If William listed himself near his neighbors, he lives somewhere in this vicinity.

As part of his census duties, William may have had to travel south to Newport, riding on the new plank road recently built between St. Augustine Road and Newport by the Chaires brothers. Later, the county commission paid William as deputy sheriff $10.54 to escort James Carter, a free man of color, out of the state. A question arises: If there were no free persons of color listed as heads of household in the county, where did this James Carter live? Was he recently given his freedom?

William was thirty-seven, and Mary was twenty-eight. John Slicer was thirteen, and Ellen was eleven. Florida (ten) was right behind her. By the time Mary was twenty-eight, she had birthed four children—Sarah (seven), James (six), Valentine (four), and Zech (two).

Living nearby are Charles I. Powell and James F. and

Henrietta Carter. William Porter and Frances Cuthbert lived next to them.

Out in Elizabeth, Mary's parents' closest neighbors were Lewis and Sarah Gaskins and Isaac and Narcissa Lamb. Nearby were Henry and Eva Kirkland and George and Nancy Bishop.

Google Maps, 1850s Elizabeth Community. Green marks new purchases of land in the 1850s. Purple indicates land bought in the 1820s, blue in the 1830s, and orange in the 1840s.

William arrived at the courthouse and tied his mare to the hitching post. The hitching post was simple, with two posts on each end with a top rail held in place by leather straps. He walked the long stairs up to the courtroom and inside got quickly to work and swore in several assistants. "Raise your right hand and repeat after me," he told the small group of men.

We know this because they required him to keep a duplicate of the oath of office taken by each man. He supplied them with forms on which they gathered information on all the families living in the county. For each sheet produced, which held about 160 names, it was William's job to produce two more copies. He had several people working for him.

The assistants received two cents a name, which was excellent pay. Each carried a portfolio, blank schedules, blotting pads, and even an inkstand. At the end of each day, they turned in their forms, which were collated and analyzed by William, using a strict set of federal rules.

Each form required everyone in the household to have an age. Many people did not know their ages, which means the census takers rounded those up or down to ages such as twenty, fifty, or eighty.

Getting people to talk about themselves was hard. Some people lied about their age, such as when they wished to conceal a birth out of wedlock. And there were those who refused to be counted. William suspected they had something to hide.

One afternoon about midway through, he knocked on a door and the lady of the house, an older married woman with grown children, answered. She invited him to sit on her porch, and he began his work. He first asked how many people lived there and their ages. Where each was born.

Later, he said, "Now, madam, at what age shall I put you down?" She hemmed and hawed but gave him no direct answer. So he asked, "How old is your husband?"

She replied, "Fifty-one."

"And your eldest son?"

"Twenty-six."

"And the next?"

"Twenty-three."

"And how old do you call yourself?"

She dropped her eyes and shook her head, "I don't know my age exactly." She added, "but it's about thirty."

William looked at her and hesitated, knowing he was entering shaky ground, "Did I understand you, madam, that your eldest son is twenty-seven?"

"Yes."

He stared at her before proceeding. "You must surely be over thirty?"

The lady shifted in her seat, pulled herself more erect, and snapped, "I told you 'about' thirty. I can't tell exactly. It may be thirty-one or three, but I am positive not much older."

He too spent his day like his employees, going door to door. It was awkward at first. One day he only made ten cents, five names at two cents a place. The distances between the houses were great, but the biggest problem was recording the information and moving on.

Jefferson County was right neighborly, plus people in the country had so little opportunity to learn what happened in the rest of the world. People wanted him to stay and talk, and so he may have. Hopefully, the rest of his employees did better at moving on than he did. The problem, though, of tarrying had to be dealt with. He would talk to his employees about it as soon as possible.

By the end of the first week, William along with the rest of his people got the hang of it. One enterprising young man may have turned in a list of 600 names, which made him $12 in pocket change. Of course, if William checked the list, he may have noticed discrepancies. The young man may have made up some of the information. If so, he would discharge him immediately.

On Thursday morning in the spring of 1850, after going for a walk, Mary hung her bonnet on the nail by the door and slipped into the front hall where six-year-old Sarah met her. "Mama," she said, "my back and head hurts."

Mary felt her head; Sarah had a fever. "Come out here in the light," she told Sarah, "and open your mouth and say 'ah'." They stepped out onto the porch, but Mary saw nothing different in her throat. She added, "Come on back to the kitchen. You can help me cut up potatoes. We're having stew for dinner today."

That night, Mary noticed Sarah hardly ate and went to bed early. By the next morning, her fever was still there; and she complained her head hurt. Mary and William worried if they should call for a doctor, but later Florrie noticed raised pink and red bumps on her back, a type of rash. Sarah had chickenpox.

Within two days, all the kids had it except John, Ellen, and Florrie, who had all had it when their mother was still alive. All the crying and itching was maddening not only to her four babies but to everyone else too. She made them wear gloves, but little fourteen-month-old Zech kept taking his off.

Mary bit off his fingernails to keep them short. She made the others bite theirs off too. Thankfully, Zech's case was the least symptomatic. She also gave them cool baking soda baths when the itching got too bad.

It exhausted John to keep the house in cool spring water. Mary, Ellen, and Florrie worked around the clock applying cold rags to their sores. Both Ellen and Florrie read to the children and played games, anything to keep their minds distracted from the itching. After about a week, it was all over except for sores which took longer to heal.

One beautiful spring day, William worked north of town and rode back down Jefferson Street. He admired the flowering oleanders in the yards of prosperous Monticello residents. The Lamar's had expanded their home, adding a second floor. This house is today known as the Budd/Braswell/Pafford/Wyche home.

Across the street was the beautiful Taylor/Palmer home. Folks built farther south toward the courthouse, three new homes within the last decade, the closest being the Denham house at the corner of High and Jefferson which he now passed. The Greek Revival cottage added to the city, and he noticed how much Monticello had changed in the past few years. Bud Rainey built a handsome home located where Gary Wright's compound currently sits today, and Smith Simkins built another gracious home on East Washington at the northeast corner of Waukeenah.

Initially, he and Mary noticed the tiny village had grown mostly north, straight up Jefferson Street, but now the growth changed. South of Adam Wirick's home, brick buildings reached toward the modern, stately courthouse and ran east on Dogwood. Darius Williams Mercantile was now a two-story brick building on the northeast corner of Dogwood and Jefferson, and across Jefferson facing Williams Mercantile was

Denham & Palmer's Mercantile, also a two-story brick building. Today, Williams Mercantile houses Vintage Treasures. Standing immediately due north of the courthouse on the east side of the street was a dry goods store owned by William Budd and later his younger brother J. T. (the store would later be known as J. T. Budd and Son). The building was probably wood. Now, the building there says 'Bank,' but it houses the Cowhaus Coffee Shop.

East and West of the courthouse but south of Washington Street were two inns, the Bless House and the Madden House, which faced north where the Rev Cafe sits today. The Academy still stood at the western end of Washington Street, but a new, finer edifice was being constructed nearby directly in front of the parade ground, a tall, stately, two-story building of brick. His own organization, the Masons, along with the Oddfellows raised the funding for the new badly-needed school.

The town added two more churches. The Presbyterians had built their church almost six years earlier in its present location, but the Baptists had finished theirs south of town on Palmer land in what had been a cornfield. Today, if it were still there, it would sit in front of the house at 365 South Jefferson Street, in the middle of US 19 south. The Baptists met there in their wood frame building south of town with a small bell tower and its earlier two doors on the front.

Monticello, First Baptist Church, Keystone Genealogical Library

Sitting on the back porch in the mid-afternoon shade, Mary was planning what she would take next Sunday for the Baptists' annual strawberry supper. There would be strawberry pie, strawberry shortcake (made with biscuits), strawberry biscuits, and strawberries served over pound cake. She was hoping to come up with something new, though, something not thought of before; but it stumped her. She got an idea. Maybe a bread pudding made with strawberry syrup drizzled over the top? She would begin experimenting right away.

Mary knew what this feeling meant. She had experienced it

five times before, but this time it was too soon. Looking down at the baby suckling at her breast, their eyes locked. She always loved this, when the little feller stared and grinned. He smiled his toothless grin, and his milk drooled.

She said to him, "You can grin and suck, but not both at the same time." He went back to sucking. She smiled at him but thought it was too soon for another to come.

Until now, every baby except James had come an easy two years apart. Even little Jesse came nineteen months after his brother Zech, and Zech came two years after Val, and Val two more after James. Six-year-old Sarah wanted to help, and she was doing what she could. The real help, though, came from Mary's stepdaughters Ellen and Florrie, twelve and eleven respectively.

She looked at Jesse. Poor thing. He would be booted out of the cradle any day now.

Later in the fall, William came home mid-afternoon and found Mary sitting on the back porch making butter with the side crank barrel churn. Her Uncle Joel Walker, who was close to her in age and now the sheriff, had left her there. They had a pleasant talk. William saw him on his way out.

Though the tall, rangy black-haired Joel was her uncle, she was the oldest of her family, and he was the youngest of her grandparent's family. They played together before they migrated from South Carolina, and now they were more like siblings.

Mary's Uncle Joel had run for sheriff. A group of the town's leaders asked him to run. His size and ruggedness from years of working cattle made him an ideal candidate for the job.

Rocking Chair on Porch with deer skin seat, Florida Pioneer Village, Silver Springs State Park, personal photo

Mary turned the crank and scanned the backyard for her chickens, who pecked their way across the sandy ground. William stopped short before interrupting her private moment. She was as pretty as ever, as she always was when she was pregnant. But he had sad news. "Mary," he said softly, and she smiled. He stepped onto the porch and sat in the chair vacated by Joel. The sad news could wait. He took over the cranking.

Mary was over seven months pregnant and into a period of general discomfort. Worried this time because Jesse and this baby had come so close together, he knew they had to be more careful. He couldn't imagine life without her. They chatted about this and that. He said, "Are you sure you're okay with naming this child Julia if it is a girl?"

"Of course. Some day she will be honored to know she was named after your sister."

"Thank you, Hon." Then he added, "Today, I heard John Gamble died."

His news surprised her. "Was he ill?"

"No, I don't think so. Did I ever tell you they were the sons of a famous Revolutionary War hero? Their father seized a fortress on the Hudson River during the war." He looked away and paused before adding, "I think it was at Stony Point. Anyway, you and I both know how many sons and grandsons of famous patriots and even founders moved here to Florida, but how few of them had the mettle to survive, let alone prosper? Very few, I tell you. Very few, but the Gambles are two who made it and did well, though they had their problems." He was telling her something she knew, but she listened quietly anyway. They chatted and enjoyed the peace and solitude of a household free of kids either gone to school or napping.

The Gambles settled two large tracts of land in what was then Leon County before this portion became Jefferson County in 1827. They arrived before Mary's family. John Gamble created Waukeenah Plantation near present-day Waukeenah, while Robert created the adjoining Welaunee Plantation, a portion of which is now Avalon Plantation near Capps. Both brothers later moved to Tallahassee, where John owned Neamathla Plantation on St. Augustine Road east of town. Robert lived in his mansion on College Avenue. John's son, also named Robert Gamble, married his cousin Laura Wirt Randall, granddaughter of the attorney general under

President Monroe. They would later move to Manatee County and become some of the first settlers there.

One early morning, William pulled around to the front door with the carriage. They were going to town. Mary came down the steps wearing her best emerald green calico with its full pleated skirt. He said, "Mary, my girl, you look ravishing today." She smiled and gave him her hand as he helped her into the carriage.

In Monticello she shopped, and they drove over to the site of the new two-story brick school. Said William, "It will be the first brick school built in the state." The Masons had made it possible, another reason William was proud to be a Mason. They built it timely.

HIGH AND GRAMMAR SCHOOL, MONTICELLO, FLA.

By the next year, Florida passed a law to establish a system of free public schools sustained by local taxation. The judge of the probate would also be the school's first superintendent, with the county commission on his school board. By the beginning of the Civil War, there would be four more schools built—at Waukeenah, Lloyd, Aucilla, and Walker Mills (Drifton), but most only went to eighth grade. All were private, including Jefferson Academy.

#

Chapter 3
<u>Before Its Time, 1852</u>

If it is going to snow in Florida, it usually happens in February, but whether it snowed on Julia Ann's day of birth in 1851 or not is unknown. What we do know is that after four boys, William finally got a daughter he could name after his sister Julia Ann Pic who had died earlier. Even better for Mary, she would not get pregnant again for another year.

Spring came with a whimper, and the entire month of February blew in with successively weaker cold fronts until it warmed nicely by month's end. Mary worried the flowers would bloom early and get hit by another freeze.

Outside her window, a wild pink azalea bloomed. She found it hard to believe she was only one year older than Sarah when her family came to Monticello. Much had changed in those two decades. In the last nine years, she met William, married, became a mother to three motherless children, and had six babies. She looked at Julia Ann, so tiny in her arms.

It was a warm day. The delicate blossoms of the wild azalea looked like someone had picked a small bouquet and attached it to one branch, a little bush of green. Each little star-shaped flower looked as if it poked out its tongue of delicate whiskers.

Native Azalea, Personal Photo

What a blessing to have this here. Out in the woods east of town, they were everywhere, especially the pink ones in the hammocks near the swamps. She missed living there with her parents, so two winters ago her dad dug one and transplanted it by her back window.

Every spring she waited for its blooms but missed home all the more when they faded. Since she lived in town, she planted althea, hydrangeas, and oleander, but they bloomed later. This plant was the first to bloom every year. Luckily, where their home was located were live oaks, magnolias, and cabbage palmetto. She loved to see them since they reminded her of her home.

    Her parents didn't live far away, and she saw them and her brothers and sisters anytime someone came to town. The home place in the community of Elizabeth was only a little more than a couple of hours to the east by buckboard and even less by horseback. Between town and her parents' home were the Bellamy fields, a wilderness of cypress swamps, pine forests, palmettos so thick it was almost impassable, and always the moss waving from the massive oak limbs over the canopied road. In the pines, she knew there would be wild dogwoods, and she wished she could make the trip this warm day to see their blossoms peeking around the trunks like white lace. The silence was what she missed most. It would be deeply silent except for an occasional wind blowing through the pine boughs. But she was going nowhere today. There was too much to do with eight children underfoot and this one in her arms.

Elizabeth, 1850s Google Earth. Road to Elizabeth between Bellamy Plantation and the Salt Road

She thought about the road to Elizabeth. It was barely over two ruts wide, but traveling by horseback was easier. Wagon wheels either bogged into the shifting sand when dry or slid off the slick red clay when not. The rains came suddenly and frequently, often with little warning. Horses and mules were the transportation of choice, but at that time women straddled neither. When she was a girl in South Carolina, though, it was different. She was glad this new tradition only came about when she became a woman.

Outside her window, there was chattering and yelling, constant clanging of metal harnesses, and the dull thud of horse hooves on dirt. Monticello's streets were dusty when it was dry and muddy when it wasn't. Especially east of the courthouse, Washington Street was a loblolly. During the last rainy spell, they laid out stepping stones so people could cross on foot (probably the intersection of East Washington and Cherry). Her house was an easy distance from the center of town, and nothing much happened she didn't see.

Julia Ann was much more interested in the noises outside, and she realized she had finished. So she pulled down the soft fabric of her chemise and bodice and handed her to Florrie, who walked into the room. Mary noticed Florrie knew when she was done.

Florrie was born Florida Mae, though she didn't much like the name. Mary didn't think it was a bad name. Florida was pretty enough. After all, it was Spanish for flowers; but Florrie, born in 1840, knew they named her after the Territory, not the flowers. Statehood happened when Florrie was five.

Mary stepped into the warm sunshine on the front porch as former Governor Moseley and another man walked by, leading their horses through the mud. It had been a rainy winter and now a rainy spring. She smiled at both and remembered when both men would have worn buckskin leggings and homespun blouses. Florida changed quickly from a territorial backwater to a growing, prosperous state. Moseley tipped his hat and continued talking to the stranger as they made their way to the center of town.

Cotton was the crop of the affluent. The town was prosperous and growing because of it and the labor provided by the slaves. The substantial cotton prices replaced the years of financial woes caused by Indian problems and economic depression. These prices also created a factorage system and the beginning of manufacturing in the little community.

Though there was no slave auction in Monticello, people bought slaves either from each other or from afar. Sometimes a neighboring plantation liquidated. William's brother-in-law by his first wife (James A. Goff) sold seven slaves to satisfy a debt he owed to John Bellamy.

Most people brought their slaves with them when they moved into the area or sent them later. This was because of the act of 1808 which prohibited the importation of slaves into the country. It was legislation promoted by President Thomas Jefferson, something he had pushed since the 1770s; and it reflected another move toward abolishing slavery. England abolished their slave trade about the same time and abolished all slavery throughout the empire by 1833. The US did not follow suit on the latter, though.

Most people in Jefferson County, when they needed slaves, bought them from plantations in Maryland, Virginia, the Carolinas, or Georgia. There was a slave broker who traveled between the areas and worked out the details. These slaves who came to Jefferson County were the offspring of America's oldest families, descendants of slaves brought into the colonies as early as the early 1600s when the initial tobacco markets thrived.

Though many of the estates in Florida collapsed during the earlier economic troubles, a few held on and became increasingly successful. Mary's family, though, did not want to hold slaves, which meant growing cotton wasn't economically viable for them. They may have objected to the use of whippings, though whippings were still used for felonies at the jailhouse for both slaves and whites. More for whites, though, because owners preferred to punish their own slaves. A marked-up slave brought less value.

The public now regarded branding as cruel, and laws prohibited it. Still, though, whippings were more commonly meted out for much less by the planters, such as for running away. Runaways were often newly-bought slaves trying to get back to where they came from and where they had family.

By now, all slaves needed a pass to travel off their plantations. After his slaves murdered local resident Richard B. Cole, the legislature passed new laws and regulations. Mary may have thought about the sermon last week at the Baptist church. The preacher talked about their moral and Christian duty to take care of their slaves. They had not only a legal duty but a moral one to house, feed, and clothe them in a proper and wholesome manner—not to do so was neglectful, repugnant, and downright inhumane. He encouraged their treatment with humility. She and William listened with interest, but they did not own slaves.

She knew it would be nice to have house slaves like the planters' wives had—one to do the cooking; another to be a chambermaid that also does the washing, ironing, and sewing; one to handle the horses and outdoor jobs like chopping wood; one to take care of the garden, the cow and to make butter; and one to serve as a carriage driver. A few plantations even had a fiddler, but sometimes the driver was the fiddler. Such a life, she thought.

Yet William was right. They had a house full of children to keep busy. John kept the house in wood. James made a fine carriage driver. Florrie, Ellen, and Sarah made great chambermaids and helped with the cooking. Val was old enough to help with the milking. All they needed was a fiddler. Maybe Zech could learn.

He was her introspective one. When preoccupied, she

noticed Zech had a habit of pulling at his earlobe. Mary arched her back and stretched her shoulders as she wondered when William would be home for dinner or if his business would keep him longer again tonight. There were no set hours for a constable, so she never knew.

One morning in September 1852, as Mary, Florida, and Ellen were in the kitchen making breakfast, Mary's brother Henry came in; and she offered him coffee. He was waiting for William. They were going to the land office in Tallahassee to purchase property from the US government.

They had run cattle for years on land north of Monticello and made improvements. Since the government had opened it for settlement, they wanted to purchase it.

William and Henry made the long trip to Tallahassee. While gingerly riding a corduroy road north of the lake (a road made of tree trunks laid perpendicular to the direction of the road across a swampy area), William said to Henry, "You surprised us when you left your dad to work at the mills." Henry and J.J. worked at Walker Mills for their great-uncle Littleberry, grandfather of Joel's brother, who owned the mills.

Henry replied, "Life for a rancher is for better or for worse. Prices fluctuate, a mule gets hung in a fence, and one false move and a dog gets gored. It leans to the worse, and all my life my dad never caught up. I turned to carpentry and took a job at the mill."

Coming back, they both stopped in Monticello before riding to their homes. Later, when Henry pulled off, William, tired of riding, drew his left boot out of the stirrup and raised it to lean his knee on the saddle in front of him for the extra short ride.

When he got to the house, he found Mary in the kitchen with Ellen and Sarah making biscuits for supper. He could hear them collectively singing, *"When I was playing with my brother, Happy was I. Oh! Take me to my kind old mother, there let me live and die."* They were singing one of Stephen Foster's new songs, *Old Folks at Home*.

Foster was at the height of his craft between 1850 and 1860, releasing ten or more songs a year. His moving nostalgic melodies and romantic melancholy ballads were widely accepted even as far south as Florida. This one was so accepted in 1935 that Florida adopted it as the state song because the home the singer sings about is down on the Suwannee River.

She looked up, and he laid a document down on the kitchen table. Pulling out a chair, he pecked her on the cheek and said, "Sit down, Mary, and see what we've got." His grin told her he was happy with it.

He had purchased forty acres from the US government. Today, it is located north of the dog track near US 19 North but fronting on Oetinger Road. Mary's brother Henry received his patent for land due south of theirs, and the dog track sits today on Henry's land. President Millard Fillmore signed the US Land Grants.

Because William had earlier registered his mark and brand in 1847, he may have run cattle or raised swine with his father-in-law, but he is not listed in the agricultural schedule of 1850. He may have simply leased the land to his brother-in-law Henry, who held the land immediately south.

It was a wonderful neighborhood. Governor Moseley's plantation was between their lands and Lake Miccosukee on what today would be Mays Pond Plantation. Former Territorial Governor Richard Keith Call also owned land in the vicinity, both on what would later become Mays Pond and Norias Plantations.

Most telling of all about their economic health was when William and Mary settled their property note. It appears the proceeds from his job as the census assistant marshal helped them to pay off the land. William's pay records can be found in the US Census Letter Book dated 1851-1852. We are unsure if he borrowed money to purchase the land or if the mortgage came after he held its title.

William and Mary sold this property only four years later to James C. P. Fife, who owned land in the vicinity. It is doubtful they ever built anything on the property other than maybe a cattle pen.

That night, William had a meeting downtown but was later than usual coming home. She heard him coming up the stairs singing at the top of his lungs. She jumped out of bed, threw on a wrap, and rushed to the front door before he woke the household. He was singing, *"I asked if she'd have so humble a lad? Said she, no finer a man could be had."*

She opened the door. He exclaimed, *"Oh Mary, sweet Mary,"* as he removed his hat and bowed so low he stumbled. She rushed to help him across the porch before he could fall backward, shushing him to quit singing, but he would have none of it. He bellowed more of the song, *"And so we did marry sweet Mary and me. Our lives were joined forever to be."* And the two of them stumbled into the hallway.

Goodness, he reeked of booze. *"Oh Mary, sweet Mary"* he sang again as they went down the hall to their bedroom. She listened for baby Julia Ann's cries, but none came. She slept through it all.

The next day on the porch Mary heard Ellen scream from the kitchen. Running there, she saw an enormous black snake halfway on top of the back steps with his head raised almost half a foot above the kitchen floor. He was a nice one, all black and shiny, almost blue. He pivoted his head from Ellen to Mary with his half-lidded gaze.

She knew he wasn't poisonous, but she also knew a bite from him would hurt badly. Ellen slowly backed up, never taking her eyes off him, while Mary reached for the broom sitting by the door she had entered. His head moved from one to the other. She crept toward the snake, stomping her feet, but he didn't back down.

Mary said, "Oh, you're a fearless one. You need to go back where you came from." She pushed the broom toward him. The serpent lunged at it, but she gave a big shove, and his body tumbled down between the steps.

When Mary looked over her shoulder, she saw all the kids standing at the door and in the hall. John, fifteen, said, "I'll go kill 'em."

But Mary said, "No, he's a good 'un. Let him be." She knew the black snake would protect their door from other less desirables. He was territorial and wouldn't let another snake take up residence. Like most everything else in Florida, she knew you often had to take the lesser of two evils.

Varmints weren't the only source of trouble. Rumors throughout the county persisted about Indian depredations upon the cattle stock in South Florida. The depredations were far removed from where the Indians lived farther south. There was great distrust between both sides. There were many Indian signs on the St. Johns River and as far north as Tampa on the other side of the state. Great alarm ensued amid the excitement.

Monticello had not forgotten the troubles less than fifteen years earlier. When local militias throughout the state formed to investigate, they found the Indians almost a hundred fifty miles north of where everyone thought they were. Again, the militias captured as many as possible to move them west. They continued to do this throughout the summer and into the winter of 1852 until the Indians went back and the militias disbanded.

William Andrews may have been part of this militia, though we're unsure if this might have been another person of the same name. Why would he leave his family to do such a chore? Maybe it was land. Our government was still less than eighty years old and still had trouble paying its bills. It continued to grant land instead of payment for its soldiers, though it was not a promise. But earlier calls for volunteers had made those men eligible.

At the southwest corner of West Washington and Water Streets, construction of the new school proceeded. They were building a *"school building 60 ft. x 55 ft., two stories high of brick."* The bricks came from the George Taylor Plantation, and Samuel Carroll's slaves supplied the labor. The Masons and Oddfellows spearheaded the fundraising for the construction costs. The building still stands, though they would later add the wings.

Jefferson Academy, Florida Memory Collection

Still, Middle Florida was peaceable; people continued to move into the county. One group of people was the second wave of Walkers (more cousins) from the Colleton District. From the western portion of the district came the Raysors and Walkers. Many of the names from this area mirror the area around Carter's Ford. Daniel Walker surveyed John M. Raysor's deed of 1844 for 2,120 acres on McCune's Branch and Willow in Colleton District.

Indexed in the same deed book are other Walkers and Carters. Besides the two communities above, this area included Schoolhouse Branch, Burnt Bay, and Hell Hole Branch. This John M. Raysor married Mary Ann Walker, and it appears she is probably the sister of James Sanders Walker who came to Jefferson County around 1853, so she was not part of the first group, Mary's Walkers.

In mid-May of 1854, William came home from work late one afternoon and found his very pregnant Mary on the back porch enjoying the rather cool day for this time of the year. A front had moved through the night before, and the day was drier than usual. She was holding one of her chickens, looking for something amongst her feathers.

He said, "Has Maggie got something wrong with her wing?"

Startled, she smiled. "You are about the quietest man I've ever known. No wonder they made you a lieutenant in the Indian War. You move around as quietly as the Indians."

He took a chair and joined her, looking into the trees and admiring her garden. "It is a beautiful day, isn't it?" She nodded, and both sat in their comfortable silence.

He broke it, "Well, we got word the Kansas-Nebraska Act passed." She looked deep into his eyes and saw the worry there. The entire family had been talking about this act since Congress first introduced it in January.

Jefferson County was strongly Democratic. The Democrats had carried the county in every election since statehood; but the Whigs, the opposition, would experience a rift in their party when the Kansas-Nebraska Act passed in mid-May of 1854, an occurrence which many say may have been the single most significant event leading to the future War Between the States.

The nation was uneasy about the slavery question, and Monticello and Jefferson County were no exception, though it was a strong slave county.

Far away, though, there was much pressure to open the Nebraska Territory, an area north of the Mason-Dixon Line (the 36° 30′ north line). Kansas and Nebraska were west of Minnesota, Iowa, and Missouri. Settlers wanted the land but would not move there until they could take title.

The south who wielded power in Congress would not vote to open this territory. They wanted no more land north of the line to be held by non-slave-owning settlers. The south knew that as more non-slave states joined the union, their power in Congress dwindled.

Without the south's votes, Congress could not agree. In the end, Congress reached a compromise called the Kansas-Nebraska Act. It proposed a southern state inclined to support slavery—Kansas. Unfortunately, Kansas was north of the Mason-Dixon line itself, due west of Missouri, and it violated the earlier Missouri Compromise which had kept the Union from falling apart since the 1820s.

A main issue behind the push was the building of a transcontinental railroad through Chicago. The people of the Midwest needed this railroad. Chicago had the most to gain, being in the center of the nation and sitting as a great lakeside port. Their congressional delegation pushed hard for opening the Nebraska Territory to settlers, even if it meant creating a pro-slavery state north of the line and violating the Missouri Compromise.

Subsequently, Congress repealed the long-standing Missouri Compromise in the Nebraska-Kansas Act, and this opened everything north of the Mason-Dixon line to popular sovereignty, where the people who lived there could determine for themselves whether they wanted slavery. This enraged many northern people and especially the abolitionists.

Illinois wanted a transcontinental railroad, the north wanted a stop to slavery, and the south wanted slavery. The Kansas-Nebraska Act got Illinois its railroad by opening the northwest territories to slavery. It got the south new territories open to slavery; but the north, especially the northeast, got nothing.

Jefferson County, though pleased with the Kansas-Nebraska

Act, worried about its unintended consequences. It was the talk of the entire county if not the entire nation.

Earlier, the south talked of secession, but this act eased some of the discontent. But at what cost, many worried, especially William and Mary.

William noticed the talk upset Mary, so he changed the subject. "Hey, they finished the railroad bridge across the Mississippi River. It is open for business. Imagine that, a bridge across the mighty Mississippi!"

"What does it look like?"

"It's a railroad bridge."

Added Mary, "Well, don't that beat all. There's a railroad that far west, and we still don't have one through this part of Florida."

She changed the subject and placed her hand on her stomach. "If this is a boy, we should name him after you and call him Henry; but if it is a girl, I would like to call her Henrietta--Etta for short." He smiled and nodded his assent.

One summer day, Mary heard Zech coughing in the next room. Earlier, he had had a cold, a lingering one he could not overcome.

The coughing continued over the next several days, though it didn't affect his energy level. He went about, playing and running with the other kids. He was only four but did his best to run with his older brothers. Still, the coughing fits would overtake him and stop him in his tracks.

Several times a day she heard him have trouble catching his breath, wheezing an intake of air, and barking the air back out in fits of coughs. "John," she said, "go fetch Dr. Palmer. Tell him something is wrong with Zech, and it may be contagious."

She put Zech to bed. He did not need to overheat any longer.

Dr. Palmer came early in the afternoon, and the news was not good. He hovered over the child, frowning. Shaking his head, he told Mary, "Zech has whooping cough, and he will be very sick for a very long time." Mary knew there would be months of severe coughing.

Sometimes his cough caused him to choke and vomit. Several times he fainted. In her mind where she kept such thoughts, she knew children even died of the disease. It was also called the croup, the hundred-day cough, or the convulsive cough. Sometimes Zech's coughing sounded like a dog's bark.

In the end, Zech lived. Luckily, people in the US now seldom experience whooping cough because of vaccinations and antibiotics.

Did Zech actually catch whooping cough? We have no way of knowing, but it was endemic in children. Someone in the family probably did get it. Diaries and journals show that most families struggled with the disease.

The turkey oaks lost their leaves, and winter came in 1853 behind the cold fronts that moved farther south. One afternoon between Christmas and the new year, William attended a mass meeting of local citizens to discuss a bill permitting voters in each justice of the peace district to decide on the availability of liquor licenses for their districts. They endorsed the bill, but it failed to pass the legislature in Tallahassee.

The legislature passed tougher licensing requirements, though, and by April 1854 a visitor reported of Monticello that he found "not a grog shop in the village" and not a person drunk on the streets. There was at least one liquor store owned by G. J. Streety, so this person must not have traveled off the main roads.

By mid-summer in 1854, Florida suffered a hot spell. This part of Florida does not get the coastal winds, and the humidity in the hot air can be stifling. Mary sat on her back porch in the breezy area between the house and the kitchen. If there was a breeze, this place funneled it, but today there was nothing but the sweltering heat. She kept a small rag in her bosom and used it to wipe the sweat from her face. Pregnant, Mary sat on a chair and fanned herself.

Tonight, they would dine in the backyard. Anything to cool down. Two-year-old Julia Ann played at her feet. Thankfully, she quietly played and didn't climb into Mary's lap.

In the evening, Henry came with good news. The legislature passed a special act for the Pensacola and Georgia Railroad, and they planned to build the first section from Tallahassee to Lake City. Monticello was getting a railroad and depot—at least, that's what people thought, since everyone expected it to come directly through town!

It would come to town, but not quite how they expected.

Running for Office

By September, everyone settled down; and Mary felt giddy. In fact, the entire household was beside themselves. In the kitchen, plucking a chicken, she told Sarah, "It was certainly fortuitous your father was the census enumerator for the county. He got acquainted with so many people."

Sarah, eleven, had her father's piercing gray eyes. "Mama, why won't Daddy take any of us girls with him campaigning?

He's asked J.J., Vollie, and Zech to go. Why not me? Why can't I go with him? I'm older than any of the boys."

Mary stopped plucking feathers and dipped her hands into a pan of water before drying them on her apron. "Come on, Sarah," she said. "Let's have a talk." She pulled out a chair at the kitchen table and sat down.

With a sigh, Sarah washed her hands and dried them as she sat down next to her mother at the corner of the table. Mary said, "There are men's doings and women's doings, and some of them aren't mixed, and politics is men's doings." Sarah looked anywhere but at her mother.

Mary took Sarah's hands in hers, resting her forearms on the table. "Sarah, you can't expect your father to carry you on these trips like he does the boys. When your father calls on a family, he will not sit down and talk with the man's wife and daughters. No. Most likely he and the father will sit down alone and have a discussion. Do you understand?"

Sarah nodded yes, but Mary was still unsure if she actually did. "Politicking and voting is not a woman's business. We do not vote. They don't even expect us to take an interest. Besides, it would be improper for him to take a daughter and not a son. J.J., Vollie, Zech and even little Jesse will one day be men; and they will vote. All of them. Your father takes them because he wants them to understand the process and how important it is to all of us and our country. There is no reason for him to take you, me, or any other female in this house."

Sarah made no reply at first but wept softly instead. Through her tears, she looked at her mother. "But I want to go somewhere other than here in Monticello. I want to see what the rest of the world looks like."

"Oh, honey, I know how hard it is to be a girl. I used to get so mad because of what my brothers got to do that I couldn't, but it is our lot in life." Weeping Sarah, kneeling in front of her mother now, laid her head in Mary's lap. Mary stroked her dark hair. "God gave us our role to play, and we have to make the best of it." She raised Sarah's chin so she had to look at her. "I'm so sorry, honey."

Sarah's sadness troubled Mary, though within a few hours Sarah acted like it had never happened. She was again her old self.

Still, Mary could not help comparing herself to Sarah. Unlike Sarah, Mary had not been exposed daily to how others lived, especially the gentle class. Mary grew up with those like her own, far removed from how others lived. They were not poor, but they worked hard and learned how to live without until times got better.

Sarah grew up exposed to so much more. It worried Mary that Sarah saw the difference.

William campaigned nonstop for sheriff, riding out each day to visit with folks all over. Today, he worked Lloyd, going from household to household. One night he told Mary, "I think the census is helping. I met a lot of folks out gathering names. People seem to know me more than I realized." He knew where every house in the county was. Because of his time as assistant marshal of the census, he had gotten to know many people.

His record as a constable gave his platform the depth of having been a law enforcement officer of the court. He was the front-runner and looked unbeatable. Mary was proud of him.

The kids enjoyed it too. Henrietta was an infant, Julia was two, and Jesse was three. Mary had three children in four years, but she wasn't pregnant again in four years, and she felt light as a feather and free. After all, she was only thirty-one but had seven children of her own, added to her three stepchildren.

Her brother Joel encouraged William to run. Joel was currently sheriff, but he and her brother David farmed together, and the needs of the farm required more of his time, so he couldn't run another term.

Joel's recent experience as the sheriff, though, worried her. A few weeks ago, an inebriated Robert Potts drew a knife on him and his assistant Asa May. Potts lunged at both of them, but Joel and Asa overcame him and took him into custody. Justice of the peace Thomas Chance incarcerated Potts. It worried her because William didn't have Joel's stature.

The next afternoon, Mary wore a dark green gown fitted at the waist with a full skirt and crinolines to give it width. It was good to be into her regular clothes. Standing in front of a small looking glass in the hall, she captured, with one of her combs, a loose tendril of dark brown hair, pushing it into place near the chignon at her nape.

Earlier, she had baked a pan of scalloped tomatoes. Her garden was in full swing, and she had a plentiful supply. She usually fried the green ones, but today she layered sliced ripe tomatoes with onions and breadcrumbs in a buttered pan, generously sprinkling each layer of tomatoes with salt and pepper. She sprinkled the top with cheese and more breadcrumbs. It baked real pretty, and William sent John Slicer down to the courthouse with the pan so Mary didn't have to deal with it later.

William and Mary filled their days with barbecues and picnics. Mary watched William many evenings as he sat at his desk writing out a speech or pacing in front of the hearth to practice it. Barbecues were held at each of the towns. They held one in Waukeenah, another in Aucilla, and one in Lloyd. He campaigned throughout the county.

Tonight, they were going to a barbecue in Monticello held for the candidates to speak about what they would bring to the county. Strangely enough, her quiet man became quite loquacious when speaking about the needs of their community.

William stepped into the hall and asked, "Can you help me with this?" It was a loose, billowing bow tie, but he had tightly bound it. She did the honors and stepped back to admire her husband.

He wore his new black formal coat with notched lapels of black velvet. It was a fashionable, loosely fitted, full-skirted coat. His vest was a deep red. The billowing white tie complimented it nicely. It all went so well. With his sandy-brown hair and his piercing eyes, he could still give her butterflies after seven children.

The morning of the election, William rose early with J.J., and they stoked the fires throughout the house. Mary immediately got into the kitchen and started breakfast.

She usually waited for the kitchen to warm, but not this morning. A front had moved through, and this October morning was chilly. She made biscuits as the stove warmed.

William walked in wearing a white shirt and britches with suspenders. He had on a work coat but had his good sorrel coat over his arm. "Mary, I got something on this coat. Can you get it out?"

She swiped the dough off her fingers one at a time and rinsed them in a pan of water. She quickly dried them and, taking the coat, she set it down and began working on the spot, using a bar of lye soap. He disappeared into the house.

He wanted to be at the courthouse before the polls opened to shake hands and greet people. We know little about what voting was like then, but we know usually there were no official ballots, and sometimes political parties printed their own, called party tickets.

A voter had no privacy because private voting booths and secret ballots didn't come about until late in the 1800s. There was some separation between the election officials and the voters, but how much is uncertain.

Most people in Jefferson County were Democrats, not Whigs. Democrats wanted minimal government and talked of agrarian values, westward expansion, and Jeffersonian principles. Whigs, who opposed expansion, supported the modernization of the economy, banks, railroads, and tariffs. There were no Republicans yet.

Campaigning was accomplished face-to-face and door-to-door, or it was carried out by giving local stump speeches and attending campaign rallies.

Election day was a big to-do for everyone countywide. There were parades, and entire families came in wagons from the farms throughout the county. They got dressed for the occasion, and Mary's family was no exception. While she was in the kitchen with Ellen helping, the kids came and went to make sure what they wore was appropriate for their father's big day.

Florrie oversaw the dressing of the little ones. The entire family planned to go to the courthouse to watch the crowds gather.

The electorate must have liked William's speeches, because he won and took office as Jefferson County's sheriff in late 1855 for a two-year term.

#

Chapter 4
The High Sheriff - A Thankless Job, 1855

William jumped into his new job. As sheriff, he became the ex-officio tax collector for the county, filling in when people did not pay their taxes. This was why he had an additional bond with the governor.

Because there were no longer county auctioneers, he also conducted public auctions at the courthouse for the property of delinquent taxpayers. He received in payment three percent of the amount he collected. The sheriff's salary depended on these fees. Since 1824, the authorities no longer sent people to jail for their debts.

In this capacity, William was also the constable and received his pay from the fees collected for each writ served and warrant executed, something done by the sheriff's department today.

Sometimes gone before daybreak and arriving long after sundown, he transported prisoners from one county to the other, or he took them between the jail and the courtroom in the courthouse. If his expenses were more than the fees collected, he could petition the legislature for funding. Since they only met every other year, though, he had to wait a long time for reimbursement.

We know William and Mary lived in Monticello by 1855 because of an 1834 legislative act which said sheriffs and clerks of the court had to keep their offices in the county seat. William's term as sheriff was for two years.

Eighteen-fifty-five was a busy year for the Andrews family. Mary thought to herself, "My husband is a quiet man, but all of this requires a gift for gab. This is so unlike him." Yet he always spoke when he thought it important. His speeches were brief and to the point, though she wouldn't know firsthand.

Mary spent most of her time at home now. This latest pregnancy had gone well, but she was big, and propriety required her to stay at home the entire hot summer and Indian summer. In mid-October, she delivered a boy, which they named William Henry after his father.

A newspaper article described Williams' business with a runaway slave. Here is a created scene using this information along with other information in the same paper about a freeze.

William owned an overcoat but seldom used it in Florida's milder temperatures. It only dropped into the teens once or twice a year and only during the colder winters. He may have kept this coat so long that he later sent for it when he went north during the War Between the States. Today, he wore it; and it was almost dark when William returned late in the day with his umbrella under his arm.

It had shed torrents of rain earlier, but now dry with the wind blowing and the temperature dropping, he hung his gun horizontally on the hall wall inside the door, resting the barrel on one peg and the stock on the other. Mary thought he looked tired, weary even. He took off his coat, and the other gun and holster he hung from the peg underneath the stock. He removed his brown wool felt hat with its tall crown and four-inch brim and laid it on the table by the door. It had a matching band of fabric around its base.

She met him there and kissed him on the cheek; it was cold. The children ate in the warmth of the outdoor kitchen. Outside the wind howled around the corners of the house, a cold, wet wind. It was airish in the hall, so she suggested they sit a little by the fire which John kept stoked the entire day.

William poured himself a drink. "Mary, it's days like today that wear me out. I've got a Negro boy at the jail. He says he's eighteen, but he doesn't look a day over fifteen." He sat in his chair by the fire. The badge on the lapel of his brown coat flashed in the firelight.

Photo Taken Outside of Jail Built in 1846. Photo taken probably after the Civil War. Keystone Genealogy Library, Jefferson County, Florida Library,

He looked at her. Mary didn't say it, but the question must have been on her face. He added, "I left him at the jail."

Mary looked through the window, listening to the wind. She said, "William, you can't leave him there. He'll freeze to death. It's getting colder by the minute."

Taking a sip of the rich amber liquor, William stared at her over his glass rim and swallowed. With a sigh, he said, "Mary,

I've taken care of him. I got old Joe to stay at the jail tonight to keep the stove stoked. I'm worried it will be hard to keep it warm, though. The wooden floors in the lower apartment are missing boards. We laid some loose boards on top to keep someone from falling through, but it is airish in there. I need to take extra blankets."

While William was sheriff, the jail in Monticello was located where Monticello's only Mexican restaurant sat before they moved across Pearl Street. He had no full-time employees, no deputies, and no jailer. But, because he could hire someone part-time if needed, to tell this story a part-time jailer was fabricated.

If needed, William also had the power to raise a posse of local men to assist in a difficult situation or bring someone to justice. They held hangings in the enclosure at the jail, but hangings of slaves were uncommon. There are no records of any hangings, white or black, at the big oak south of the courthouse.

There was an article in the newspaper about how much the jail needed to be repaired. Also, we know pot-bellied stoves were the newest way to keep a building warm. William or the earlier sheriff, his wife's Uncle Joel Walker, may have bought a brand new pot-bellied stove. Black cast-iron wood-burning or coal-burning stoves were round with a bulge in the middle. It could keep the downstairs warm, and there were a couple of cells there. He probably placed the boy in one of those.

On the flat top of the stove, William probably kept a pot of coffee ready for anyone who stopped by for a visit or business, but he also may have had an office in the courthouse like the more contemporary sheriffs used to have.

Jefferson County's Courthouse while William was sheriff.

Pulling a burgundy wool shawl tighter around her shoulders, Mary sat opposite him in front of the fire. "Who does he belong to?"

Stretching his back and leaning forward toward the fire with the drink in his hands and his elbows resting on his knees, the firelight danced on his face. The room smelled of burning pine pitch "He says he belongs to someone in South Carolina, but I can't believe he got this far by himself. I think he's trying to get back to South Carolina."

"Maybe back to his mother?"

"Maybe so. I've posted a letter to the sheriff where he claims he came from. Sent it on the stage today. We'll see what response it gets. I also gave notice to the surrounding counties."

The letter probably went by stage. The stagecoach line ran from Tallahassee to Jacksonville, stopping at places in between like Monticello and Madison. It stopped every night at a stage stand, reaching its destination in five or six days. This means his letter probably took three days to reach Jacksonville before going north to South Carolina. He may have held the boy for weeks, awaiting a reply.

Most of the early settlers in Jefferson County lived in a land beyond the reach of law enforcement. Virgin forests stood, outlaws roved, unknown health conditions prevailed, and deep swamps concealed. All these straightforward, determined, and self-reliant people had were the standards of the communities from which they came. They defended themselves, their families, and their properties by any means available. They had their own concepts of justice.

In time though, the people of Jefferson County wanted a system of law that provided them the freedom to raise their families, hold property, and roam about in security; but they found enforcement weakened by the wherewithal of the accused to flee to environs unknown. Catching criminals was a problem because large portions of the county were still uninhabited, as they are today. Escaped criminals took to the woods and swamps and often left no trail.

There were still lots of environs in which to flee in Jefferson County—the forests, the river bottoms, and the deep swamps. Lakes, rivers, bays, hammocks, forests, and swamps all intersected the county. With dense forests and vegetated understories, outlaws took advantage of many places to hide, as everyone learned during the last Indian war.

Traditions created problems too, where some offenses were expected to be handled directly by individuals without waiting for the law. The most frequent crime was assault and battery, of which indictments were many. It cut across society, and getting a conviction was difficult because of community standards of conduct in such matters.

Frequently, they dropped the charges, or the penalty was so minor it wasn't a deterrent. False imprisonment was less common, but there were several cases. Murder was an ordinary offense, but the county had few premeditated cases. Sometimes, it began as assault and battery but ended in death. There were cases of murder that grew out of brawls. Several murderers fled to avoid arrest.

The need for good sheriffs grew as the territory grew into a state. The need for a strong jail did too. In 1848, when Jefferson County constructed an adequate jail, they built a two-story, brick jail at the cost of $3,897 at the corner of Madison and Pearl Streets, surrounded by a tall wall.

Sheriffs received 37.5 cents per day for maintaining prisoners at the jail. A primary job of the sheriff was transporting prisoners between the jail and the court, a distance of about three blocks. Escape from the jail occurred, but unfortunately, because of the county's environs, they hardly ever recaptured the escapees.

Mostly, his prisoners were white. It was unusual for him to hold slaves because masters usually dealt their own punishment. But if they jailed slaves, such as the boy, they reimbursed the sheriff 25 cents a day. By state law, they allowed a slave "half a pound of salt meat or beef per day and a peck of good Indian corn a week." It appears prisoners had to prepare their own food.

As sheriff, the county paid William using existing fines and "special" fees. They expected him, during local elections, to transport election returns to Tallahassee, drawing four cents a mile. It was his job to notify road commissioners of their appointments made by the county clerk. For every notice he delivered, he received fifty cents and mileage at ten cents a mile.

He also rendered services to the probate judge, to act as an administrator ex officio for a deceased person's estate. They compensated him for summoning grand and petit jurors.

Citizens expected the sheriff to use raw frontier punishment for enforcing the laws. He was paid $2 for whipping a prisoner under a court sentence or containing a person in a pillory. They paid him $3 for nailing a prisoner's ears to a post, $5 for branding, and $10 for the ultimate punishment, hanging. The punishments were handed from the judge to the sheriff for the sheriff to handle. They meted out punishments of all kinds behind the high wall in the enclosed jail yard.

In May, William's older daughters rushed in a flurry of skirts and shawls to meet other female students at Mrs. Ferguson's home, the headmistress at Jefferson Academy. Ellen, sixteen, wore her best sage green gown and Florrie at fifteen her dove gray one. Their skirts were full to the ankle but were not the bell shape which came later. Both rushed down the porch stairs, through the front gate, and into the street, talking a blue mile. The rest of the family hurried to dress and leave for the parade as the young women of the Academy planned their annual march to the courthouse for their May Party.

At the courthouse, a large crowd gathered as William, Mary, and the rest of their children flowed into the flood of people to welcome the "Queen of May" and her court. They crowned Miss Williams queen, and later the crowd walked to the College Green, which may have been another more eloquent name for the area back of the school which was once the militia's parade ground. They spread a banquet. There was fried chicken, turkey, green peas, chicken and rice, biscuits and marmalade, and cakes, including a pound cake with sweetened wild strawberries for topping. Mary had sent her plates of food earlier by James and Val.

Christmas came, and the family gathered in front of their home's hearth to decorate a tree, a German custom learned from the Lightseys. Recently added may have been two of the modern kerosene lamps which helped light the room, adding to the candles on the mantle. Over the hearth, Mary decorated with boughs of pine while at the table which William usually used for his desk, Ellen, Florrie, and Sarah, eleven, painted pinecones.

Together, the family added the pinecones, bird feathers, and red holly berries to the tree next to the hearth. Julia Ann, three going on twelve herself, added bird feathers. She reached as high as her arms allowed. The boys had collected feathers all year long.

From Zech, Mary took three-month-old Henry, who was beginning to quarrel, and she sat in the rocking chair. She handed him a wooden spoon, which he clumsily grasped, satisfied for the moment. She watched all the surrounding activities. Zech stared about the room, pulling on his earlobe, and stepped forward to help his sister Sarah add holly with its berries to the hearth.

Christmas Eve was always family time, and they later

exchanged gifts. The children sat on the floor with their backs to the fire, which huffed and popped. Earlier, little Etta threw in sticks of lighter until someone realized what she was doing. It was a roaring fire, and the room was aglow. Their shadows danced on the surrounding walls.

Later, Mary sat next to William in chairs facing the children as Mary opened a gift from him. He wrapped it in old newspapers and twine. She pulled from a small box a beautiful indigo portemonnaie made of satin with a silver clasp. With her upturned mouth forming a knowing smile, she opened it and looked into its satin-lined cavity and met his eyes. She pressed the little clasp, creating a sharp click. He knew she loved it.

She and William gave each of the girls a new dress. In fact, they were store-bought dresses of calico. Florida was booming, and so were the Andrews. The girls opened them all at once and jumped up, holding their dresses in front of them, twirling, squealing, and chattering their thank yous.

The boys got various items of need, such as spurs and hats, but eighteen-year-old John Slicer got a brand new saddle. It would come in handy since John had lately been working for Old Jesse. They passed John's old saddle to the youngest boy, barely old enough to ride on his own. Jesse got the hand-me-down.

Several weeks later, Mary and William got up as the sun peeked into their curtained window. It was a day like any other. William got dressed while Mary pulled on a wrapper and went to the kitchen to start breakfast.

Ellen met her there, and Mary said, "Good morning, Ellen. Did ya sleep well?"

Ellen replied, "I would have if Florrie hadn't talked all night. I hope she finds her a deaf husband someday, because if not, he'll get no sleep." She grinned and winked at her stepmother.

Ellen put on a pot for coffee when Mary said, "I can manage here. Can ya go ahead and get the kids up?" Ellen nodded and disappeared.

Mary loved these early quiet moments in her kitchen. The night before, John Slicer had got the wood cookstove ready. All she had to do was light it. She sat in front of the grate of the open stove, watching the flames kick up, feeling its immediate warmth while she drank a glass of cold milk left from the morning before.

The drafty old log kitchen warmed, and she waited for the coffee pot to boil before adding the coffee. Next to the stove were split logs of dry, aged oak cut into one and two-inch wide pieces, ready if she needed them.

She heard the girls talking and laughing in the house, but as she leaned down to close the flue damper so the hot air could circulate around the firebox, she heard a commotion in the house. Looking toward it, she slid a pan of bacon off the fire and went inside to investigate.

The commotion was coming from the boys' room, and William was there questioning James.

John Slicer was missing. He wasn't in his bed or anywhere they could see. Ten-year-old James was saying, "Daddy, I swear. I thought he went to bed. He came in late after everyone was asleep, and I heard him messing around, but I fell asleep."

William frowned. This was unusual. The boys had curfews, and though John had pushed his boundaries a few times, he was always home by the time they got up. Lately, they had not been policing his curfew. After all, he was eighteen.

Later, at the courthouse, William discovered John Slicer and a man had gotten into a drunken fight the night before. The other man was critically hurt, though Dr. Palmer said he could possibly survive.

John Slicer disappeared suddenly and completely. William sent messages to everyone he and Mary knew, but John vanished into thin air. They kept waiting, but he didn't return. He took Jesse's saddle and left behind the new one he had gotten for Christmas.

Several weeks later Mary quietly observed William as he sat in front of the fireplace staring at the flames. He hadn't read to the family in weeks. The boys filled in the gap, and James was reading something in the newspaper.

Her household grew somber and was mournful as the weeks turned into months. In the spring, while William was home for dinner, she quietly watched as he took a strap to six-year-old Zech and scolded him about a missed chore.

"Zech, what's wrong with you? You've gotten where you're as sorry as our town drunk. He sits around waiting for others to do his work." He paced while Zech whimpered.

William added, "He thinks others will feed and clothe his family, but you know as well as I do those children walk around here in rags, and it is as much an embarrassment for them and their mama as it is for the town. All because their daddy shirks his duties." Zech, crying, looked at the floor as his tears splattered on the oak boards at his feet.

"Look at me," said William. "Do you expect others to do your chores for you?"

Zech gulped air and said, "No, sir."

William added, "Well, go on and get'em done." Zech left the room almost at a run by the time he entered the hall.

Later, after William was at work, Mary brought Zech into her kitchen. They sat at the table, and she reached for a biscuit from a plate covered with a white cloth. She said, "Honey, you know your daddy is still on edge about John, don't you?"

He nodded as she turned the biscuit on its end and made a hole in its side, pressing its insides with her finger to make room for syrup. She added, "But you still need to pay attention to your chores. Being slothful is a sin of omission, and people who are slothful ignore the special graces our Lord gave us, such as compassion and kindness."

She took a little jug of cane syrup and poured a dab on a saucer. She took a pat of butter and creamed the two together with a fork. Taking a knife, she scrapped the creamed butter and syrup into the hole in the biscuit, which she handed to him. He immediately took a bite of the tiny dessert.

She continued, "Today you might overlook your chores, but later when you're older, you may even overlook your charity to others. Do you understand?" He nodded as he nibbled on the biscuit.

Mary added, "You need to pay special attention to what is expected of you."

Mary thought about William and his own special hell since John Slicer left. She added, "Your daddy loves you, but he's worried if you shirk your chores now, it will only get worse." Zech was now looking down, fiddling with the biscuit.

"Look at me, Zech," she added. "Your Father does not want to see you afflicted when you grow up because he failed to teach you right from wrong while you were young. Do you understand?"

Zech nodded. After he finished the biscuit, he asked if he could go. She nodded and watched him bound from the room. Mary got a cup of lukewarm coffee and sat at the table. She couldn't get William or their household off her mind.

Outside, Zech joined his brothers and a couple of neighborhood boys hard at play in their make-believe comings and goings. With stick swords, they crashed through the hedge in the back, shouting and stabbing at each other. Today they were pirates, extra noisy ones. William was at work, and she noticed lately the boys played quieter when he was home.

William disappeared into a cocoon he built for himself. The little fellows didn't understand what was going on, and now when around him they grew somber. Everyone moved around their home as if walking on eggshells.

Weeks later, there was a reading and concert in the courthouse upstairs in the courtroom. The lecture was about General Washington, and the concert followed with strings, a flute, and a drum with music from his era. The rousing pomp and circumstance of the faster tunes brought about stamping and knocking from the audience. Mary looked at William, but he wasn't himself, though he was smiling. She knew William would have otherwise shouted and stamped in time, but he hardly moved. It was as if he couldn't let himself find enjoyment.

A few weeks later in Monticello, William stepped into the courthouse where there was a mass meeting to select delegates for the upcoming Democratic Nominating Convention to be held later in Madison. William Bailey sat at the east end of the courtroom along with Daniel Bird, who was acting as secretary. The meeting was long, and William stood in the back with Jesse because sitting long made them both restless.

There was a long discussion about the Kansas-Nebraska Act, but everyone agreed. What was good for the northwestern states and the south infuriated the north. The Kansas-Nebraska Act provided for popular sovereignty, which meant Kansas could decide by popular vote whether they wanted to be a slave state, and they were fighting about it in Kansas. Both sides of the slavery debate saw Kansas as an ideological battleground.

The room praised President Franklin Pierce for his appointments in Kansas aligned with pro-slavery views. However, northern abolitionists and non-resident slavery proponents flowed into Kansas territory, both with the goal of influencing its politics.

Monticello's men learned Kansas was bleeding with a series of violent confrontations. Even the abolitionist John Brown himself was there, and Henry Ward Beecher, the husband of writer Harriet Beecher Stowe, took with him a shipment of wooden crates labeled "Bibles" but which were in fact Sharps rifles. Afterward, an anti-slavery group in Kansas formally rejected the Kansas legislature and elected their own legislature based in Topeka.

After this, Kansas was the site of dual governments, the other in Pawnee, Kansas. Said Bailey in the front of the courtroom, "President Pierce refused to recognize the new government!" The crowd of men roared, whistled, and applauded the action.

Border ruffians from Missouri, a slave state since 1821,

flowed into the new territory while abolitionists joined Free Staters. Bailey added, "The partisan violence is mostly along the Kansas-Missouri border."

William leaned toward Jesse and said, "The Lord knows I wouldn't want to be the sheriff there!"

By the end of the long meeting, the town elected forty delegates to attend the Madison convention which would be held in April.

Summer came, and many times Mary, William, and the rest of their family wondered if John Slicer had gone south. The swamps of South Florida provided a haven for those who wanted to disappear, though the situation between the settlers and Indians there heated again. They discussed it ad nauseam at her kitchen table, the dinner table, and on the porch in the evening until mid-fall, when Mary was pregnant again.

She could stand it no longer. One Indian Summer night while she and William sat alone on the front porch, she seized the opportunity. "William, you and I both have got to change our attitude toward the other children. We cannot do anything about John's disappearance. He is gone, and we can't change that. But we have our other children to consider, and they are losing the sparkle in their eyes. They are suffering as much as we are."

She placed her hand on her stomach and added, "I would hate for this next little fella to come into our family with so much sadness." Wide-eyed, he looked at her belly and then at her face.

She had not told him until now. William grinned, and she placed her hand on top of his. He continued to rock, and she knew nothing more needed to be said. He needed time to think.

Their rocking chairs quietly creaked back and forth until the yard darkened and the crickets and cicadas sang.

The next evening the family sat on the porch, and William read aloud a new book entitled *The Life and Voyages of Christopher Columbus*, by Washington Irving. He began, "*Christopher Columbus, or Colombo, as the name is written in Italian, was a native of Genoa, born in the year 1435, of poor but reputable and meritorious parentage.*"

James said, "Where is Genoa?" As William explained, Mary realized he was already trying.

By 1856, while William was sheriff, the family prospered like the town. The mid to late 1850s were good for Monticello and the surrounding county. There were no Indian problems in all Middle Florida, though they fought farther south. Florida's general land office extended its cadastral survey into their reserved lands. With settlers close behind, war broke out once again in 1856, a war of smaller battles and skirmishes downstate.

To the settlers, south Florida was open territory. By 1855, as settlers continued to push farther south into the state, the US Army destroyed a Seminole plantation west of the Everglades. The Indians struck back near Fort Myers, and the Third Seminole Indian War began.

Jefferson County men joined the ranks of several companies during 1856, including the Carters, Walkers, Howells, Oglesbys, Driggers, Parkers, and Williams. Many of these men, including Isham Walker, served in Captain John W. Brady's company. It is possible Mary's brother George W. at twenty-three joined Capt. Robert Bullock's Company of Florida Mounted Volunteers on September 11th, 1856 for six months. They raised the volunteers to suppress the Seminole uprising and were stationed at Fort Mellon, present-day Sanford on the St. Johns River.

According to records, George's horse died from injuries on November 13th, 1856 while scouting; they remounted him on the same day. Discharged at twenty-four as a corporal on September 10, 1857, they reinstated him on June 1st the following year when the unit's former corporal Elias Jernigan deserted.

Mary couldn't help having a soft spot in her heart for her brother George, who was more like her own child than a sibling. George was born during the Indian uprisings of the Second Seminole War when she was 14. Mary always felt George was hers, mainly since her mother reeled from the extra responsibilities of the Indian attacks and Mary's father's absence. It left little time for her children, three of whom were six and under. She had seven children when George was born.

Mary remembered how he did everything earlier than the others—how he tried to form words as young as three months. Now, he was a man and going away to war. Mary was as frightened by this prospect as she was by her own boys.

Fort King National Historical Park map, Personal Photo of Marker

Many of the towns in north Florida grew into small cities. By the end of the year, Florida's general assembly carved Taylor and Lafayette counties from Madison County.

Monticello was no exception to the growth in Middle Florida, which was untouched by the problems in the peninsula.

Adding to her main street running north and south, smaller roads developed off the main, such as Dogwood and Pearl Streets which built eastward for two city blocks.

To vanish months earlier, John Slicer, according to family lore, rode northeast after he and a man got into a fight, leaving the other man seriously injured. John fled because he thought he had killed the other man. So, instead of embarrassing the family further, especially his father, who was a lawman, he left for Blackshear, Georgia. Blackshear is west of Waycross and east of Valdosta.

At the time he disappeared, John Slicer's father William was a constable and may have been sheriff. In this story, he is the sheriff. One wonders, though, why John fled to Blackshear, and there is no explanation except Mary had second and third cousins living there. It was a rapidly growing area of Georgia. Settlers were still moving into the region.

John arrived as the new county of Pierce formed from Appling and Ware Counties. Many families from Colleton County, South Carolina, moved into the area nearby. Walkers, Carters, and Lightseys lived in the next county from Blackshear, and John may have sought their help.

Because of other family lore, though, it is uncertain if William and Mary knew he was there. One wonders if the family kept his whereabouts from William because he was a constable and/or sheriff and the information would have placed him in an irreconcilable situation.

In Blackshear, about 116 miles northeast of Monticello, John changed his name to John Livingston. He also met and married Emily Dowling. They married on a Sunday on his 19th birthday, March 2nd, 1856. She was seventeen. By May 1857, their first son was born, so they named their baby son William Henry after John's father William. They may have originally named him William Henry Livingston, though.

William and Mary also welcomed their newest addition. Laura R. Andrews, their ninth child, was born May 11th, 1857 in Monticello. Several weeks later, a comet illuminated the sky. Fearful, people had called it a doomsday comet, but William read in the newspaper the comet appeared as far back as 1456. Still, people worried about the comet's heat and advised anyone who would listen to have no refuse near their homes in case of incineration.

By the fall and still no sign of John Slicer, Mary noticed the differences in her husband. Though he worked to control his temper with the children and to spend more time with them, he was still visibly more withdrawn.

Thirteen-year-old Sarah was with Julia Ann and Etta running an errand, and the boys were gone too. The house was quiet with the baby Laura and the toddler Henry sleeping. Mary seized the opportunity and napped herself, a much-needed nap since she was pregnant again for the tenth time in less than fifteen years.

A couple of blocks away, the boys ran into their sisters. "Julia Ann," said Vollie. "I know how you can get that thing on your lip to go away."

Five-year-old Julia Ann bowed her head and raised her hand and handkerchief to her mouth, trying to hide the ugly, oozing fever blister. Sarah, who was standing nearby talking to girlfriends, noticed the teasing and pulled her five-year-old sister into the folds of her skirt. "You boys go on. Leave her alone."

"But Sarah, we were trying to help," said Vollie. Around him stood Zech, Jesse, and several similar snickering neighborhood ruffians. He added, "All she has to do is run down one of those red-headed Hamricks from Elizabeth and kiss him." The boys erupted into laughter, and Julia Ann burrowed her face far into Sarah's skirts.

The mob of boys moved on, talking and ribbing each other. Sarah knelt and took her handkerchief to see if she could help, but the fever blister oozed. "Come on," she said, and they went into the house. "Mama will know what to do."

Later, after the children were in bed, William and Mary sat on the porch talking. "Mary," he said, "I will not run for sheriff again. I've decided it."

She replied, "I'm not surprised. It is a thankless job."

The moon cast moving shadows on the street in front of the house. The fragrance of the tea olive shrub near the porch was strong. In the night's silence, they could hear their creaking chairs above the crickets and cicadas. She added, "I think the worst was all your duties unrelated to protecting people. So much paperwork."

He nodded. "And worst of all were the taxes, or at least the collecting. I have to take people's money even when I know that times are hard."

After a few minutes of listening to the night sounds, Mary found herself deep in thought. His news not to run was no surprise. The night he whipped George Riley weighed heavily on his mind. The local court found Riley guilty of manslaughter, and his punishment was two months in jail with thirty-nine lashes to be administered by the sheriff.

She also remembered her father's comments about William's strife over the disappearance of John. He said William may be questioning his own role as a father. He may be blaming himself.

"A penny for your thoughts," said William.

"Oh, I was wondering what you planned to do after the sheriff's office?"

"Well, I don't know, but something will come up."

She smiled because it always did.

Within a week they were at Elizabeth with her mom and dad. Her father's sister, Aunt Mary Jane, was widowed. Mary's Uncle Stephen Lightsey had passed away, and they were at the cemetery next to the church. It was a windy day; Mary's dark blue dress billowed and ballooned, as did all the ladies' skirts.

The men stood holding their hats as the preacher prayed at his grave. William looked down the line of his children to Mary at the other end. Her profile with her bowed head made him ponder the fifteen years they had been together. So many pregnancies. The last one was harder, and she was getting on in years. Though pregnant again, Mary's dress with its high waist showed nothing. After this pregnancy, though, he vowed to himself to be more careful.

In November, William came in one afternoon with big news. The nation had elected its fifteenth president and vice president, James Buchanan and John Breckinridge. President Buchanan basically accepted the Southern view of slavery, but the vote to elect him was close. Much of the country disagreed with his view.

Also, because William did not run for a second term as sheriff, in the same election Jefferson County elected someone else for his job. William served a two-year term as sheriff, stepping down in the fall of 1857.

Several days later, while the family sat around the fireplace, as was customary, William sat at his desk and with the kerosene lantern read from the paper. "The Supreme Court agrees with the south. Dred Scott and his family are to remain slaves. I guess this endorses slavery."

Silence ensued, and he looked at his children. A few stared at the fire, and others stared at him. He added, "It also says there is a rumor the family of his original owners plans to purchase all the Scotts and free them."

He added, "But who knows if their owners will agree to the sale? They haven't in the past." The fire cracked and popped in the silence.

Ten-year-old Vollie asked, "Daddy, Britain freed their slaves by buying their freedom from those who owned them. Why don't our government do it?"

William quickly corrected, "Why 'doesn't,' you mean? It's because the south has a powerful voice in Congress, and they don't want to sell their slaves. Like Dred Scott's owners don't want to sell theirs. It would never pass Congress. Slaves, to a majority of Congress, are property; and many consider it a property rights issue."

In the silence, the burning oak logs popped and cracked. William stared at the fire and worried if the war would come. "If it does," he thought, "I hope it comes sooner than later." He looked at his four sons James, Val, Zech, and Little Jesse, ages twelve, ten, eight, and six respectively. He looked at Mary. She was staring at them too.

Later, the news at the dinner table was all about the railroad. They hired 370 slaves to clear a route connecting the St. Marks rail in Leon County. It would move eastward through Jefferson and Madison. Meantime, a shipload of rails arrived in St. Marks on January 25th, and they sent them by the St. Mark's rail to the intersection of the new rail line.

The people of Jefferson County saw the need for better transportation. Locally, as early as 1834, Florida's citizens bought more than $100,000 of stock in the Florida Peninsula and Jacksonville Railway Company. The venture failed because this rail was never built. Now the people of the state were building the Florida, Atlantic & Gulf Central Railroad, which was run by a five-member board.

Despite having two Jefferson County residents on this board, they were unable to convince the remainder to run the railroad through Monticello. Monticello was too far north, only eight miles from the Georgia line. The county's local people were livid and threatened to pull their considerable financing.

One night in 1858, the following spring, the household arose to the frantic ringing of the courthouse bell. William quickly pulled on his pants and boots. Simultaneously, Mary pulled on a wrapper as the kids flowed into the room. Ten-month-old Laura still slept with them but was wide awake.

William grumbled, "This better not be another calf tied to the bell." He realized all his boys were there, standing in their long underwear. "At least it's not my boys," he thought.

It wasn't a calf this time, but it was much worse. Downtown Monticello was on fire. That night, the business district of Monticello burned to the ground. Portions east, west, and south of the courthouse were untouched. Also untouched was the Presbyterian church. All the men within the sound of the bell could do nothing for the business section. So much lost!

The next afternoon, Mary and the children walked downtown to see the outcome. From the courthouse, they could see all the way to the Presbyterian church. Everything in between was a pile of smoldering devastation.

The aftermath of a similar Monticello fire years later in 1875. View from the Courthouse to the Presbyterian Church, Florida Memory Collection

#

Chapter 5
To Take One's Leave, 1858-1859

In the fall of 1858, the family hunkered down as wind and rain lashed the walls of their home. Earlier, they had closed and fastened the window shutters because everyone was certain this storm would be a good one; and it was. Outside, it poured buckets.

At the fireplace, they listened to William read. He was almost shouting. "It says here, *after only 24 days, the Butterfield Overland Mail Coach rolled into San Francisco with mail from St. Louis.*" He looked up at the kids. "It took only about three and a half weeks. That's a record!"

Said eight-year-old Jesse, "I bet I could ride it faster!"

Shaking his head, twelve-year-old James said, "Probably not, 'cause you'd need sleep, let alone fresh horses all the way."

Jesse thought about it—when a gust hit the house and made it shudder. Everyone sat up extra straight. The rain on the roof was thunderous, and William shouted: "This one's blowing like great guns!"

The next day the Andrews felt sorry for their friends and neighbors, especially those who depended on their cotton crops. The hurricane soaked Middle Florida's cotton and ruined it. Trees were down everywhere. For the Andrews there was minor damage.

Later in November, when their Indian summer lasted into winter, the railroad tracks reached Capitola, thirteen miles from the St. Marks rail. There was general excitement throughout the county, but people were still mad about the railway bypassing Monticello. In retaliation, they withheld their monetary support for the line.

With winter near, Mary's father prepared his fields for the coming year. To help, James and Vollie skipped school. Mary rode with them to Elizabeth to spend time with her mother, taking Sarah, Henry, Laura, and Joseph with her.

She tried to visit once a month. Because Jesse frequently came to town, she saw her dad often, but not her mother. It was also good to be her mother's child again. To be home was nostalgic and a good feeling—manna for her soul.

The next evening, she and the kids and her parents went to a party at the Kinseys northwest of her father's home. Almost all of Elizabeth was there. Outside under a 'lean to' stood a table of refreshments with bench seating both inside and out, though it was chilly. A fire was indoors in the fireplace and outside in the yard.

Inside, they began the Virginia reel; a row of boys, including her James, faced a row of girls, including her Sarah. The head couple danced through the others to take their place at the foot. Mary's father lit his old cob and went outside to the fire surrounded by men.

On a bench, Mary sat between her mother and sister Susan. Her mother said, "Sarah is turning heads, Mary."

Mary watched her daughter as she twirled, and she noticed Jacob Hartsfield was definitely interested. "Well, she's only fourteen, but I guess we need to watch her closer."

The entire household was aware of Sarah's changes. Contradictory and disagreeable, she was restless and always dissatisfied with herself. Any challenge resulted in her flight to anywhere her family was not. Mary thought her behavior absurd.

In December, the legislative session in Tallahassee met, and in response to the events at Harper's Ferry, Governor Madison Starke Perry declared the nation *"headed into disruption."* He called for the reorganization of the Florida militia, and Florida's general assembly responded to his call.

William came home one evening full of news. "I guess this means we are one step closer to a break with the Union." The comment flew right over the younger ones' heads, but Ellen, Florrie, Sarah, James, and Vollie took notice.

James spoke, but the look from his mother told him to drop it. There would be no more war talk tonight at Mary's table. William changed the subject; but Zech, who was unusually bright at nine, looked from face to face before seeing his mother's. He noticed the quandary and looked at his plate.

Jefferson County divided itself into militia districts and enrolled men for militia service. Some districts were justice of the peace districts. They included not only individual militias but also patrols. They made three men in each district responsible for enforcing patrol laws that guarded against the unlawful movement of slaves, keeping watch for abolitionists, and more.

Meanwhile, the Jefferson Rifles reorganized and drilled regularly on the College Green behind the school. Its green turned again into a trodden dirt ground. Mary's brother Henry was a Jefferson Rifle. She saw him more regularly in town. He made a habit of stopping for lunch, and she was glad for the company.

It was an unusually warm January in 1859. As administrator, William sat long hours at the living room table working on

David Woolf's estate papers. Sunlight from the window fell across his notes.

Though no longer sheriff, he still did this job for his old friend. Woolf must have been a friend, because years later William's next to the youngest son Henry traveled to Texas with several of the Woolfs and his Aunt Susan Pillan's family. Woolf Creek runs close to Elizabeth, though today many spell it Wolf Creek. Mary brought William a cup of coffee and tiptoed out.

Though home more often, his household chores and community work kept him occupied. His employment at this date is uncertain. The railroad may have previously hired him. For the past year, the railroad had moved across the county, now drawing close to Walker Mills, which Mary's brother Henry owned and which is today known as Drifton.

Days later in late January, Henry, J.J., and George came to dinner. Her brother William was not there because he had married Amanda Porter the year before. He was the first of her brothers to marry. Their daughter Clifford had been born the previous November.

Mary looked at Henry, thirty-five and unmarried. Handsome like their father, dark-haired, and tall like the Carters, he passed a plate of biscuits to Sarah who was sitting to his right. "I rode to Braswells yesterday, and they are laying cross ties there." His excitement was because Braswells was only 2.7 miles west of his mill.

The railroad's progress amazed everyone. A few days later, William and Mary rode on a Sunday afternoon to see the spectacle. She still wore her Sunday clothes, a full skirt of dark ochre and a white blouse. Her navy blue bonnet shielded her face from the sun. Once there, they sat in the buggy surveying the work. "This reminds me of when we came down from South Carolina," she said. "They were building a railroad from Charleston to Bamberg. That was thirty years ago. Time surely flies."

Said William, "And now Monticello will have its own railroad and depot." Monticello won its dispute with the new railway. The company agreed to run a spur from Walker Mills to the east side of the city. The entire county was excited with the transportation possibilities it provided. The new railway was their link to the Atlantic ports as well as to Gulf ports. The rails also provided an easier way for new settlers to move into the county.

A Buggy Ride - James Arch Andrews, grandson of William & Mary, family photo

On March 17th, all her siblings were there by her side as

Mary watched her father kneel and cup his hand on their mother's cheek. It was over. His Elizabeth, his wife of thirty-seven years, perished.

It was more than Mary could take. Overcome and speechless, she slipped from the room and stepped into her family's central gathering place.

Something seemed wrong, though, about entering this room without her mother. Mary laid her right hand on the long table, feeling its smoothness—the worn, smooth wood of all those years of palms and fingers and plates of warm goodness and steaming foods.

She glanced at the hearth and almost expected to see her there, her mother leaning over it, with her hand on one hip, stirring a big, steaming pot. She remembered her mom's excitement the day her dad brought home a cast iron stove. She had earlier eyed the invention at Palmer's store, but there wasn't enough money. Her father waited until the harvest of a lucrative cotton crop, and he and the boys brought it home for her birthday one fall afternoon.

She wasted no time. By the next evening, the men had installed it. That night, instead of lifting and moving the hot, heavy iron cookware from the hearth as she had done since she was a child, she and her daughters cooked standing up, without bending or squatting.

All those years. Here where the family met to dine, to worship, and to visit with friends. Those moments when their dad read before retiring for the evening. Thirty-six-year-old Mary closed her eyes.

Something shifted inside her. She shivered and pulled her shawl closer. She dropped into one of the straight-backed chairs, laid her head on the table, and sobbed. She felt it in her core. Today, her family's central gathering place was cold and empty, and her mother was not there to provide comfort. Nothing would ever be the same.

It is uncertain what took Elizabeth's life, but in 1859 there was an American pandemic of cholera, which spread via contaminated water. Cholera caused a sudden onset of profuse vomiting and diarrhea, followed by rapid death. It had stricken Monticello before in 1832, when the *North-Carolina Free Press* of Halifax on September 18 said, "*The sickness that prevails now is an epidemic or Cholera Morbus.*" The article was about Monticello and Jefferson County. Cholera was usually a quick death, but Elizabeth's death appeared to not be as quick. She had time to tell her family that she wished to be buried in the churchyard cemetery (according to her obituary which ran in the *Family Friend*). She could have died from malaria, which was more common for their area.

All the next day, people appeared at their home, bearing their sympathy and plates of food. A few came in buggies, others in buckboards, and a good many on horseback. Her parents had lots of friends and colleagues. They came from all directions, using the roads and walking paths which ran from house to house in Elizabeth.

Inside, Jesse sat in a chair by his wife's coffin, a simple pine coffin he and the sons made. Outside, the children laughed and played, oblivious to what was happening amongst the adults. Jesse noticed none of it. He stared blankly and received his guests with a weak smile and expression of gratitude for their coming. Outside, the adults gathered in small groups throughout the sandy yard and on the porches. They filled every available table in the house and on the porch with food.

That afternoon, they followed the coffin into the churchyard cemetery to a nook of shade and dappled sun. It was cool but comfortable underneath the spreading oak hammock. Standing beneath, with all her brothers and sisters surrounding her, Mary looked up into the branches covered by their green resurrection ferns and spotted there a cardinal, a female cardinal with its reddish-brown wings. It looked down at her, and Mary remembered her mother's words. A cardinal means someone who has passed wants you to know they're thinking of you and looking out for you. Looking up through tearful eyes, Mary smiled at the spiritual messenger.

Weeks passed, and Mary felt like she was walking through water. She cried when alone but kept the family home going. Earlier, she overheard Zech complain that his cornbread was dry as an old maid's kiss. He got his ears boxed by his dad for the comment; even so, it made her smile. They missed her, and she knew she had to snap out of this sadness she kept locked in her mind. It wasn't like her to wallow in this feeling of hopelessness anyway.

He was right about her cornbread. Corn is not ready to grind into meal until it is dry enough, yet she used it anyway. As her mama said, it makes a stubborn bread. She thought a lot lately about her mama's sayings.

Mary knew what she had to do. She needed to go see her father and remember the wonderful memories. He probably needed it too. That night, standing in her white cotton gown, she said, "William?"

In the pale candlelight, he turned to see what was the matter. He knew she had something important to say.

"I need to get away. I want to visit daddy for a couple of days." Standing in his long underwear and still wearing his white cotton blouse hanging to his thighs, he instantly agreed. He felt it too. The next morning, she took the buggy. Joseph was still nursing, so she took him with her.

It was a beautiful day, and from her carriage she took her time guiding the horse. In a dyed-black dress with its fitted bodice forming a V over her trim waistline, she had her figure back from birthing Joseph. The dress had a full skirt with a high boat neckline and long bell-shaped sleeves with black cotton lining to cover her arms. The ride on what is now known as Bassett's Dairy Road was relaxing. She needed this.

She waved at the Bellamy slaves, who all waved back, as she made the left turn headed straight to Elizabeth. Later, she got to her once-favorite part of the trip, the oak hammock that housed the old church and the cemetery—where her mother lay. She stopped and stared at the newly banked grave but did not get out. She wanted to save it for later with her dad.

The little church may not have been there. Older members of the family who were still living in the 1960s, such as Judge Terry Lewis's grandmother, said the church burned in the 1850s. Mary may have only seen the graves left behind, because they may have built the next church on what we call today Bassett's Dairy Road, where it still sits.

She called to Nellie, slapping the reins against her backside, and moved on eastward through the canopied lane.

At her father's home, Mary pushed open the front gate and could not help noticing her mother's flowers. Her garden was so special, and it reminded her so much of her mother's many hours there.

Jessie stepped onto the porch and read her mind. "Imagine the flowers in heaven. The thought gives me peace I'll see her again." He stepped down the stairs. "Mary, I've gotten so many letters of sympathy. She was truly loved, and not only by all of us."

Mary saw a stricken man, a shell of what he had been. "Daddy, let's ride to the cemetery."

Without hesitation, he joined her in the carriage and encouraged Nellie to pull around. "You know it is good your mama is there right beside my mama and daddy. I've been there regularly. She and I talk." He looked at Mary's round eyes and grinned. "Well, I do the talking, and she listens. I like to sit and think of her beyond the blue sky."

"Daddy, I've always thought their spirits were there looking down from the oaks."

"Either way," Jesse said, "it gives me peace."

When they got to the cemetery, he helped Mary down from the buggy. At her mother's grave, she saw someone had placed flowers there and had a large log turned on its end for sitting. She instantly knew her father had done it and transplanted a tree near the log, a dogwood he dug up. She dropped to her knees as her black skirts billowed on the ground and added flowers of her own, picked earlier, a bouquet of goldenrod, her mama's favorite, because they lasted so long and were so plentiful.

It was fall. Back at her family's home, she and her dad joined her sister Jane, who fixed dinner. The three of them sat down to ham, peas, and potatoes. Mary thought it a sweet conversation about the wonderful memories of their mother. It did her heart good.

Later, on the porch, their dad took a nap while the two sisters sat with their brother William. Mary had news they hadn't heard yet. "William told me yesterday the railroad got 35,000 tons of iron rails and three new locomotives."

"How far will that get it?" asked her brother.

"Enough to extend it forty-five more miles, or to near the Suwanee. They think they can finish the new line by next summer."

A few days later after supper on their porch in Monticello, William read the paper to Mary and the kids. "It says here John Palmer's store has *'Just Received per Steam Magnolia, sugar-cured hams, super-fine flour . . . tomattoes, Scottish ale. . . lager beer in bottles,"* and even *"mint julips in bottles."* He looked wide-eyed, surprised about the latter.

Mary frowned and shook her head. Five-year-old Henry wrinkled his nose and asked, "What's a mint julep?"

Mary said, "Something for grownups."

He fell quiet again because it was a cue to quit asking questions. Though they did not universally practice it, for some subjects his parents believed children should be seen and not heard.

William read, "Herring, Fennell, & Shehee has *'embroideries, collars, & sleeves,'* plus *'a large assortment of bonnets, trimmed and untrimmed.'* It also says here there's *'a large supply of hoop skirts,'* and even mourning goods." He stopped and looked again at Mary. "Mama, I believe the people of Monticello have money to spend."

"Too much, if you ask me." Yet she planned to go to Herring, Fennell, & Shehee's the following morning.

The next day, Mary and Ellen walked to Herrings. Ellen was twenty. Lately, John Davis, who was three years older, spent a lot of time courting her. (John's mother would become Mary Grantham, wife of John Grantham. There is uncertainty, though, about John Davis's father. There were two county men who could have been his father—Benjamin and Dennis.)

Inside the store, they saw bolts of fabric on a counter. Mr. Herring moved toward them. Said Mary, "Good morning Mr. Herring. Do you have any fabric in British English gray?"

Herring pulled out bolts. While they looked at his selection, another customer entered the store. It was Betsy Howell Walker, Uncle Joel's wife. Betsy, who had been Mary's friend for years and was about her age, quickly joined them. There was a rush of greetings, hugs, conversation, and an invitation to supper.

Later, as Mary and Ellen left Betsy and Mr. Herring, Mary noticed the display of mourning clothes near the front. She was still wearing hers from her mother's passing but had lately noticed the worn skirt. Still, she would only be in mourning a few more months, or so she thought.

After dinner that evening, Mary, Betsy, and Joel sat on the porch chatting over glasses of cold buttermilk. Almost all talk was the possibility of war. Mary was glad the children were not there to hear it. They also discussed the state Democratic convention to be held next month in Monticello.

By mid-June of 1859, the town had crowds of people shoulder to shoulder on its sidewalks and streets. The air shimmered in the smoldering temperatures, climbing by 9 o'clock in the morning. Joel said, "The devil himself must have exhaled upon this land."

Side by side and dressed in their black dress suits, Joel, Jesse, and William walked on the wooden sidewalks, tipping their hats to ladies who floated past in their dressier gowns. Tall and rangy, Jesse spoke as he wiped the perspiration from his forehead: "Surely rain's coming. The humidity is rising."

Monticello hosted the Florida Democrats and their state convention. Future Governor John Milton of Jackson County was its chair while Charles E. Dyke, editor of the *Tallahassee Floridian*, served as its secretary. Jefferson County alone had sixty-seven delegates, which included its largest planters, merchants, and professional people from throughout the county.

Even so, there were other political issues boiling in Middle Florida. Jefferson County's Democratic leaders, some of the wealthiest and most influential planters in the state, opposed the Whig's principles of state-supported banks and high protective tariffs on manufactured goods. They also believed in the state's rights theories of John C. Calhoun and felt Florida possessed the right to secede from the Union whenever its citizens called for the action. Many Floridians considered Jefferson County the "banner" county for the Democratic Party of Florida.

Mary and the girls were downtown among all the people in their finery, their stylish buggies and clothes. Said Florrie, "Don't you just love the new belle styles?"

All Mary thought, though, was how everyone else had to take to the streets to keep from brushing dust against those fine skirts. The women with their bell-shaped skirts sashayed up and down the wooden sidewalks in the shade of the roofs overhead.

Still, she admired the gowns. There were colors she had never seen in fabrics. They called one mauve, and it was all the rage. All her older girls, Florrie, Ellen and Sarah, were ecstatic.

Sarah begged for a mauve short-waisted jacket to wear with her light brown dress.

Monticello and the county boomed. Stores were well supplied. The warehouses waited for the next cotton crop; and families were in town, making their required purchases. Mary remembered the earlier days when the Indians roamed amongst them and Monticello was simply a frontier town. It was a simpler time and life, some of which she did not miss, but some of which she did. She thought of her mother and how much she wished the two of them could stroll together again. She missed her mother today, and her father was off with William.

The next day William waxed on ad nauseam about the proceedings. "They endorsed the Dred Scott decision and also President Buchanan's defense of our Constitution." He and the boys were unstoppable, and neither she nor the girls could get a word in edgewise. Mary was so tired of it. "They voted on the Kansas question and endorsed Governor Perry."

Zech pulled at his earlobe and asked, "What's the Kansas question?" All the daughters rolled their eyes, but James about busted a gusset explaining its significance. The women were sick of all the political talk. It was all they had heard for weeks.

Early that fall, during the first cold snap, a relief from the monotonous heat, William and Mary sat in front of the fireplace in their room. William said to Mary, "Earlier tonight, I didn't read aloud something that bothered me. Entitled 'Horrid Disparity,' it said a preacher reported on Ocala and how its saloons were full of soldiers to receive their pay for the last

Indian War. Well, while one soldier was there for several days getting gloriously drunk, someone went to his home on business and found his wife dead. Mary, she had her baby, and it was still alive. That poor woman birthed her own baby by herself and faded away."

He stared at the fire reflecting on his face. "They say we cannot prohibit men from drinking without withdrawing their liberties, but I swear—" His voice trailed off; and in the silence she heard his rocking chair stop creaking. He sighed. "Something needs doing soon. The drinking is out of hand."

Mary said, "Was the baby still attached?"

"I don't know. The paper didn't go into details."

She felt tears stinging her eyes, and she dropped her head. Life for women was a hard go.

William stared at Mary, who at thirty-six was still pretty but whose eyes crinkled at their outer corners and whose richly dark black-brown hair still had no gray. She combed it out for the evening, and it lay dark and wavy on her shoulders. "I didn't want the children to hear this, but I knew you would hear it from your family or friends tomorrow, so I saved it. If we don't get a handle on this problem with drunkenness and its effect on families, I daresay eventually they will outlaw alcohol all together." She nodded.

"Remember when they limited the number of toasts at the Fourth of July celebrations? That was only the beginning. If people can't control themselves, the government will do it for them." William probably knew it had happened in other states. Laws were being enacted in Ohio, Illinois, Rhode Island, Massachusetts and New York. Vetoes and the courts intervened, but it wouldn't be much longer before they stuck.

Fall came, and another cold front moved through. Trees lost their leaves, except the evergreen live oaks and pines. Mary arose early for the solitude.

Sitting in her kitchen, she drank leftover cold milk and planned the day's meals, an apple cobbler for dinner today and maybe apples to sweeten the ham, though she hesitated to serve two apple dishes together. Yet this would finish the dried apples. She pulled out the apple basket.

Whereupon Julia Ann bounced in, and all Mary's peace disappeared. She loved teaching her girls to cook, but Julia Ann's mouth never stopped. "Mama, want me to help you with those apples?" The stream of verbal consciousness began.

"Sarah Ann Fulford's mama won't let her help in the kitchen. She says that her mama doesn't want her girls to work now because they'll work for the rest of their lives. She wants them to be children while they can still be children. Anyway, I told Sarah Ann I liked to help with the housework." Julia Ann stood with a smug look on her face.

Mary said, "Well, her mama is right about working for the rest of their lives, but still, how will they ever—" Julia Ann cut in and changed the subject before Mary could even finish.

"Julia Ann, you must stop cutting people off when they talk. No one will want you around if you do all the blathering." Julia Ann stared at her wide-eyed. "When you are talking, you aren't listening. People like to talk as much as you do." Julia Ann looked at her shoes and teared up. Mary dropped to her knees in front of her.

"Honey, you don't want to be snubbed by people. No one likes a bore. People who talk too much are boring. Practice listening to other people talk." She held the sobbing child and wished she didn't have to be so frank with her, but it was true.

They tried to get Julia to understand this about herself. Mary stood and took Julia Ann's hand.

"Come on, let's make apple cobbler together. Get me flour, baking soda, salt, lard, sugar and cinnamon, and I'll get the milk and chop the apples." Mary put on bacon and broke the eggs. They still had breakfast to make.

"Mama, can I chop the apples?"

"Sure."

Julia smiled, and Mary noticed she bounced back quickly. William said it was a trait of his mother's.

Later that morning, Mary noticed two-year-old Laura was lethargic. As she put her to bed, she saw that a red rash had formed on her face. Mary knew what it was—Laura had the measles.

She and Florrie quickly sent the other children to Elizabeth Lightsey's home a few blocks away on West Dogwood. Elizabeth and Clara had had measles earlier, and someone who had it couldn't get it again. Again, their home was a safe place for the rest of their children.

They hung blankets to cover her windows. In candlelight, they worked with Laura, who was sicker than usual. With water freshened from the spring, they took turns dabbing her flushed face constantly. In her sleep, Laura frequently cried out.

Her eyes watered as her body, mouth, and face covered with spots and her fever peaked several times. She lay in bed, mostly listless or achy and crying. Overly concerned, Dr. Palmer came several times.

William took his turn and wiped her face with a rag; and from the constant sweating, her straight, sandy blond hair kinked. One minute she shivered, and the next she burned up. Her face reddened with each cycle as she whimpered and cried. Dr. Palmer came again.

"She needs lots of water." But it got harder to keep Laura hydrated. Late one night William dropped to his knees beside the child to pray, and Mary joined him, feeling his body next to hers.

Throughout the night, the child hardly stirred. Mary and William barely slept. They took turns dripping water into the child's mouth from a rag. It looked hopeless.

"Mary, I'm going for Dr. Palmer again."

She nodded in agreement, and he stepped into the hall as a bird flew past. He glanced at Mary.

"When did this bird get in?" But he saw raw fear in her eyes. If a bird flies into your home, death follows. He closed the front door as the town crier called midnight. Mary heard his horse's hooves disappear, though the good doctor only lived four blocks away on Palmer Mill. The two of them returned within moments.

The measles, a viral disease, presents flu-like symptoms and a red rash around the hairline before it moves to the body. Children usually survive. A few die of pneumonia, encephalitis, or diarrhea. For children it has a high morbidity rate, meaning it is common, but it has a low mortality rate.

Adults, though, don't generally survive, because their mortality rate is high. Death occurs from pneumonia and brain inflammation or meningitis, which is why they quarantined Laura to keep other adults from contracting it. In this story, Mary and William had had it previously.

Today, measles are long past because of inoculations. Probably all of Mary and William's children had measles, mumps, and chickenpox. Later, these diseases would protect their children while many adults who never had them would die, especially among the enlisted men during the civil war. Laura survived the measles.

In October, William took a stage to Tallahassee for business. It rocked and swayed while he listened to a verbose stranger with a New England accent. "I'm headed to Tallahassee from Jacksonville. What about each of you?" The other passengers answered, but the stranger wasn't interested. He jabbered about the sufferings of the colored race.

Being well-traveled, he considered himself well informed on politics and the political economy, so when his fellow passengers became silent, the traveler taught them a pedagogical lesson. He felt it his responsibility to give them his 'unprejudiced' opinions on matters of which he had been an eyewitness, or so he said.

William opined that men who talk too much seldom have much to say.

The stranger described the cruelty of overseers in Mississippi, hundreds of runaway slaves in the Georgia woods, the opposition to Negro education, and how some in South Carolina opposed even their Christianity. When he looked outside, his fellow passengers, William included, exchanged worried glances, some with anger. Clueless, the man waxed about the horrors and misery inflicted.

"My friend, what do you do for a living?"

"I am a commercial agent for a northern house with connections in the south. I seek and recover bad debts."

So he's a 'wrecker,' thought William, a man who goes to

bankrupt estates to see what they can resell. The downhill side of slavery, a system that sells its bond servants, breaking up families and moving men and women against their will.

A single woman passenger could stand it no longer. "I believe Negroes remain where they're fed well. They rarely attempt to escape."

Another passenger said, "Not until they commit a crime—and even then, many stay for the whipping, being more afraid of starvation."

From the look on the stranger's face, he was unmoved. The uncomfortable conversation continued all the way to Tallahassee.

After William returned, he and Mary talked about the experience. "Mary, stagecoaches will soon disappear. In the north, they're only used where trains do not run."

They discussed Monticello's new depot and the tracks between it and Walker Mills. Though the railroad passed far to the south, the company built a spur to connect the town to the main line. Its brick depot, probably similar to the one still in Lloyd, was almost complete. It was a masonry vernacular one-story brick building. It provided the county access to Atlantic and Gulf coast seaports.

Lloyd Depot, built within a year of Monticello's Depot, still standing, personal photo

Monticello continued to grow, as did all of Middle Florida when the railroad sought to connect Tallahassee to Lake City, which was previously called Alligator. They may have involved William from the beginning of the railroad, but it is uncertain until the local newspaper wrote about him in the fall of 1859. It described him as the depot agent.

The railroad came to Monticello, but Tallahassee had a railroad line for years. The first in Florida, it extended from Tallahassee to St. Marks. William and his first wife Elizabeth probably used it when they came to Tallahassee in 1837. Its first cars were drawn by mules and its later cars by steam power. Its major freight was cotton.

As early as 1852, Congressman Edward Cabell, who years earlier asked William to work on the census, worked on the planning for a trunk and central railroad line running from

Pensacola to the St. Johns River. He first planned it to follow the Bellamy Road through Waukeenah in Jefferson County.

In 1856, the legislature made the road possible through the Internal Improvement Fund, but the subsequent road did not follow the Bellamy Road as planned. Instead, it followed a more workable route through the heart of the county south of Monticello through Lloyd, Aucilla, and Walker Mills, which Mary's brothers Henry and J.J. now owned.

Upset because the railroad bypassed Monticello, the city's people threatened to withhold their local funding, which was significant, so the railroad added a later branch, a 4.5-mile spur ending in Monticello.

While the rest of the country fixated on John Brown and the Harper's Ferry fiasco and the coming November presidential election, Monticello focused on its first depot and train service. The *Family Friend*, in its October 29th issue, announced the 'Grand Opening' for November 5th, 1859 and encouraged the town to turn out for the first ever *"iron horse"* to come to Monticello.

For a mid-October, it had been cold all week long. Mary couldn't remember when it had ever been this cold this early. William and James arose each morning and built a roaring fire in each bedroom's fireplace, including the oven in the kitchen outside. By the time she and the girls got up, the chill was off, though the rooms were still cool. Outside, frost glistened on the fences, shrubbery, and rooftops.

That night, after the children's bedtime, she and William sat in front of the hearth. "Well, they found *Sambo*. Your cousin David Walker found him while on business in Albany."

In the firelight's warmth, she nodded. "So where is *Sambo* now?"

"He's at the jail. Mary, you can't tell me they don't want their freedom even when their owner treats them well. I can't believe Thomas Palmer ever hit another person in his entire life."

"Poor *Sambo*."

Unprepared for the early cold, she and the older girls darned and knitted socks and mittens. William and the boys made a trip to her dad's, where they spent the day splitting logs, which they brought in by buckboard.

They nested and stacked them on the fence line. It had been a busy week for all. It was a job done every year over several weeks, but it was usually accomplished without this haste because no one expected such an early cold snap. Outside, Mary watched two cows walk down Palmer Mill Road. Steam rose off their bodies.

They had a good fence. Cattle and errant mules still wandered around town, knocking over anything in their way. Mr. Chase at the newspaper complained in his last issue that they knocked over several gravestones in the city graveyard.

We know from the 1860 census that William and Mary lived next door to Martin Palmer and several doors away from Dr. Palmer, who lived at the corner of South Jefferson and Palmer Mill. The Andrews's home could have either faced Palmer Mill at the corner of Washington Street or faced Washington Street, though it could have been farther away. There were fewer houses on the streets then. For example, between Martin Palmer's home in the 1860 census and Dr. Palmer's, there were only two households listed—William Budd's and Margaret Budd's. Today, between those two homes are six households and a government building behind the old high school.

She remembered when they offered William his new position with the railroad. It was a wintry day like this. Midday, someone knocked on the front door. Removing her apron, she opened the door to a smiling Edward Cabell. Returning the smile, she bid him come inside from the cold.

Edward Cabell was a man of medium height and build, with dark hair which parted and swept to one side. He had light-colored eyes and was a handsome man. Dressed in a heavy, black, wool frock coat with a white shirt and a black cravat tied at his neck, he stepped into the hall as a wind rushed in after him. Mary closed the door as he removed his hat.

"How do you do, Mrs. Andrews? Is your husband home?" Before he finished his request, William stepped into the hall.

The two men retired to the parlor at the front of the house. She knew Mr. Cabell and William had talked earlier about a possible new position at the railroad; and she remembered how much she hoped Cabell, who was president of the Pensacola & Georgia Railroad, had good news.

She knew William loved a challenge, and Monticello's first depot certainly was demanding. As its new agent, he devised the systems needed for its expected commerce.

Today, everyone was talking about next Saturday. Exciting times for Monticello, they had almost finished the new depot. William worked nights lately, while cotton came into the depot to await the first train.

Earlier in the pale morning light, Mary noticed William's excitement. With a grin on his face, he tiptoed around the bed, trying to keep quiet as he dressed. He stumbled on a chair, and she heard whispered expletives. The first rays of daylight and the fire he built bathed the room in a rosy glow. He dressed while she snuggled into the covers, waiting for the room to lose its chill.

It was Saturday, November 5th, and as he explained earlier, he wanted to get to the depot as soon as possible. Its warehouse was full of several wagon loads of cotton waiting to be loaded.

Before, people took Jefferson County's and South Georgia's cotton harvests to Tallahassee, where they loaded them on the train and took them to St. Marks. Or they took them by wagons south to Magnolia on today's Old Plank Road. In either port, they stacked them into oceangoing ships that sailed for domestic and foreign markets.

For the railroad, 1859 was a good year for cotton, unlike the last year when a hurricane roared through and destroyed the crop. William hired several men to load, who planned to meet him at the depot before 6 pm for the train. He needed to be early, though, because they expected the entire county too.

Everyone wanted to welcome the train and see the new depot. People had stopped in ever since they installed the telegraph. It followed the rails, and its operation mesmerized even the most sophisticated. It was not unusual to see at least half a dozen people standing by the window to get a glimpse at the telegraph operator as he took and sent messages.

By mid-afternoon, a crowd formed. Waiting, they scattered everywhere, stacked many layers deep around the depot. People even climbed trees, sat on their horses, and stood in their buckboards for a better view. William's own family came into the depot and waited in his office. He would later place them in an advantageous spot.

A few minutes before 6 pm, they heard a click-clacking sound mixed with a chuff, chuff, chuffing far off to the south.

Its shrill whistle echoed through the woods, and a bell clanged. The rumbling and bells drew louder.

The crowd grew quiet, and there it was—a speck in the distance on the track. The train was barely visible in the woods below Monticello. From its huge front funnel-shaped stack belched black and white smoke. Again, its whistle pierced the late afternoon air.

Most of the town's children and the enslaved had never seen such a contraption. Someone had draped it in colored streamers and wreaths of flowers. The crowd erupted into shouting and applause. A small band standing at the northern end of the platform struck a song.

Giddy with excitement, Mary and her squealing children stood south of the platform. She held baby Joseph, who cried with all the noise Next to her was Florida holding two-year-old Laura.

William suggested their position since they could not join him and other dignitaries on the platform, and it was a pleasant spot to watch the approaching train. On the platform, she saw William with his top hat looking every bit the successful man he was.

The James Rose, facing north, rolled to a stop beside the depot, squealing its brakes on the shiny new rails as its engineer released its steam. Those closest pressed back into the crowd. The entire town roared again. They would nickname the engine "Old Bailey" in honor of Jefferson County's entrepreneur General William Bailey.

The spur ran to Walker Mills, now called Station 3 by the railroad and later known as Drifton, where it connected with the new railroad. It ended in Monticello with no further rails north. North of Monticello was Albany, Georgia, and the terminus of the Georgia railroad. For years, there would be no connection except for a stage line which ran from there through Thomasville and Monticello, ending at the depot in Walker Mills.

Later, Mary sat quietly as she nursed baby Joseph. He had reached that magical age when a baby stares and grins. He finished eating, but she wasn't ready. She tickled his face and wondered if this would be her last baby.

William was often busy and tired. He didn't come a-calling as often as he once did. He was almost forty-eight, and she wasn't a spring chicken either at thirty-seven. She was tired, too; and they had discussed it. She didn't need any more children. Her body was plainly worn out.

She looked at Joseph, who was still not asleep. He stared at the embers. She wrapped him and herself in her navy shawl and softly sang, *"Old King Cole was a merry old soul, and a merry old soul was he. He called for his pipe and he called for his bowl and he called for his fiddlers three."* Joseph nodded off.

Four days later, on a Tuesday, William came back just after leaving for work. Inside, next to the hearth and talking to Florrie as she ironed a shirt, Mary realized something was wrong. William looked pensive and hesitant. "Mary, you need to go to Joel's house. Betsy needs you."

She reached to touch her face. "Oh my goodness, is he getting worse?"

"He's gotten much sicker and is fading."

She placed the iron on a metal plate and took off her apron. Barking orders, she was out the door within minutes.

Several weeks earlier, Mary's Uncle Joel, who was closest to her in age and was more like a brother than an uncle, became ill. His wife Betsy, Mary's closest friend (whose mother was a Lightsey from Colleton County), sent their son eleven-year-old George Berry to let Mary know. Mary returned with him to sit with Joel and help Betsy with the household, especially with their one-year-old daughter, Florence Augusta. That was in September, and since that time Joel got better, but not much.

William rode to Elizabeth to fetch Jesse. The two raced into town along with David and Littleberry. Later, their sister Mary Jane followed with George and J.J. All spent the rest of the evening there in a vigil while the women and Dr. Palmer tried to save him.

Around 10 pm, there occurred a fearsome clap of thunder, though there was no lightning seen. It shook the household, rattling windowpanes. They all ran out onto the porch in the warm evening air, but there wasn't a cloud in the moonlit sky. They wondered if what they had heard was an explosion, but there was no burning light in the sky anywhere.

Worried, though, William said, "I think I'll ride to the depot and check things out."

Added George, "I'll ride with you." The two walked to the hitching post and left. However, George returned shortly with no news of what caused the disturbance.

A little after midnight, Joel, at thirty-six, died.

While everyone was still with Joel's body, Mary slipped outside into the night air. She felt lost and an overpowering urge to flee. Taking a deep breath, she moved down the steps from the porch into the dark moonlit street. Listening to the night bugs, she walked.

Instantly, she felt stooped and struggled to stand up straight, to fight the urge to wither. With her head high and shoulders squared, it was all she could do to get a hold of herself. She tried to push away the dark thoughts and dwell on the wonderful memories of Joel as a child. Oh, that wonderful day the two of them held on to a branch for dear life while Henry dragged them behind his horse.

She chuckled but again remembered Joel was dead, and she cried by the time she reached home. First her mother and now her childhood kin and friend. On the porch she sat and listened to the evening sounds, longing for any refuge it gave from the overpowering sadness.

She had felt more like herself after mama died, but now this. Fighting against the urge to sink into bad thoughts, she questioned: How can it be Joel is dead?

She heard footsteps in the dark. William came home to check on her.

#

Chapter 6
Happy, Healthy, & Prosperous, 1860

Last evening at the depot, William and George found only the night watchman. Relieved to find no explosion there, William and the watchman retired to a cup of coffee, but neither could figure out what had happened. The next day, when William and the sheriff stopped for fresh oysters at the new restaurant by James Rogers, he learned a meteor hit somewhere in Madison County.

The *Family Friend* reported in its following issue, "*Many of our citizens were startled on Tuesday night last about ten o'clock, by what they at first supposed to be a heavy clap of thunder, but which, on ascertaining there was no speck of cloud in the heavens, was found to be a report of the explosion of a meteor. Persons by whom the luminous body was seen at the time of its burning asunder, represent it as being 'a splendid spectacle'—reflecting a light for a few moments that almost rivaled that of the noonday's sun.*"—Madison Messenger of the 4th inst."

Later that winter, by the fireplace, the family gathered and read. The children decorated the mantle with boughs of pine and painted pinecones. They put up a tree, but Mary hardly noticed. She went through the motions with little joy.

Still, the family tried to keep any form of normality. With everyone hungry for news, Monticello's new local newspaper did not disappoint, as William read from the table with the kerosene lantern.

Mary remembered her mother's thoughts about reading. People no longer sat and talked. Everyone now had to have something to read, but in her day, they talked or told stories from memory. No one had to have a newspaper or book to be entertained. Both her parents felt the art of storytelling eventually would cease because of all the newspapers and books.

Later, the family sat and talked. Mostly, they remembered Uncle Joel. Mary reminisced about his youth. Said William, "He dropped out of the race for tax assessor and collector, though he hated doing it."

Later, they discussed the death of a two-year-old child in Macon. Said Mary, "We cannot be too careful about our children. Who knew eating friction matches would kill a baby?"

Susan's husband Isaac came down with his own illness. By the second week of January 1860, William and Mary were again at a graveyard, this time in Madison. Isaac Pillans died, leaving Susan with at least five children ages three to fifteen. Mary stayed a few days with her while the capable twenty-year-old Florrie ran the Andrews's household.

Thankfully, Susan's oldest, John Clarence, fifteen, helped her hold their family together, a household of boys and one girl. Susan's youngest, Lizzie, three, the same age as Laura, went home with Mary to stay for a while.

With another tragedy in Mary's family, she stopped in Elizabeth. The fresh air and change of scenery lifted her spirits, as did her visit with her father. Worrying about someone else's problems always helped her with her own blues.

Winter came and went as the January 28th, 1860 issue of the *Family Friend* reported the delightful weather in January "*led to believe that Spring has usurped the throne of Winter.*" It also reported a Democratic meeting would be held at the courthouse in Monticello on Saturday at 11 am to elect delegates to serve in April at the state convention in Tallahassee, where delegates would be elected to the national convention in Charleston. The paper said, *"In all probability, the approaching "National" Convention will be the last ever to assemble..."*

But as is often the case in Florida, the weather turned on a dime, and it disintegrated again with freezing temperatures and blustery winds as one arctic front after the other pushed through. Florida's humidity made it seem extra cold.

William enjoyed his work at the depot. He did not miss the labyrinth of the sheriff's responsibilities. More straightforward and easier to deal with, the day-to-day challenges of being a railroad agent provided methodical work.

The day warmed into the 70s, normal for this part of Florida. The air cooled in the evening with frost on the ground and warmed by mid-afternoon. Sitting at his desk in the depot office, he wore one of the new sackcloth jackets, a three-piece navy suit with two cloth buttons, two exterior pockets at the waistline, and another interior left breast pocket. Underneath his matching notched-collared vest, he wore a bleached white muslin shirt.

The suit, made of cotton and lined with the same, was cooler than his old, heavier coats. It being impolite to appear in shirt sleeves before a lady other than his wife, he owned two of these suits. All the shopkeepers and bankers wore them now. Much more sensible for Florida's heat, its style is still a mainstay in today's business world.

The depot sat on the west side of the tracks, between Pearl and York Street at the end of High Street, according to an 1884 Sanborn map. These narrow-gauge tracks, also called the

Branch Road, led south to Walker Mills. The depot was probably similar to the one still standing in Lloyd.

Lloyd Depot, Oldest Depot in Florida Still Standing, Florida Memory Collection

According to the company's minutes dated 1858, the railway company, strapped for cash, had thirteen depots to build. Most likely all the depots were similar, cut to the same mold, some larger than others, except for Tallahassee. They made the capital city depot architecturally roomier.

Tallahassee Depot, 1880, Florida Memory Collection

Last fall the railway company finished construction of the depot's long, rectangular brick building with its two gabled ends. It included a waiting room and office at the south end and a large freight room, covering two-thirds of the building, at the other.

The freight room stored commodities such as cotton, supplies, and produce awaiting the next train. They stacked this freight high against its walls, leaving a lane for wagons to pull through. A dusty haze hung in the light which entered through its two wide doors.

At the north end, a large door stretched wide enough for a wagon to enter and be unloaded. Inside, men unloaded the wagons, usually pulled by two large draft mules. Over this north-facing door, outside and with an eyebrow of bricks, it read MONTICELLO. This gabled end had a brick wall below but a wooden triangular gable and shingled roof above. His children thought its door looked like a gaping mouth, but William thought of it as a new gateway for the county's abundant agricultural commodities being shipped to other parts of the country and the world.

On the sides of the building, the eaves overhung the long walls below. On the side opposite the tracks, they stuck out only a few feet, but on the track side, the roof line projected eight feet beyond the brick side of the building, allowing enough space for a train to pull alongside and for freight and passengers below to remain free of the elements.

When the train arrived, a long tunnel of motion and industry was created between the depot and the train as people and animals moved back and forth between the station, over the platform, and to the cars through a haze of steam created by the parked locomotive. At the north end of the platform, a long ramp ascended and was used for rolling a hand truck of luggage.

William's office had room for his desk, a clerk's, and a ticket window overlooking the walkway and tracks. Underneath this window, another desk for the telegraph and operator sat.

The waiting room was partitioned from the office by a tall wall, which rose short of the ceiling. This gabled end of the station included two large nine-paned windows, giving the waiting passengers an unobstructed view of the oncoming train. Because Monticello's terminal station had only one train that made the trip daily on the singular branch road, the train usually came into the station backward, pushing its cars before it.

Inside at the ticket window, passengers came to do their business while the freight men came to do theirs at a back door on the eastern side of the depot. The ticket window had iron bars. A weight inside the window could lift or lower to allow packages to pass through. In the waiting room on the south end of the depot were benches around its perimeter, where men, women, and sometimes children waited.

The windows and doors of the depot provided cross-ventilation. In the winter, though, a large black barrel-shaped cast iron stove, which resembled a big man's pot belly, easily warmed the entire office and waiting room. The stove sat on the inner wall about halfway down. Its pipe entered a square tube of bricks which disappeared into the ceiling.

Sitting on a brick base, the stove used coal, the same as the train engines. Though the waiting room and office smelled of fresh-sawn wood, one also detected a strong hint of oil and sulfur. The stove emitted a ticking sound made by the burning coal, while below, the floorboards creaked under the weight of its moving occupants.

To the left of the stove, hanging on the wall, a board said: "Arrival of Train" and "Departure of Train." Here William or his clerk posted a paper showing the time for each. The train left Monticello daily at 4:30 am headed to Tallahassee. It returned around 6:30 pm headed the other direction for points east or as far as the railroad reached. In time, though, they simply posted a sign under Departure. It said, "30 minutes after arrival," but most people could not read, so they came to the window anyway. After a while, changing the departure was senseless.

The floors were hard, unfinished, and wide-planked oak; the interior walls and partition were unfinished yellow pine. The outdoor brick platform on the train side ran the length of the station. There were benches outside, too, for the waiting customers.

Supervising a crew of six men, William negotiated and kept track of the area's stock, which shipped to markets north, east, and west. Parts south of Middle Florida were mostly uninhabited. The warehouse stored incoming and outgoing cotton, grains, baggage, supplies, and even the mail, all going both directions, away from town and into town, the same.

Everything north and nearby that had once been shipped over the old muddy and dusty wagon roads was brought to this station and shipped by rail. Busy days, such as during the cotton harvest, required dawn to dusk effort with little chance for rest. On those days, Mary or a kid brought William his lunch. However, in February, with no cotton to ship, William found more time on his hands—only to deal with the railroad's debt problem.

Almost dark, William came home after a long day. He apologized to Mary, but the editor of the *Family Friend* had spent time with him earlier to discuss the railroad tax, about which everyone in the county scurrilously argued. He and the editor also began a new game of chess, a game William learned in the coffee houses when he was young.

William explained this was not a tax but simply a debt. During a referendum, Jefferson County's citizens saddled this voluntary debt upon the county. Thence, the county received an equivalent for the money, stock in the railroad. William explained until he was blue in the face, but all Jefferson County knew was that they had something to pay, and no one liked it.

William added, "I have to get up early to go to the courthouse tomorrow. The state tax assessor will be there to receive the tax returns for the year." Out in Elizabeth, at James

Walker's house, the tax assessor set up the following Wednesday. Mary saw William was weary from his long day.

A few days later, on a wintry day, the skies threatened snow. Julia Ann and Laura were in the kitchen helping with supper. Said Julia Ann, "Mama, will it snow?"

"No, it doesn't get cold enough here to snow. It only rains."

"I wish it would snow. I wish I could see it."

"Well, now it's too dry to snow."

Julia Ann wrinkled her forehead. After the rain moved through the night before, temperatures dropped into the low 20s. To Julia Ann it was a puzzle, because in the north, when the temperature dropped to below freezing, it snowed. So why didn't it snow in Florida? She wasn't the only one. The rest of the kids were confused too.

William explained, "Ahead of the front, it is warmer and more humid but too warm to snow, so it rains. When the front pushes through and it gets cold enough to snow, the front takes its moisture with it. Thus, behind the front, it is too dry to snow." It puzzled the kids, but still, it almost never snowed.

In late February, Mary walked into the parlor, where she and the girls were working on Ellen's trousseau. In the room, warmed by a day-long fire, Sarah sat to one side in front of the hissing fireplace with Ellen sitting on the other. Betsy, Joel's widow, came to help. Between them, they hemmed a hoop petticoat. Earlier, Ellen had accepted John Davis's proposal for marriage.

Julia Ann talked nonstop, giving hardly enough time for anyone else. Until Mary said, "Julia Ann, there is a bag of potatoes in the kitchen sent from Elizabeth. Bundle up and take them over to Ann Lightsey's." She hoped the extended errand would keep Julia Ann from under foot.

The petticoats gave the gown a bell-shaped skirt stylish for their day. Mary picked up her scissors but dropped them. They stuck in the floor. She looked at the girls and then toward the door for someone coming. They all laughed.

About a month after Uncle Joel's funeral, one evening in front of the fire, Ellen and John offered to postpone their wedding, as convention required. Though Joel was not Mary's brother but her uncle, he had become like a brother; and many in the community thought he was. Mary said, "We've discussed it, and you should proceed as planned."

William added, "We believe that eventually there will be a war. This war might keep the two of you from ever marrying. We think you should go ahead regardless." So decided, the family pushed aside convention and moved ahead with the marital plans, something that would happen repeatedly in the years to come. So much that was considered unacceptable because of propriety or etiquette would be the norm by the end of the war.

The next day, Sarah ironed one of the finished muslin petticoats by the front window while Etta hung another from the top of the door. All dressed in black, they were still in mourning for Uncle Joel, but they proceeded with their plans for Ellen.

On the first day of March, taking the buckboard, horse, and a picnic lunch, Mary, Ellen, Florrie, Sarah and six-year-old Etta rode to Mary's father's house to gather smilax. Jesse could have managed it alone and would have, but Mary wanted the girls to have the same experience she had when decorating for her wedding.

The five females walked from the house to the woods, with Jesse leading his horse alongside. They moved past the field toward the river swamp, all the while looking for smilax, a tender green vine with lobed leaves and tendrils.

Photo of Smilax

The woods were deep and shaded with a sun-dappled floor, and the bright spring green canopy swayed in the breeze overhead where the birds trilled and warbled, peeped, and cheeped. "There, Daddy, look in that water oak. There's smilax draped between it and the tree next to it," said Mary.

The higher vines, the freshest and without the brown spots, were the best ones. Using the horse, Jesse stepped into his saddle and even knelt in it, balancing from his knees to reach for the vine which he pulled. He took the knife sheathed in his belt and cut the vine, letting it drop to the floor of the forest. Mary and the girls anxiously watched, but the horse never flinched.

A good day if only for a chance to forget the sadness, the girls listened to their mom and grandfather tell them stories of a time long past; and if they had heard it once, they heard it a dozen times. "Watch for the snakes. You know they're crawling now."

All the tender green smilax vines they cut would make a wonderful garland to hang over the fireplace. Jesse had earlier cut white spider lily fronds and wood fern. They loaded everything in the buckboard, but not before sprinkling the smilax with water. They loosely stuffed it under the seats so it would stay out of the sunshine and remain fresh.

"A madhouse," thought William. Women everywhere decorated the parlor and dining room. Betsy Walker sashayed by to help Ann Lightsey. "Hello, William!"

"Good morning, Betsy. Where's Mary?"

"In the girls' bedroom with Sarah." Fourteen-year-old Sarah, emotional all week over her dress for the wedding, wanted a new one, but Mary stood firm. Being Ellen's day, pretty Sarah would not upstage the bride, or so Mary said to William.

William couldn't see how, anyway. Ellen's new gown for the wedding fit her beautifully, a beautiful dark green, fitted with a V waist and a fashionable full, bell-shaped skirt.

That afternoon the family gathered along with John Davis's family in the Andrews's parlor. The day before, Ellen and John had applied for a certificate of marriage and were about to tie the knot.

They stood in front of the mantle decorated with the delicate green smilax and white roses cut from Ann Lightsey's garden. Amongst the decoration were several lit candles.

Mary and the girls also decorated the front door and the front gate. They kept the rose buds for Ellen's bouquet and used the fully opened roses on the hearth. On the dining room table and sideboard, they spread more smilax.

Defying convention again, Ellen wore the dark green satin gown, a delightful contrast to the white rose buds she carried. Tucked in her bouquet of roses were three little satin black ribbons for the memories of her mother, grandmother, and uncle.

Julia Ann constantly chattered throughout the bustle of the pending wedding. William noticed her smiling dimples, and he knew she loved every moment of this. There she stood off to the side in a rose-colored dress reaching to her knees with her white muslin pantalettes and stockings peeking out beneath. Of all his girls, Julia Ann reminded him so much of his mother.

With Ellen's green satin and lace bonnet framing her face, William thought her beautiful—and from the look on John's face, the most beautiful girl ever. William looked at Mary, and she smiled at him and noticed his misting eyes. He smiled and took her hand in his, pulling her closer. They linked arms and watched as their oldest daughter married. They had not had the honor of marrying off John.

Mary thought about Ellen's mother and hoped somehow she looked upon her oldest daughter on this most special day. W. H. Strain, the current judge of the probate, married Ellen and John on March 2nd.

Nothing tells about the wedding or even where they moved to live, but a John Davis worked for a family of Fulfords in

Taylor County in the census records for 1860. Ellen probably moved there with him. It is certain, though that she did not live with Mary and William when the census enumerator visited them later in September.

We also know John, of prime age to go to war, soon disappeared from any later records. He vanished with as few records as found when he appeared. Records show a John T. Davis who joined the 6th Regiment Florida Infantry at Mt. Vernon Arsenal near Chattahoochee and who died in Knoxville on December 29, 1862, but whether this is Ellen's John Davis is uncertain.

A couple of weeks later, William must have been working long hours at the depot. In the March 17th issue of the *Family Friend*, it read, *"The business done upon the Monticello Branch Road during the past six months has been immense. . . . Our Depot Agent, Mr. W. H. Andrews, is busy all the time from early morn till late at night, loading and unloading. . . . The salary allowed the Agent at this depot, is not in proportion to the service rendered, and we think it ought to be increased."* It appears they appreciated his labors.

Lloyd Depot Warehouse Door (wide enough for wagons to be pulled through), personal photo

One extra warm day in late March, William sat on the porch with Mary and all their family, listening to him read the paper. He cherry-picked the articles when he noticed a notification. He said, "Well, I'll be. *Out of the whole grand army of the Revolution which fought under Washington and his Generals, there are now living, throughout the entire country, only one hundred and sixty-five.*" He said, "My dad fought in that war, and he's been dead for decades."

Mary added, "And my grandfather did too."

In April, Mary, wearing a full butternut skirt and white blouse, accompanied William as they walked to the courthouse to purchase land from Elizabeth Hurst, a first step to building a home of their own. William felt her joy. It was unusual for her to gush like this.

Oddly, Mary is the only grantee on this land, located in the woods on the west side of Jumpie Run Plantation where the Jefferson Arms Apartments sit today. The property only contained two acres, though, and the family may have purchased it to build a future home.

The property was near the railroad station, a short ride for William. It was well out of town, and Mary may have wanted to live in the countryside again.

Did William feel that if the country went to war and the south lost, properties owned by those who bore arms against their government might be confiscated? Or if he didn't return, would the property bypass probate?

Sadly, though, the war, less than a year away, meant the house would never get built. The property sits only about a mile and a half from the courthouse.

The railroad, though, continued to build east toward Lake City. By May the crews started laying tracks westward between Lake City and the Suwanee River, where the eastward tracks reached.

The nights, though late in the spring and unseasonably cool, gave the family more time around the fireplace, with Mary and William in chairs and the kids on the floor. William, usually by the table with the kerosene lamp and the *Family Friend* spread before him, watched his kids stretched all which-a-ways. Thirteen-year-old James lay on his stomach with his chin propped on his clasped hands. Fourteen-year-old Sarah sat with her back to the wall and her legs stretched in front underneath her full dark purple skirt.

Everyone got real quiet, waiting. Ten-year-old Zech, who sat with his legs crossed Indian style, asked, "Daddy, anything more about Pike's Peak?"

William searched through the four pages and said, "Yep,

here it is. *A correspondent of the Boston Journal, writing from Brown County, Kansas says the roads in this—"*

But Florrie interrupted: "I thought Pikes Peak was in Colorado?"

"It is," said William, "but they may have late snows and need to wait for it to melt. *The roads into this vicinity, leading west from the river, are white with the wagons of Pike's Peak emigrants. They are camped in large parties along the waters of almost every creek, waiting for the grass before proceeding further.*"

The kids loved to hear about the gold rushes. The one in California even lured William, but thankfully he didn't go. There were several men, mostly young men in Monticello, who went; but they returned empty-handed. Digging for gold was hard work, and by the time they got there, they missed the easy gold.

Mary listened as William read, and she worried that maybe their own boys would fall for this someday, the chance to get rich quickly. It sounded too good to be true, but the young were often optimistic fools.

"*Meanwhile, the reports from the mines continue very conflictingly, and though many are sanguine, the information is by no means satisfactory. . . .*" Thankfully, she thought, they are writing about both sides. I hope my boys are paying attention.

Finished, William folded the paper and rose. "It says here the Odd Fellows are celebrating their fortieth anniversary, twelve of which at the Jefferson Lodge #3 here in Monticello. The town will fill again with outsiders."

Said James, "Nothing like when the Democrats came to town, though."

Mary agreed. "This town was splitting at the seams."

Over a month later, she could not remember the last time when she was so excited. Maybe when they moved to Florida; she wasn't sure. Sitting next to William and their eleven children together, they took up almost two rows of seats in the railroad car. They were going to St. Marks. In fact, over five hundred residents of Jefferson County were going. Everyone laughing, giggling, and talking. So noisy in the cars, one could hardly think. Still, she enjoyed watching the world go by.

Excited to see her children's faces, she watched James and Vollie, who stood near the back of the car with several other boys their age. William forbade them from leaving the car. They had heard of too many mortal accidents where people foolishly jumped from one car to another.

Little two-year-old Joseph stood between her and the window with four-year-old Laura between her and William. Under Mary's seat sat a picnic basket packed for the day. She monitored James and Vollie, though, especially watching Vollie as he conversed with those around him. Witty, charming, and the center of attention, especially with the young girls, he might be only eleven, but he showed a propensity to captivate a female audience.

Palmetto Pioneers

Valentine (Vollie) Andrews, Family Photo

The May 19th issue of the *Family Friend* reported, "*On last Wednesday morning, at an early hour, there was a general outpouring of the homes of Monticello and vicinity—men, women, and children. A railroad train had been chartered for an excursion to St. Marks. . . . was speeding over the track, like a thing of life, with its joyous, merry, laughing freight,—every heart bounding with happiness and prospective enjoyment. . . . passed Tallahassee at lightning speed, and arrived in St. Marks . . . making the trip in two and half hours.*"

They remained in St. Marks for almost five hours. By the river, they ate the picnic she prepared. William, she, and the children all rested after dinner on blankets they spread on the ground.

Since all the news came from Washington, Sarah, fourteen, had questions for her father. "Daddy, tell us what it was like to live in Washington when you were a boy."

Lying on his back and staring into a canopy of trees overhead, William replied, "Well, first, you know I was from Georgetown."

"How close is it to Washington?"

"Not far. A small stream called Rocky Creek separates the two villages and empties into the Potomac. Georgetown sits like an amphitheater on one bank with its pretty wood-covered view of the opposite bank. A bad wooden bridge across the creek allows passage between the two towns. It wasn't unusual to see senators on their way to session crossing that bridge."

"What was your mama like?"

"She was a pretty woman, but most importantly, she was a smart woman, who owned and ran a tavern. This is how I got my education. She paid for it, and every time I got home from school, she put me to work in the tavern."

"What was the tavern like inside?"

"Oh, there were several kitchen tables, about five, if I remember correctly. My sisters and I helped serve. We bused plates of food from the kitchen and cups of tea, coffee, and other libations. Uncle Jesse and I kept its fireplace going all the time in the winter. We lived in the other house which sat on fifteen acres."

"Daddy," asked James, thirteen, "What about Alexandria?"

"That's where my mother came from. The bridge between Alexandria and Washington crossed the Potomac, a wide river. It sat upon crossbeams, and it took nineteen minutes to walk from one end to the other. To use its two sidewalks, you had to pay six cents each way. At night, they lit it with lanterns. It also had two drawbridges to let boats pass underneath."

Asked nine-year-old Jesse, "What's a drawbridge?"

William explained, and he noticed several of the younger children and Mary were sound asleep. He felt a nap coming on himself.

Leaving around 2 o'clock in the afternoon, the family boarded the train. The paper reported, *"Between sailing upon the river, walking, talking, love-making, etc., all appeared to enjoy themselves. There was nothing to mar the pleasure of the occasion."*

After dark, they arrived home, tired, dusty, and completely exhausted. Both Laura and Joseph were sound asleep, carried by Florida and James, respectively. They were late, though, because an accident detained them at the Chaires Depot.

The baggage master, who sets the switch, neglected to do his job. On the return, the excursion train, being the first to pass, lost its locomotive, tender, and one boxcar. The paper said, *"Much excitement and confusion ensued; but fortunately, upon investigation but one person was found injured . . . the fireman."* It did not explain how everyone got to Monticello, except it was after 8 pm, three hours late.

In late spring, William took Mary to lunch at James Rogers's restaurant for her birthday, and they may have eaten venison, the special for the day. Mary enjoyed dressing up and joining him for a meal away from home. She had not been to this restaurant yet, and he came by before noon to pick her up in the buggy.

She waltzed through the front door with her full skirt in sway, wearing her navy blue dress with full sleeves and white undersleeves. The dress had a square neck and was fitted at her waist, where she had added extra crinolines to give the skirt a more fashionable bell shape. Her hair, which she pulled up and back, cascaded to her nape in curls. Obviously, Sarah and the girls helped her with her hair. Grinning, he helped her into the buggy, but she hardly needed him, she being a healthy woman physically.

Mary's birth date is unknown, but from the 1860 census, it appears she was thirty-eight in this year. Though approaching middle age and after having ten children in fifteen years, she still appeared attractive to William.

William may have bought her a windmill for her birthday. People gave practical presents. Windmills had four blades and a tail to turn them into the wind to pump water. They built one at the depot in order for the train's steam engines to resupply with water. He may have gotten a good deal because the railroad required several to be built across north Florida. For days she heard the men hammering in the backyard as they built its tower.

Mary loved it. The clanging and creaking were as much a part of her day now as the lowing of wind in the pines. But tired, she took a seat on the back porch. She let her weight down, heavy into a chair. In the growing dark, bats darted across the sky, soundless, erratic, flickering, and swift.

Mary's girls got supper ready for their brothers, who had not yet come in from their chores. She rested, something she had begun doing lately. William worked late at the depot, and she enjoyed the solitude. She heard voices inside and out as the woods silhouetted against the reddening sky. Everything dimmed. She saw a star and another. She liked to think they were her mother and Joel saying hello again.

In June on a Friday, everyone woke to violent wind and a thunderstorm that shook the rafters. Their boys, who slept in the attic bedroom, came running downstairs as the house shuddered and shook. William stepped on the back porch with a lamp, on the leeward side of the storm's winds. The rain hailed and hammered against the roof overhead. He quickly stepped inside and tried to shoo everyone to their beds, but it was no use.

Half of them, the little ones, piled into his bed with Mary. He sighed and crawled in with them.

"I guess my dad and brother's corn and cotton crops are ruined if this gets to them."

"I reckon so."

Asked six-year-old Etta, "Will it ruin the parade tomorrow?"

"No, I don't think so."

Added Mary, "Now, y'all all go to sleep." Outside the hail stopped, but the rain continued in buckets.

Weeks later, the family dressed early in the morning to be ready for Captain Partridge's parade. Wearing her green checked dress, Mary held Laura's hand firmly. There were so many people in town and so many horses. The men and boys with their steeds ripped through the dust-clouded streets. Even little Laura mimicked her mother, holding a handkerchief to her face. Extremely hot and humid, everyone wanted to see the military parade. Captain Partridge's company of cavalry comprised over seventy-five men, all uniformed. They made a fine display.

James and Vollie left earlier, and Mary noticed Sarah, who looked much older than her fifteen years, wore her best dress for the occasion, the lavender one. Goodness, Mary thought to herself, she must have on every petticoat in the house. Sarah used that special walk designed to float her skirts back and forth like a bell. Oh dear, she needed to have another talk with her soon. Sarah walked ahead of the family with a friend—and she turned heads, heads of the male variety.

#

Chapter 7
Every Set of Three is Complete, 1860

By the end of June, in the sweltering heat, the Democrats held their convention in Quincy. They put forth John Finlayson's name (from Jefferson County) for governor. However, the delegates leaned toward John Milton, of Jackson County, a strong secessionist from Marianna. Finlayson pulled his name and threw his support for Milton.

Because of the heat, Mary moved slowly to conserve her energy, and she longed to spend a day in the country with her father. Sadly, with William's long hours at work, the management of their household fell to her, leaving precious little time for a trip to Elizabeth.

The oppressive month crawled until its end when William traveled to a grand demonstration of the masonic fraternity in Tallahassee. President Cabell approved a half-price ticket on the railroad for any mason who wished to attend.

According to a newspaper column, William, a mason, belonged to one of the oldest masonic lodges in Florida, Hiram Lodge #5, a regular and recognized lodge in Monticello, chartered through the Grand Lodge of Florida by the United Grand Lodge of England.

The Grand Lodge of Florida shows no records of William's membership, but when someone came from another lodge outside of the state, the local lodge rarely included them in their roll. The initial lodge where they joined included them in theirs.

William may have become a mason while living in Washington, DC. However, Wesley Pippenger, a genealogist from the area, investigated but could find no records in either

Washington, DC or Leesburg, Virginia. According to census records, William disappeared from this area before he married his first wife. He may have joined wherever he lived.

After dinner the family gathered on the porch, and James read from the *Family Friend*, "Preparations, we understand, are being made in neighboring towns, to celebrate appropriately, the approaching Fourth of July. We are pleased to witness this continued evidence of patriotism by the people, and are hoping every town and hamlet throughout the length and breadth of our Great Republic, will contribute to the National jubilee."

Jesse looked at his mother, as the other children listened. "He means our town doesn't he, because nothing yet is planned?" She nodded.

"In these days that 'Secession' is the cry in the south…many persons object to celebrate the Fourth of July from the fact that it is the anniversary of a national event in our history, and one that… formed… the American Union—a Union which they hold in abhorrence. Such is not the case. The day is not celebrated upon any such grounds, but as the birthday of freedom—freedom from British oppression and arrogance… that farmers, tradesmen and merchants—the representatives of an enslaved people, resolved 'to sacrifice their lives, their fortunes and their sacred honors' in a noble attempt to rescue a downtrodden and oppressed people from the dominions of a tyrannical king…"

Jesse interrupted, "So I guess what we celebrate is not the union itself?"

William said, "That's right. Our celebrations are for our independence from Britain. Our freedom to rule ourselves."

Added Sarah, "It won't be the same without a celebration."

The newspaper summoned the town through various issues

to rise and plan another glorious fourth. Monticello, well known for its Fourth of July celebrations, waited as its leaders discussed whether there should be another one in 1860, especially with an expected war between the states on the horizon.

Usually, Julia Ann would have asked fourteen dozen questions by now, but Mary noticed she was flushed and quieter than usual. "Julia honey, come here a minute."

Julia, wearing her golden yellow gingham checked dress that stopped below her knees, got up. Mary remembered when Julia had first asked, "Mama, when can I wear long skirts like you?"

"Soon enough, dear, soon enough."

Julia Ann didn't bound but walked and sat in her mother's lap, leaning her head on Mary's shoulder. Her legs dragged on the floor. Mary placed the back of her hand on Julia Ann's forehead and felt other parts of her body. The child was hot. "Julia, I think you need to go to bed."

She knew Julia was sick when she went to bed with no dissension. As Mary followed her, she realized the rest of the kids were staring at her. Julia Ann's spell would last about two weeks this time, as the malaria continued to take its toll.

By mid-summer, all the talk in the county if not the state and the south centered on secession. The men especially talked about it nonstop. The women did, too; but they tired of it. At sewing and shelling circles, the ladies tried to change the subject and dwell on normal activities; though it was harder to do. These were not normal times.

Intensely hot, as a heat wave hung over the south and without a cloud in the sky, William and Mary sat on the porch in the heat at twilight. Inside, it was stifling. William said, *"The 'Family Friend* says several people in Charleston died because of this heat."

"I guess we're lucky we don't live on top of each other like they do in the cities."

He nodded his head, thinking about Washington, and how hot it could get. The younger children were in the backyard, catching fireflies squealing and giggling while the older ones were walking.

In fact, there were many people stirring around, walking in the pale evening air. Henry and JJ joined them. The conversation turned to the election, and William asked about the new Davis Academy created at Walker Mills.

Said Henry, "The program went well. You would have been impressed with the students' addresses, especially David's. William, he said to tell you how much he appreciated your help writing his speech."

According to the July 14th edition of the *Family Friend*, Mary's brother, David, delivered a speech entitled "Passing the Rubicon". David used the metaphor "to cross the Rubicon" to reveal what he believed would be an irrevocable step that would commit the nation to a specific course. The speech, about the consequences of electing a black republican compared the events to Julius Caesar, who indeed crossed the Rubicon River and started a five-year Roman civil war, which resulted in the end of the Roman Republic. Caesar won and proclaimed himself dictator for life.

The conversation moved to Col. Blackburn, whose forty-three-year-old wife had died of typhoid. All four had attended the funeral.

William said, "I think half the county showed up." During a

pause, the four listened to the circulating sounds of the crickets and cicadas. "Well, we sent our railroad application to the general assembly today."

Said Mary, "Why didn't they want a connection with the Savannah Florida Railroad?"

Added Henry, "Though Savannah appears closer, a connection with the South-Western Railroad near Thomasville would serve our purposes better, providing a straighter shot through Albany to the northern rail lines. All Savannah offers is a seaport, and we can send our products to Europe through St. Marks. The line through Thomasville would open new markets and increase competition between the ports and the railroad. We might get better prices for shipping."

Conversation ceased again, and they listened to the cicadas--except Mary, who realized the kids were awfully quiet. She thought she had better investigate.

In mid-July, Mary and her brood hurried toward the courthouse. At almost 10 am, the especially excited Zech and Jesse kept a firm hand on five-year-old Henry, as they talked a mile a minute and moved at almost a run. Mary had trouble keeping up. Ahead were William, James, and Vollie in an immense crowd in front of the courthouse, where stood the Jefferson Rifles, the local militia.

Eighty-five men, including several of her brothers, fell in lines in an area marked off to hold back the crowd. Sarah said, "Doesn't Uncle Henry look grand?" Mary thought so. At thirty-six, with his lofty height and broad shoulders, he was still a young-looking man.

The captain gave the command. Every man stood at attention

with his chest out, neck braced, shoulders back, feet aligned, and gun at his side. They formed perfectly straight lines. She saw her older boys stood at attention too, practicing the stance.

Though dressed in street clothes, the soldiers made a fine-looking lot. The captain led a drill, and the men performed for the crowd as a drummer kept time. The captain yelled 'Fall out', and the men fell out of formation and climbed the stairs to the courthouse. They were there for a short meeting before going to the parade grounds for more practice.

Jesse and Henry rattled about the militia all the way home. William and the rest of their sons joined them for a few minutes, but William peeled off for the depot. Mary noticed thirteen-year-old James's eyes sparkled as he talked nonstop about the Rifles. He had asked William how old a boy had to be to go to war.

James and Vollie worried her the most. She thought to herself, "When this war happens, they most likely will get James, but maybe not Vollie." At ten, she felt certain they wouldn't get Zech. All three boys, though, were itching to go.

Later that evening, William sat in his usual chair on the porch in the balmy, but cooler late afternoon, thanks to the earlier 4 p.m. thundershowers. Quietly, their neighbors gathered on their respective porches. William was holding the paper, and the kids automatically chimed in asking him to read. In the lamplight he looked around at the brood. "I think several of you can begin doing the honors. John has left us, but Florida you can read." He handed the paper to her and pointed to an article.

"*During the recent fighting in Catania, Sicily...*"

One of the little fellers broke in. "Where's Sicily?"

She replied, "Southwest of Italy in Europe. It's an island."

William added, "An island in the Mediterranean Sea north of Africa."

Henry chimed in, "Africa's where the darkies are from."

"...*one of the nuns shot from her window a member of the Royal troops. She fired with such precision of an Alpine huntsman, never missing. The Colonel ordered his men to fire in platoons repeatedly against the windows, but in vain. The heroine remained unmatched, and still kept firing away, killing her man with every shot. Wow!*," she said as she looked up.

Mary added, "My mama was good. When Daddy left for the Indian War, we knew she could pick off an Indian in the same way. Daddy taught her and all of us how to shoot, because we didn't know when we might get attacked. But he said Mama had something special. She took to it right away, but later she admitted her dad taught her how to shoot."

She smiled at William. "Granddaddy said your daddy was an excellent shot, too. That's another reason I married him." The boys rolled their eyes, but the girls giggled. They never doubted their parents loved each other.

Mary got up and asked if anyone wanted something to drink and moments later she appeared with a tray of crockery cups. She moved about the porch quietly. William watched her float by. Her long sweeping skirts of checked cotton swished as she moved.

She was wearing a dark lavender dress she had made herself with fabric from Palmer's store. The bodice fit her well at the waist and her full sleeves with a dropped shoulder were fitted at the top and the bottom near her wrists. A white cotton under blouse with a small ruffle at the wrist and at the top of the neckline added to the stunning, everyday dress. William admired her taste. He thought her still a beauty at thirty-nine.

A few days later, William worked late again. In the evening, Mary sat on the porch alone with a full moon casting long shadows across the yard. It was peaceful outdoors. She loved the solitude especially after the kids were in bed; but lately, William worked long hours. She contemplated going to the depot but decided if work kept him, he didn't need her in the way. In her rocking chair, she listened to the insects' mating calls.

The next night William came home to Mary's apple dumplings. They were in the dining room, gathered around the big wooden table. Seven-year-old Julia Ann talked nonstop, "I made the dumplings. Mama made applesauce and added it to a pan with water, and I added the brown sugar and cinnamon." She held court, and no one else could get a word in edgewise.

She continued, "She let me make the biscuit dough and drop it in spoon by spoon." She grinned from ear to ear and reminded William so much of his mother and sisters. Shorter, like Florrie and Ellen had been at her age, and pretty like his mother, Julia Ann had chattered since the day she uttered her first words. Wearing a dark green checked dress, probably with fabric left from one of Mary's, it reached below her stockinged knees. Her light brown curly hair fell softly around her shoulders.

Later, after the kids were in bed, he and Mary on the porch talked until late. William said, "Julia Ann is a chatterbox. Where does all the jibber jabber come from?"

"I don't know, but it didn't come from my side! The Walkers are a quiet people."

"Well, we had talkers but nothing like her. If she were a boy, I'd think we were raising a politician."

The closer fall came, the more anxiety and angst was felt over the national election of a new president, especially the black republican. Abraham Lincoln, fifty-two, ran against three other men Judge Stephen A. Douglas, forty-seven, John C. Breckenridge, thirty-nine, and John Bell, sixty-five. People worried Douglas and Breckenridge would split the votes, giving Lincoln the win. Douglas, nominated by the northern Democrats, ran against Breckenridge, nominated by the southern Democrats, evidence of a country splitting long before the vote or the war.

The people of Monticello backed Breckenridge, a sentiment most apparent when on Tuesday morning, suspended from the upper portico of the courthouse, was an effigy representing Douglas. On its breast was pinned a paper that read, "*Stephen A. Douglas, The Traitor, to the South, the Union, and the Democratic Party.*"

By early September, Mary saw her tomatoes and beans were finished, as well as her okra and potatoes. Standing in her garden next to a tall okra plant about her height, she was removing its more mature okra pods, testing each with her knife, when she heard someone at the front door.

Wearing a light gray cotton dress fitted at the waistline and forming a V over her smooth stomach, she headed around the house toward the front as she removed her long white apron. She liked these dresses fitted at the waistline, and thank goodness she wasn't pregnant. After ten children, she wondered if she would ever be pregnant again. Also, these full skirts were actually cooler than the more fitted ones of earlier years. She walked around to the front of the house, tucking a loose tendril of hair over her forehead and feeling the wind her skirts allowed.

She arrived in time to greet Mr. Blackburn, who stood at their front door talking to Sarah. "Well, hello Mr. Blackburn. What brings you to our humble abode?"

"Tis the census," replied Mr. Blackburn.

"It's a hot day to be walking the streets. Sarah, fetch the two of us some water. And Mr. Blackburn, have a seat right there by the table on the porch. Mr. Andrews is at the depot, but I believe I can supply the information you need."

He started asking questions right away. "How many people live in the household?"

It appears Mary answered the questions, because for William's place of birth she replied 'Virginia', yet in other censuses, especially the 1850 one, William, the deputy enumerator himself, recorded his place of birth as the District of Columbia.

According to the census, William and Mary live in Monticello with real estate estimated at $300 and his personal estate at $100. They did not list William in the agricultural census, which indicates he no longer needed to augment his income to provide for his family.

Because of this federal census taken on the 7th of September 1860, we know William, forty-nine, a railroad agent, lived in Monticello two houses from William Budd. Next door was M. Palmer, a forty-two-year-old female with no occupation listed and several boarders. On the other side were various merchants, teachers, and even a livery stable owner.

The Andrews' home was near the McCants, Rhodes, Streetys, Palmers (including Dr. Thomas and Martin Palmer), Partridges, and Budds. This was the working class of Monticello. Because several of Monticello's old antebellum homes are still standing including Martin Palmer's and Dr. Palmer's we know William's home probably sat somewhere southwest of the courthouse, possibly on Palmer Mill Road near the west end of the parade ground, which was directly behind the high school, which still stands today.

In William's home, thirty-eight-year-old Mary with his daughter Florida, (nineteen), born of his first marriage, joined his and Mary's ten children including Sarah (fourteen), James (thirteen), Valentine (eleven), Zachery (ten), Jesse (nine), Julia (eight), Henrietta (six), Henry (five), Laura (four), and Joseph (two). Both John and Ellen had married and left home. Apparently, William and Mary did a good job of safely raising their children. None appears lost, yet. A thirteen-year-old white male, named T. Weitz or Welty, lives with the family. He appears to be no relation but needs further research. There are no slaves listed, though they may have hired day help for the household.

William, Laura, Joseph and possibly Henrietta only knew Monticello as their home. The older children probably began their lives in Elizabeth. All the children ten years or older were of school age in 1860. Sarah, James, Vollie, and Zech all attended school, another sign of the family's prosperity. The three younger ones of school age did not attend—Jesse (nine), Julia (eight), and Henrietta (six). With no public school, only private, the four older children probably attended Jefferson Academy, which cost money William and Mary obviously paid. They may not have been able to afford to send the other three. Florida is nineteen and out of school but still living at home at the time of the census.

Mary's fifty-nine-year-old father Jesse, listed in the 1860 census, lived near the Lewises, Grubbs, Clarkes, Kirklands, Lambs, and Bishops, all families out near Elizabeth and

Aucilla. His closest neighbors were James and Winifred Lewis and John and Margaret Polard. Nearby was Nancy Kirkland. Jesse's wife Elizabeth had passed and several older children had left home. Still living with him, though, were Jane E. (twenty-eight); William (twenty, probably William Berry); George M. (his age given as fourteen but is probably an error since George would be twenty-four by this date); David L. (seventeen); and Ann E. Polk, a fourteen-year-old unknown female born in Alabama, who may have been hired to help with the household, but again needs further research. The latter four are listed as attending school, but most likely George was not still in school. (see Appendix 4)

Jesse is listed in the 1860 regular census with no real estate and only $200 in his personal estate. Yet, according to the 1860 Jefferson County agricultural census, a direct contradiction to the population census for the same year, Jesse is listed as having 150 acres of improved land and 250 acres of unimproved land for a total of 400 acres. He also had $2,500 cash value in his farm, $50 in farm implements and machinery, and $664 in livestock.

No longer living with Mary's father were: Henry, JJ, William A, Sarah, Joseph, and Archibald J, all of whom had left home. JJ and Henry live in Dwelling #524 next to their sister Sarah "Susan" Pillans and her family in Dwelling #525. Others nearby include the Ritters, Turnbulls, R. A. Walkers, Blackburns and Baileys. All were families listed as living in Monticello.

Listed as living with JJ and Henry is George, (twenty-five); Archabald, (twenty-three); and David L., (seventeen). The census listed George and David L., twice, living with both their father and their brothers. Henry's property is listed as $8,000 in real estate and $12,000 in personal estate, a goodly sum for an unmarried thirty-five-year-old man. George and Archibald are listed as having $300 each in personal property. Susan, thirty-four, has no property listed, but has $1,200 in personal property. Her husband, mentioned earlier, had already passed away.

Joseph, eleven years younger than Mary and missing from the two dwellings and not listed as living with either of his two sisters or brothers, may have passed away by July 13, 1860. Mary and William named their youngest son, born in 1858, Joseph Edward Andrews. A research question exists. Did Mary's brother Joseph die before 1858?

A couple of weeks later, Mary was in her kitchen with little four-year-old Laura making gingerbread. In the corner on a pallet two-year-old Joseph slept soundly. Julia Ann napped inside. She tired so quickly lately. Mary worried.

Kneeling on a chair seat at the table, Laura bent over the bowl , with a wooden spoon, her thick blond hair pulled back and tied with a yellow cotton ribbon. Though chilly outside, the toasty room held its warmth from the dinner they had cooked earlier.

Mary said to Laura as she licked a little molasses from her finger, "Now mix real good the sugar, molasses, and butter and I'll add an egg."

While Laura mixed, Mary pulled together flour, nutmeg, and ginger in another bowl. The two of them added the two mixtures alternately with buttermilk and soda before pouring the final mixture into an iron skillet. Afterwards, Mary sat and drank a cup of coffee. She got lost in her thoughts. While on the floor, Laura played with a kitten, which had taken up at their house.

Thankfully, Mary had not been pregnant since Joseph's birth

two years earlier. At thirty-nine, she knew it could certainly happen again, but she and William had several conversations about how her body was tired. She worried about having another child. Still not alone, she sat there and enjoyed the few moments of solitude, as Laura played quietly and Joseph slept. Mary noticed she felt less chronically tired as the months passed. Life was better than she could remember, though she missed her mother terribly.

Julia Ann bounced into the kitchen, leaving the door ajar; and a bird flew in, almost like it had followed the girl. Mary frowned at the bird, but said nothing to Julia Ann. Together, the three of them tried to chase the bird out; but it tried to fly through a window. It hit the upper portion of glass and fell to the floor, dead. Upset herself, Mary consoled both the little girls as they cried about the lost bird.

Later that evening, William laid the paper on the dining room table. As he rose, he told Mary and the kids that he had to go to the courthouse. Usually, he left immediately after supper for such a meeting, but tonight he tarried. This meeting, about paying off the indebtedness of the county's railroad stock, strained the railroad's relation with the town people. No sense in getting there early so people could bend his ear. They had done that for days at the depot.

Everyone, agitated by how the road had earlier bypassed the city, still fussed about the Monticello spur and depot built only to get Jefferson Countians to help fund the venture. Everyone knew Monticello had money, and the railroad lacked funding without Jefferson County's help. Quietly, William slipped out the front door while James read the paper in his stead.

After William returned and he and Mary were getting ready for bed, Mary told him about the bird and Julia Ann. He listened quietly as she brushed her long brown hair, but he didn't like to put much stock in superstitions. Still, he quietly wished Mary had not told him.

To Mary, all that human agency and Dr. Palmer's medical skill could give, were administered to Julia Ann. They lingered and prayed she might be spared; and often Mary thought, "If it be Thy will, Father." But sometimes, Mary wondered if the prayer was simply another plea to save her child. She knew about her Father's will. Nevertheless, this was her baby.

Dr. Thomas Palmer

They moved Julia's bed into their room, a brighter and sunnier room. They placed it near their window so she could see the roses outside. Then from Julia's room across the hall, William carried the feverish child, her gown drenched in sweat.

Down the street, they heard building noises—hammering and chiseling. Julia said she liked to hear it. He watched Mary working with their child like a ministering angel, so strong and cheerful, yet two creases had formed between her eyebrows. She held a cold rag to Julia's fevered brow.

Several days earlier, they had taken Julia for a ride one afternoon to get air, and they returned with branches of pine, which now decorated the windowsill in their room. Julia liked to stare at the soothing resinous boughs. Later, as Mary combed Julia's soft brown hair, she noticed her baby's eyes had an unearthly brilliance to them as they occasionally looked toward the heavens.

In the hall, Dr. Palmer, who had been in attendance earlier, suggested she had but a short time to live. Both Mary and William thanked him for his candor. After they showed him to the door, William held Mary. They cried silently together.

"She asked me earlier today if she was dying. William, how can I answer such a question honestly?"

"So what did you say?"

"I said, 'Are you afraid to die?' and she told me 'No, I'm going to live with God, Grandma, and Uncle Joel.'" Mary sobbed, and the two of them stepped outside on the porch farther away from the rest of the family.

Within three days, with the end near, Mary knelt beside Julia's bed as life slowly ebbed. There were no tears. William noticed she hadn't cried since the incident on the porch. He watched her continuously dip a rag into cool water, wringing it and placing it on Julia's head. Nearby, the stalwart, bushy-bearded Dr. Palmer kept a like vigil while Zech brought in another pan, fresh from the rain barrel in the yard.

With the setting sun, William, who stood near the window in the room, saw a bank of threatening clouds on the northwestern horizon. Earlier he had paced, but now numb and helpless he sat in a chair watching his wife, Betsy Walker, and Sarah minister to Julia. Mary's sister Susan had come over to help with the children.

The other children came to pray, and on their knees their stockinged feet were lined in a row parallel with both sides of the bed. Dr. Palmer stood at her head, leaning against the wall, staring at the child. In the room, quiet except for occasional sobs from the children, everyone listened to her breathing, hardly breathing themselves. A sacred hush enveloped the room. William looked at the opened window, framed by white curtains that hung still, down each side. To him it was a passage to heaven. Outside, God's creation waited silently.

Julia sunk lower with each passing moment. With his face buried in her covers, Jesse laid his hand on her leg. He and Julia, closest in age, were closer than the others. William glanced at the bank of clouds and noticed they had moved half again, closer. They heard the first rumble of thunder, and he closed the window, as a strong wind blew the pine needles into the room and onto the floor below.

A little later, when the lightning flashed and the storm intensified its fury, Julia ceased to breathe. Mary buried her face in the bosom of her child and emitted a moan like an animal trying to escape. William rose, knelt, and laid his face on Mary's back and the children did the same to surround her and him with their love.

Mary pulled herself away and helped the rest of her family up. She hugged each one, talking especially to the younger ones. Always amazed at her strength, William watched her put the rest of their children ahead of her own feelings. She tried to comfort them.

Tearing up again, William turned from the scene and stepped to the window. He stared outside and thought about how his little girl's departure to Heaven would be through this beating rain and whirling winds where he could no longer protect her. It was unbearable. He turned to Mary and the children to assure them Jesus had her now. She no longer suffered.

A little later, he watched Mary lay two roses on Julia's heart, two roses taken from a bouquet cut earlier. Ann Lightsey and Betsy Howell Walker were already there to help Mary with preparing the child's body for burial

During the trip to the graveyard the following day, William and Mary in the buggy with Joseph took the lead. A buckboard with their children followed them to Elizabeth. All other times, the trip had seemed short as the family talked, sang, and told stories while ambling along the sandy and clay roads. Not today, though. In the silence, all they heard was the metallic clanging of the buckboards and bridles, creaking wheels, an occasional snort from the mules, and wind blowing through the pines. The front had passed through, and today the temperature had dropped. The day was dry, windy, and cooler. William and his boys had on their overcoats and the women their cloaks.

Present-day photo of the road to the original Elizabeth Church site and cemetery, Personal Photo

James followed in a second buckboard with the small wooden box. From time to time, William glanced at Mary; but she sat stoic with a detached look upon her face. He reached over Joseph and took her hand.

She looked at her brother Henry and saw a profound sadness in his eyes. As they approached the churchyard cemetery with its oak and pine canopy, she saw her father standing ramrod straight. In his hand he held a bouquet of sky blue lupine. He looked old; his rancher's face etched by the endless sun. Surrounding him were all her brothers, sisters, uncles, cousins, neighbors, and friends.

Her father helped Mary from the buggy, and they embraced. There in the shade, with a light breeze moving through, her family surrounded her and William.

Right behind her father stood her brother, Henry. He hugged

her, and she could not help heaving with sadness. Henry, always there, since she could remember. Their closeness in times like this was epic, their fraternity being a long story.

She watched over Henry's shoulder as William reached to her father with a firm hand, and he squeezed William's shoulder. She let go of Henry and recognized so many of their friends and distant family who were there from Monticello, a crowd much bigger than any expected.

Current Photo of Elizabeth Churchyard Cemetery, Personal Photo

Monticello had suffered two funerals that year that affected the whole county. There were few obituaries in the paper, yet there was one for Mary's mother and now her daughter. Their family wasn't alone in their grief, though. Dr. Palmer's wife had recently died of fever, a continued fever. The widower later found himself free to play his role as a valued physician during the coming war.

"Omne trium perfectum," thought William, "Every set of three is complete." Still, he lost count of the threes. So many deaths lately. Standing there under the graveyard hammock yet again, he couldn't help wondering. Who would be next? (See Appendix 3.)

#

Chapter 8
Imminent Enmity, Fall, 1860

The same day Julia Ann died, William's $3 notice in the *Family Friend* read, "Look Out for the Tredegar. Persons receiving freight at the Monticello Depot must invariably send their money to pay the freight bill." This advertisement shows William was still the depot agent in the fall of 1860.

William's sister still lived in Virginia, where the Tredegar Iron Works was located. This iron works company made most of the iron used in railroad building and would play a significant role during the Civil War. It was one reason Richmond became the capital of the Confederacy.

Fall moved forward, even though their little girl died. Mary made several trips to the cemetery and to visit her dad. What had recharged her before no longer helped. Her father's health faded, and he looked far older than his fifty-nine years. Now she visited because she worried about his overall health. Sometimes she visited because she worried she would lose him.

At home, the children and William's position at the depot kept the family busy. Running a household for eleven people consumed her time and mind. One good thing was that it kept her mind off the sadness. In fact, the work was so mind-numbing she frequently felt guilty for not shedding more tears.

Still, maybe God's intervention was by design. Her ability to move the sadness further into the recesses of her mind prevailed. So far, it only surfaced when she stopped to rest when her mind stopped operating in the here and now. She missed Julia Ann's industry and chatter.

For William, the death of his child did not stop his world from spinning either. He probably sought refuge in his work. With no sick leave or bereavement leave of any kind, people expected each other to return, pick up the pieces, and go forward immediately.

Monticello boomed throughout the 1850s and remained so for a dozen or more years. Through the *Family Friend*, several stores advertised every item imaginable.

At Johnson, Williams, & Co.'s "Railroad Store" for staple goods, Mary and her closest friend and Uncle Joel's widow Betsy sought a *"new style of bustle, made entirely of steel and so light."* The stores had goods for men, and William may have shopped in them for *"cutlery, saddlery . . . woodware, tinware, trunks"* and maybe even *"an umbrella."*

Whether at John S. Divine's or Budd's store on the courthouse square (in the building that today says 'Bank'), William, as a politician in the county, probably shopped at all Monticello stores.

Budd's Store on the Courthouse Square (now Cowhaus Coffee), Florida Memory Collection

Obviously, people still had money to spend, and William remained gainfully employed with at least four known jobs during the 1850s—constable, census enumerator, sheriff, and railroad agent. His ability to read, write, and cipher was still important in providing for his family.

Boomtime

Between 1850 and 1860, the county grew by 28%, as reflected by the 1860 census (See Appendix 4). Other parts of the county grew too. Aucilla was populated enough to have the Aucilla Academy chartered by the legislature in 1840. According to the *Family Friend*, on a Saturday in May 1860, their students orchestrated a presentation attended by the community and their parents. In addition, they held a May Party on the same day.

The newspaper only listed four schools in the county—Jefferson Academy, the Waukeenah Academy, Aucilla Academy, and the Davis Academy at Walker Mills (Drifton).

Dressed in mourning, fifteen-year-old Sarah passed by Palmer's and headed to Herring, Fennell, & Shehee's for their fancy dry goods. Though sent for flour, she lingered among the embroideries, collars, and sleeves. Lately, women had added lace collars to their dresses because forty-year-old Queen Victoria, a fashion influencer of her time, had recently worn them.

Mr. Herring, busy with other customers, bid her to help herself. She looked through his large assortment of bonnets, trimmed and untrimmed. He also allowed her to try on ladies' shoes, but the hoop skirts fascinated her the most.

Oh, how she loved watching the ladies sashay on the sidewalks, their hoops skirts moving like a giant bell. She wanted to wear hoop skirts, but her mama didn't see their utility. No, throughout the morning Sarah added extra crinolines belonging to her sisters, one at a time, hoping her mama wouldn't notice. Her skirts were always fuller and rounder, but not as much as she liked.

"Ok, Miss Andrews, what can I do for you?" said Mr. Herring.

Smiling, she replied, "Mama needs flour, please."

He stepped around the counter and headed for the flour barrel. "Have you heard about the new patterns for sewing?"

She hesitated, "No sir. What are patterns?"

Mr. Herring showed her the latest. Called patterns and made of paper, on the front of the pattern package was a picture of a woman's dress, certainly different from what the ladies in her family made.

As he handed her the package of flour, he added, "I miss your little sister, so full of life, always inquisitive."

Said Sarah, who felt the tears begin, "We all do. An enormous hole exists in our house now. Daddy said she filled a void we didn't know we had."

Holding the small package of flour under her arm as she walked toward the front, she noticed Shehee's had a complete assortment of ladies' mourning goods on a counter. She thought of her sister, and it made her sad again. Outside, as she walked on the covered boardwalk, she thought about her grandmother, Uncle Joel, and now Julia Ann. So much sadness.

Later, she told her mother, "Mr. Herring said you could cut the fabric to fit the pieces, and it shows you how to sew them together. Mama, we can have dresses similar to the wealthier planter ladies who get their dresses from the north."

Monticello's business section expanded during the 1850s. The Simmons family built their store, a brick building on the east/northeast corner of the courthouse square, later known to all who grew up in the 1960s as Simmons's Drug Store, but now part of it is a retail storefront.

The Masons and Oddfellows raised the dollars for the new Jefferson Academy brick classic revival building, which sat stately on the southern border of Monticello, as the alma mater later sang. West of the new school building, the older wooden academy building still sat in the middle of West Washington Street, where it boarded teachers. The parade ground, now behind the new school, was the site of increased activity. Gone was its beautiful green, trampled under the constant movement of boots as Jefferson County's men and boys prepared for what most thought would be war.

Monticello Home Guard, Behind Monticello High School, about 1917-1919. Before the construction of the band building/courthouse annex, the area behind the school may have still been used for a Parade Ground/militia practice area.

By 1860, they had built several even grander new homes. On the south side of East Washington Street stood the beautiful and spacious Dilworth House, and about a block east of it, the William Budd Home, where the Carswell family lives today, the patriarch, a descendant of the Gadsden family mentioned earlier.

Scott Dilworth Home, Personal Photo

William Budd House, Personal Photo

Across the street and closer to the courthouse, Smith Simkins built his home.

Simkins House - Personal Photo

West of town, near Dr. Taylor's, a man built a spacious wood-framed house, known for generations as the Pasco house, named after the new Waukeenah Academy's Harvard-educated headmaster who had recently moved into the county. He would move to this house after the Civil War.

Pasco House - Personal Photo

A mile east of town on Palmer Mill Road, the Palmers added a textile mill and brick kiln to their existing grist mill and tannery. Both would be useful during the war and become part of a manufacturing hub for the county.

Besides the Methodist, Presbyterian, and Baptist churches, the Episcopalians built their church at the corner of Waukeenah and East Washington Street, where Brenda Sorenson has her accounting office today. In addition, farther east on Washington Street, before the railroad tracks, the Methodists built their pastor a parsonage. Currently called the Bless House, it sits at the dead-end intersection of East Washington and Railroad Street.

Christian Bless House - Personal Photo

The business that Sarah liked best and made a point to walk by, even though it was not on her way home, was Mr. Ellenwood's Ice Cream Saloon. Her father had taken all of them there a week ago, and he called the creamy frozen treat a delicious luxury. Etta ate hers so fast it made her head hurt.

The county and its merchants were so successful that there was talk of a railroad spur between Thomasville and Monticello. Said William, "There's talk of a branch forking off the South Western Railroad with a branch leading to Bainbridge and Quincy and a branch leading to Thomasville and Monticello. At last, our town is growing."

On the morning of November 1, a local militia paraded and drilled at the courthouse. Mary stayed at home, but all her older children and William went. She enjoyed the peace and quiet as she moved from room to room. Later, sitting in her rocking chair in front of the fire, she drank a cup of coffee and thought about what she would do if the men in her family went off to war. It had been on her mind constantly. She could hear Joseph and Laura playing peacefully in the hall.

Days later, William attended a mass meeting at the courthouse. People from throughout the county, including her father, met there to discuss the country's condition.

The presidential election would change everyone's lives forever. The *Family Friend* endorsed the National Democratic Ticket with John C. Breckinridge of Kentucky as president and Col. John Lane of Oregon as vice president. William would vote at the courthouse, but in Elizabeth they voted at "Walker's Precinct," maybe in Jesse's home. "James S. Walker's Precinct" south of Aucilla and an Aucilla Precinct, too, existed.

On November 5th, William walked to the courthouse to vote for a new governor, congressman, and president. Again on the portico, he approached a window. Inside, three election judges sat at a writing desk. They had met early that morning and swore, kissing a Bible, to conduct this election honestly. Upon the table sat an old cigar box sealed with a hole in its lid.

William may have taken one of the small sheets of paper, and even though they knew him, he stated his name, "William Henry Andrews." He watched while one judge checked his name off on a list of residents. William wrote his choice for governor, folded the paper, and stuffed it through the hole into the cigar box. Or he may have arrived with a ballot prepared, maybe even printed.

Though it appeared a scene of order and probity at the window, a scene of disorder prevailed back of William. Around the courthouse, men with their horses, mules, carts, wagons, and buggies filled the road. He probably heard singing with the laughter and the roar of many voices.

The scene outside the courthouse included a type of gauntlet through which everyone passed. The men were half-tipsy as spirits were making the rounds. Mostly, the men, through good-natured jesting, called on each other to vote for their favorite candidate. Every newcomer was questioned about his vote, and when received, the crowd applauded or hissed. A few declared their candidate and followed their declaration with a brief speech.

As the day continued, the whiskey flowed. Elections were big days for small towns and cities everywhere, not just in Florida. Later in the day, William may have encountered the Walkers from Elizabeth and Walker Mills.

The judges tallied their votes, rechecked their lists, and sent the results to the capitol in Tallahassee. Statewide, John Milton of Jackson County won the governor's seat with over a thousand votes. He would not take office until October of the following year. An extremist, what people called a fire-eater, Milton held the belief that individual states maintained the right to withdraw from the Union if they felt its personal interests were infringed upon.

Lincoln wasn't even on the ballot, so he received no votes in Florida.

Days later, the southern people were deeply concerned about the election of Lincoln, even though he promised he wouldn't interfere with slavery where it existed. He was elected by the north, not by the south. Even his party was a northern Republican Party. The southern people talked about secession in the taverns, courthouses, and state houses.

Late that afternoon, Mary with her daughters stayed home, but her older boys and William went downtown for the returns. In the distance, she heard guns firing, drums beating, crowds shouting, and fireworks until late at night.

The next morning William, hungover, came to the kitchen early and gave her an account of what happened. Large crowds gathered around the town's four wells, the one west of the courthouse, another on the east side (today under the store next to the northwest corner of the courthouse parking lot), one northwest of the courthouse (today under Wag the Dog), and one on Dogwood Street (under the building now at 175 E. Dogwood St., Gary Wright's office).

He said the jubilant crowd grew too rowdy, and those older like himself worked to retire them to the hotels and several private dwellings, where several gentlemen, including Colonels Dilworth and Blackburn, addressed the crowds to restore quiet. "Young men did the shouting and carousing, our sons included. At about 9 pm, one man fired a roman candle which hit Mr. Slanter in his left eye. He may lose it. The carelessness made us reign them in; thus the impromptu meetings at the hotels and homes."

Four days later, on Friday, November 8th, the *Family Friend* published its newspaper a day early with the results for local and Florida returns. They reported Breckinridge carried Florida. However, the more populous northern states elected the Republican Abraham Lincoln.

The evening before, Monticello had received word of Lincoln's election, probably due to the telegraph. Numerous citizens assembled at the courthouse. W. O. Girardeau, esquire, addressed the courtroom crowd and counseled them to be calm and cautious in their deliberations. Colonel Blackburn, in favor of a dissolution of the Union unless the state could have equal rights, followed, urging them never to give up their rights. He called for every state to rally around a common standard.

Though immaterial, Monticello resident James Patton Anderson represented Middle Florida as a presidential elector for Florida's delegation to the national electoral college.

In 1854, the Republican Party grew from hostility to the Kansas-Nebraska Act; a coalition of anti-slavery Whigs and Free Soil Democrats created the party. Both groups opposed the expansion of slavery into the western states.

Free Soil Democrats got their name by pushing for a free market system. They believed in giving free land (free soil) to farmers (free labor) instead of allowing wealthy planters to buy the land and purchase slaves to manage it. Free soil, free labor, free men. In short, this slavery debate wrecked the Whig Party and split the Democratic Party. The residue of both created the Republican Party.

Trouble instantly brewed across the south and throughout Florida. Monticello resident Dr. T. M. Palmer visited East Florida and reported that everywhere he went, he heard talk of secession. He said when a Charleston steamer sailed into the Fernandina port, local men boarded the vessel and raised two more flags to join the ship's Palmetto flag. One flag with two stars, representing South Carolina and Florida, flew; another said, "Florida goes with South Carolina."

The southern people had three choices—resist by revolution, secede and form a Southern confederacy, or continue with the new president and preserve the Union. They called those who chose the latter option submissionists. The submissionists felt the South could survive a Republican presidency. Most southern people, though, eventually chose the second option.

The following Monday after the election, the *Family Friend* reported a mass meeting of *"the largest concourse of people we have ever seen in Monticello"* assembled at the courthouse. The crowd called Major David Walker to the chair and F. R. Fildes, the paper's editor, as secretary.

This David Walker could be Mary's uncle, David S. Walker, or her distant cousins, both of which were named David M. Walker. Mary's cousins did not live in the county during the Second Seminole War, but her uncle, who was only in his early twenties during the Indian war, probably isn't this Major Walker. The title of major could be a more recent title he received in the militia.

The purpose of the meeting was to *"determine what action should be taken by the Sovereign State of Florida, now that Abraham Lincoln and Hannibal Hamlin were elected President and Vice-President . . ."*

William quietly listened, getting there early to sit with Henry, Jesse, and J.J. The courtroom was packed to the gills, with men standing everywhere and spilling onto the upstairs portico. He estimated, as did the paper later, that there were over three hundred men present. The Walker men were well represented with William, hat in hand, and his father-in-law beside him, along with several of Mary's other kin. It was cool with the north-facing windows opened, and none of the men removed their coats. They sat shoulder to shoulder.

The chair appointed a committee of fifteen to prepare for business. The fifteen retired to another part of the building to hold a sub-meeting of the larger conference. William watched as Colonel Dilworth, Dr. Peeler, William Girardeau, Blackburn, Murphy, the lawyer Teat, Alvin May, Colonel Raysor, Dr.

Lamar, Smith Simkins, Captain Hill, Captain D. Bird, the lawyer Ulmer, and Dr. Treadwell left the room. Some had worked earlier on a draft so the committee would be short in their deliberations.

In the meantime, Mr. Davis from Tallahassee declared he wished to wait on the committee report before adding Leon County's sentiments. Leon County wished to learn what Jefferson proposed first.

The crowd turned their attention to Dr. Russell. Afterward, the lawyers James Ellenwood and B. W. Edwards came forward. All three urged secession. During Mr. Edward's address, the committee returned with its preamble and resolution.

Blackburn took the stage, "*WHEREAS, The Northern or so-called free States of this Confederacy have violated the Constitution that binds us together and makes up the terms of our Union, by a total disregard of its limitations . . .*" William knew where this was going, and his thoughts wandered. He thought about his old home place of Washington City, the fledgling republic's capital city where he roamed as a boy. He may have been sad that his hometown would be on the other side of this conflict.

Blackburn continued reading from the document in his hands, "*3. That our Governor and Legislature, so soon as they shall convene, be requested to call a State Convention to take into consideration the most suitable means of protection against Northern aggression, insult, and outrage.*"

After reading the document, the colonel yielded the floor to Colonel Dilworth, who spoke at length. He said, "*Take careful consideration of the document and study the great issues presented. Unless you are fully prepared to stand by and carry it out to the letter, you should not endorse it.*" A deafening applause drowned out the doubters.

Major Walker asked Mr. Davis from Tallahassee to speak, and Davis concluded his remarks and said, "*The time for the South to form a separate nation has arrived . . . but Florida should not take the lead in the matter due to our 'meager population' among other reasons.*"

When he finished, Major Walker spoke. "*Any person present, opposed to the resolution, step forward and speak your piece.*" Heads turned as everyone scanned the room, but no one responded. As they read the report a second time, William fidgeted. Sitting so close to each other for hours, all the men felt uncomfortable. Major Walker himself spoke for over an hour. Jesse rose and went to the back of the room where his brother James and several other Walkers stood.

The bi-partisan union here interested William. He later told Mary, "I never thought I would see the day when the walls completely disappeared between the men of all parties, especially the Democrats and the Whigs, but they were in lockstep tonight. I guess it took a big common enemy to do it. Even Fife, usually quiet but nonetheless a Whig, said it best, "*all party lines are now obliterated.*"

They called for a vote, and the crowd unanimously adopted, in a voice vote, the preamble and resolutions. Thunderous applause was followed by deafening shouts. As they left the courtroom, William noticed the overall enthusiasm of the crowd which wended its way down the stairs and into the square below. He probably could not help thinking about what this meant for the nation as this same scenario played throughout the south. Lincoln's election had taken place less than a week earlier, and it would be months before his inauguration.

Days later, around the stove, William and John Cuthbert sat alone one afternoon at Budd's store as J. T. Budd uncrated new inventory in the back. "William, I don't know how anyone can survive without slave labor. I know you and Mary's family have always gotten along without it, but you do realize, don't you, that Monticello wouldn't exist without slavery? This area couldn't have grown as it did." He paused, and William nodded his head in assent.

Cuthbert sat forward in his chair and added, "Our economy depends heavily on agriculture, particularly cotton, and slavery. You yourself wouldn't have come here if not for the economic growth of this area, and this area would not have grown without our slaves."

Cuthbert House

News about happenings in Madison included a *"plot of insurrection discovered amongst the negroes"* last Monday. They discovered a plot to destroy the town of Madison by fire. To begin with, a house burning on the outskirts would draw the citizens away from the town's middle so other men could set fire to every house and building. The paper reported a white man overheard two slaves talking about the plot. Authorities placed many slaves under arrest, but the newspaper said, "*what disposition was made of them, we know not.*"

William knew Cuthbert was right, but it still didn't make the institution right. Somehow through the years, especially since his Elizabeth died, he came to the same conclusions as his father-in-law and wife. Yet he knew that if it came to this awful war, he would join with his fellow Floridians to fight for the economic stability of his home, family, and state, all of which depended on this peculiar economic system. He didn't like it, but to do otherwise was to tear everything he worked for apart. He knew he wouldn't do contrary to his neighbors. The additional question of the defense of their homes and their liberties brought the issue back to slavery.

That evening William came home with news about Walker Mills, which people called Station 3 because of the railroad there. "Mary, Daniel Ladd's store burned to the ground early Thursday morning. He lost all his stock and goods, and it appears to be arson. Your brothers are worried about their mills."

"Do they have any idea who did it?"

"Not that I know of."

The militia men of each county met in their courthouses or churches, where they talked and planned. They attended meetings before the big votes centered on whether to join the war effort. Monticello's was in the courthouse with standing room only.

Discussions followed about the color and cut of the uniforms as well as the name of the unit. They bandied all kinds of names. Monticello Rifles, Jefferson Dragoons, the Middle Florida Soaves or Hussars, Jefferson Indian Fighters, Jacksonian Fire-eaters, until they settled it. Because the boys came from throughout the county, the first militia group of Jefferson County became the Jefferson Rifles.

Almost half formed with native-born Floridians, the Jefferson Rifles became the Florida unit with the highest percentage of native boys. As more boys and men joined, another militia group formed and called themselves the Jefferson Beauregards.

Throughout the state, in the late fall and winter, Florida militias organized in the towns and cities as much for its social aspects as for its military. The Jefferson Rifles and Jefferson Beauregards formed in Monticello while Tallahassee established its Lion Artillery. Both young and old blades joined the local militias.

The local militia may have called themselves the Jefferson Rifles or Beauregards, but most of the men only had the old flintlocks they carried during the Indian wars. Others had Bowie knives, belt knives, and sabers. Everyone carried a pocketknife.

William and Mary's son James joined the Jefferson Rifles. At dinner one evening he described drilling behind the schoolhouse on the parade ground. He said, "I'm not sure we'll ever be ready to take on anything serious, Dad. A quarter of the boys are skylarks, spending their time preening in their new uniforms for the gaggle of girls who stroll by continuously between the school and the parade ground. Half of the boys are showoffs with little to show off with. There's another group that lacks the sense God gave a goat."

"James!" Mary leveled her eyes at him. "Don't use God's name to swear!"

James rolled his eyes, but not until his mama turned her head. She had turned her motherly attention to Zech, who used his spoon to launch a pea at Vollie when he thought she wasn't looking. It hit Vollie on the side of his head.

The reference to skylarks did not escape William. He had recently read Shelly poetry to the family, something he had been doing again. He pondered this. If he left for war, he would miss reading to his family, which he did for those who could not read, especially Mary.

In Tallahassee, though, the state wished for a more central perspective. Before too long, they formed four state units—First Florida, Second Florida, Third Florida, and Fourth Florida, all infantry units. In Jefferson County, though, they still considered themselves local; and the men and boys joined enthusiastically, excited about every drill.

The following Saturday, the 10th Regiment, composed of the militia of Jefferson County, paraded through town in a grand display, headed west to the parade grounds for Major General G. W. Parkhill and Brigadier General Bird's review. Earlier, Mary alerted William that several sewing circles planned to present flags to the two cavalry and the rifle companies of Monticello. When there, the 10th Regiment, made of seven units, including the Jefferson Guards, the Waukeenah Guards, the Jefferson Beauregards, and the Jefferson Rifles, assembled in lines and awaited review.

Mary took the children downtown to the assembly. Getting there through the city's crowded streets, she and the older daughters made sure they protected the younger ones from the hordes of horses, mules, wagons, and buggies. Amid the throng, dogs barked, children squealed, and people everywhere shouted and moved about. She always looked for a runaway horse or a buggy, both of which could break free of their moorings and dash madly through the streets, dangerous for the grown-ups, let alone the little ones.

The units marched and drilled for weeks. According to James, they drilled as squads and in company formation to accustom each man to orders and formations such as marching in columns or in a "company front." They taught them how to face properly and dress the line. Mary noticed a whole new language invaded their home. "Dress the line," she thought, "I do not know what that means." Nor did she ask, either. All the men would have quickly replied with at least half an hour's explanation.

Of course, dressed in full uniform today, Major General Parkhill and Brigadier General Bird, in a regimental drill, moved about the lines, inspecting and encouraging them. Followed by speeches came the presentation of the flags. Miss Scott approached the Jefferson Rifles, where Mr. Gill stepped forward to receive the offering.

Next, mounted sidesaddle, Miss Williams came forward and, after a quick speech, presented the ladies' flag for the Cavalry Company. Her deep indigo skirt draped across and down the horse's other side. Captain Partridge stepped forward and received the carefully crafted flag for the Jefferson Guards. Mary noticed her daughter Sarah was positively green with envy. Mary and the children stood in the back in the shade of the two-story brick schoolhouse, almost a decade old. Chatting with their neighbors, they talked mostly about Governor Perry's call for secession from the nation.

The colonels barked commands as dust clouded their

trudging boots. They marched to the rattle of drums and the lilt of a fife. The units showed their carriage, proud to be doing their part.

The only men in the crowd were old with white beards who wished they were young again and the younger boys who wished they were older. Most of the latter worried the war would be over before they would have their chance to fight.

In late November, Florida's legislature convened in Tallahassee and adjourned less than two weeks after convening. They voted in Senator T. J. Eppes, a descendant of Thomas Jefferson, as senate president, and the first order of business was a declaration: the body would not elect a US senator. Why elect a senator when the state might break from the union? A letter from Congressional Senator D. L. Yulee let the body know that if the state seceded, he would come home and support it.

On November 28th, they passed a convention bill with only one dissenting vote to decide whether Florida would secede and another bill for the governor to purchase arms. Afterward, having done their business, they adjourned.

Incessant news about militias and secession filled the rest of December, leaving little time for the holidays. Amid many announcements of men running for office in their militia units, regiments, and brigades, G. W. Taylor of Monticello became a candidate for major of the First Regiment of Cavalry embedded in the Second Brigade of the Florida Militia. He would run against W. Murphy of Waukeenah. The election would take place on Christmas Eve.

Around mid-December, the newspaper officially announced Florida's votes for president, though everyone knew Lincoln won anyway. Breckenridge led with over 8,000 votes, Bell with over 4,000, and Douglas received only 221. William told Mary they elected a Mr. McClelland from New River County to carry the votes to Washington. Lincoln, not on the ticket, received no votes.

The Florida Baptists met for their state convention in Monticello and voted for secession, and later, the Florida Methodist Episcopal Conference, which also met in Monticello, did the same. Meantime, the *Family Friend* asked why Florida should wait for other states to secede first.

Good news, though, was the railroad's completion all the way to Lake City, where it connected with the Central Railroad to Jacksonville and Fernandina. Earlier, Colonel Blackburn said he intended to baptize the waters of the Gulf with those of the Atlantic, a most interesting and expected event that would never take place because of secession.

At the depot, William watched as the clerk changed the railroad schedule. Now, the train ran east all the way to Lake City. For Monticello, it arrived and left twice a day at 9:30 am, heading to Tallahassee, and at 6:20 pm, leaving for Lake City. This meant that each day, someone in Monticello could leave on the train at 9:30 am and get to Tallahassee by noon to tend to his business between one and three pm. Afterward, he could depart Tallahassee by 4 pm and arrive home by 6:20. The railroad now had more than one locomotive.

The next evening James said at supper, "Several of the older boys are home from the northern colleges. They have no plans to return."

In the quiet that followed, the family passed plates of food. William added, "These are strange times."

Cindy Roe Littlejohn

Before Christmas, the news came from South Carolina on December 20th. They had seceded. Many in town celebrated, but Mary couldn't see the festivity in it. The Indian wars had left so much bloodshed and strife.

Two days later, on a Saturday in mid-December, William and Jesse again went to the courthouse to select their county's delegates for the secession convention. They came early for a good seat because they expected standing room only. Everyone assembled to nominate four delegates for the secession convention which would meet on January 3rd after the New Year. These four selected men would vote on whether the state should sever its ties with the US government.

Many illustrious names were on the list of nominees—Dilworth, Raysor, Lamar, Major Walker, Anderson, Murphy, Fife, Palmer, Bird, McCants, and Taylor. After the meeting, Jesse returned with William, and the two sat on the porch talking over pickled mullet.

William had earlier advertised in the December 15th issue of the local paper that he had *"mullet and roe fresh pickled in tight barrels"* for sale. People were told to go to the depot to get it *"cheap for cash."*

Two days later, on Christmas Eve, the militias voted for their officers.

After their Christmas supper's leftovers and because it had been unseasonably warm, Mary and William sat on the porch surrounded by their children, along with several of her brothers and Henry's Julia. Henry said, "Well, we've modified the mills for the war, as have Palmer, Bailey, and others. Mr. Bailey makes uniforms, and Palmer's tannery works nonstop to meet the needed leather supply."

On the creek that runs east behind today's The Porch on the Green east of town, Palmer's Mill and Bailey's Mill sat on this creek farther downstream, southeast of where the sidewalk ends on US 90. However, with no US 90, Palmer Mill Road was the only road leading to the mill. One can still see the roadbed behind the homes south of US 90.

Added J.J., "Yesterday, we loaded lumber on a train headed to Fort Clinch, but we're a little worried about the boiler in the older mill. Old and rusting along its lap joints, it will have to do. No way to get another one since they make them up north."

In Walker Mills, Henry and J.J. owned at least two mills; one processed lumber and had a boiler. The town will remain Walker Mills until well after the War.

Henry operated his mill, but the enumerator listed him as a carpenter in the 1860 census. He listed J.J., Archibald, and George as carpenters too. J.J. is listed as Henry's partner in several documents, but unknown is whether Archibald and George only worked for their brothers' mills or worked for someone else, such as Jordan Fulford, a house builder and general carpenter. Jordan Fulford eventually married Ann Lightsey's daughter Clara after the war, so the families were close.

No photos of Palmer's Mill exists, but a photo of Ulmer's Mill does, north of Waukeenah in Jefferson County, Keystone Genealogical Library, Colorized by Bill Price

One night late in December, William paced before the fireplace as Mary darned a sock for Zech. In a mass meeting, Leon County had called for the state convention to meet and secede.

He said, "Mary, our state is like a magazine ready to explode. Our Republican president provided the spark, but our people were about to bust a gusset anyway. The north will inaugurate him, and he will exercise his federal rights over the states. I don't know what has happened to the people in Washington, but I think they've lost their way. Why would they lord their federal rights over the states when the states put this nation together to begin with?"

William paced, and Mary rocked in the chair she had received from him a few years earlier for her birthday. Today, the temperature hardly reached 50 degrees. Thankfully, the boys kept the fires here and in the kitchen stoked all day.

William continued, "No one wants a monarch, and yet they've brought in a president who will be one. They pushed this abolitionist thing too fast, and the south won't take it sitting down." The fire in the hearth burned a warm glow. The children readied for bed, and Mary's hair lay softly on her shoulders. He paced in his white muslin shirt, dark pants, and stockinged feet.

To understand what the times were like for Mary and William, one must understand the nation was shy of its eighty-fifth birthday. Thomas Jefferson had only passed away thirty-four years earlier. Florida as a state was only fifteen years old. There was a smattering of Revolutionary War soldiers still living, though far advanced in age.

Though Florida was destined to secede, there were Floridians such as Richard Keith Call who cautioned against secession. He warned seceding might be considered treason, if not high treason, against their constitutional government. Call urged Floridians: *"Wait then. I pray you to wait."*

The next day Mary was in her kitchen in the late morning, working on dinner when William came in early from the depot. Cleaning up after their earlier breakfast and planning their noonday meal, she thought it odd. "What are you doing home?" She noticed he had a peculiar look on his face. He looked stricken, and instinctively, she felt something was terribly wrong.

Silently, he pulled a chair from the table and said, "Mary, I need you to sit down." Staring at him, she rinsed her hands in the bucket of water on the counter and dried them on her apron as she sat. He walked around, took both her hands in his, and squatted to look her straight in the eyes.

What came forth next, she hardly heard. "Mary, there was a boiler accident at Walker Mills. Henry is in terrible shape."

She jumped up. "We need to get to him." They brought Henry's scalded body to his young recent bride, Julia, and Mary knew the girl needed all their help.

Henry's injuries were mortal, and he died a few days later. His death notice appeared in *The Florida Friend* in their January 5th, 1861 edition. It read, "*Mr. Henry Walker, who was recently injured by the bursting of the boiler at his steam mill, a few miles from town, died on the 27th ult.*" Henry's death may have been one of the county's earliest fatalities attributed to the War Between the States.

#

Chapter 9
Mr. Andrews Goes to Tallahassee, 1861

Building since the 1830s, secession did not happen overnight. South Carolina, unlike any northern state, talked about seceding as early as 1832.

Many issues divided the north and south, such as state's rights, trade regulations, industrial economies, agricultural economies, sectional rivalries, congressional control, and even chivalry versus puritanism. The breaking point was slavery and a Constitution that said "all" men are created equal. Before the Civil War, most white people, north and south, did not believe the black man was equal, something which rears its ugly head today.

Most southern states thought the US Constitution was a contract among the states that could be abandoned at any time. They thought they had the right to secede.

Politically, everything happened quickly after President-Elect Lincoln's election in November. As a result, Middle Florida talked incessantly about seceding. Most Floridians wanted out, but the questions were how and when to do it. These questions hovered throughout the holidays.

A few days before the general assembly recessed in early December, the governor's office sent word that a southern convention, also referred to as the Montgomery Convention, would meet on February 4th. In Montgomery, they circulated a proposed proclamation for a new government. Before adjourning for the holidays, Florida's general assembly extended its session into February to ratify certain acts expected from Montgomery. The legislators planned to return, after their state convention adjourned, for other business, including rules for militias and providing a state uniform and flag. They still had much work to do.

By mid-December, Florida's Governor Perry set a date for a special convention to decide whether Florida should remain in the Union. War seemed imminent.

Florida's legislature recessed on December 1 on a Saturday at noon amid intensely cold weather and did not reconvene until January 7th at noon the following year—a recess of thirty-seven days.

Before the new year, Monticello received word about significant changes in Charleston where federal troops evacuated Fort Moultrie and increased occupation of Fort Sumter. To Mary, the movements throughout the southland were like a chess game, and she worried about her family in South Carolina. Charleston was much too close to Carter's Ford for comfort. It appeared fighting could happen in Charleston any day.

People called those who were quick to call for secession "fire-eaters." It thrilled fire-eaters when South Carolina took the lead and seceded on December 20th. People called the rest of the secessionists "cooperationists." There were some who did not want secession, but the flood of secessionists drowned their voices.

We're not sure which name William and Jesse considered themselves. Several of William's sons and several of Jesse's would fight for the Confederacy. Many southerners opposed to secession would not bear arms against their brethren. They found themselves drafted and fighting for the Confederacy regardless of how they felt.

As 1860 gave way to 1861, southern states began to seize federal property within their state lines, including US courts, customs houses, post offices, arsenals, and forts. They would seize the US mints in Charlotte, Dahlonega, and New Orleans. By the end of 1861, they would almost remove all US governmental presence within their boundaries

Middle Florida heard that Virginia and Maryland by force of arms attempted to prevent the inauguration of Lincoln as president. The people of Baltimore planned a reception to assassinate him before he got to Washington, but he hurried through their city before they knew he was there. Though there is little evidence this actually happened, there was much rumor.

Under the lame duck President Buchanan, the North executed a plan. A steamship left Boston the first week of January and carried troops and munitions to the Tortugas, off the southern coast of Florida. The president ordered the forces at Fort Leavenworth to Fort McHenry in Baltimore and sent a steamer from New York Harbor with fuel and provisions to Fort Sumter in Charleston.

All of this swirled in the initial months of 1861 as William was appointed to a position with a ringside seat.

Florida's secession convention went into the House chambers in the capitol on January 3rd with John C. McGehee chairing, a staunch secessionist from Madison County. The four delegates from Jefferson County were William Dilworth, Patton Anderson, Dr. Thomas Palmer, and Thompson Lamar. At the depot, William, privy to any telegraphic messages received, listened to the latest rumors. All day, he thought about earlier conversations with his father-in-law, about how important and proud they had been to vote for Florida to join the union in 1843. Now, within a decade and a half, they were trying to sever that union.

Governor Perry and Governor-Elect John Milton strongly supported secession; the convention's delegates debated inside as well as outside the convention, on the streets and in the taverns of Tallahassee.

Floridians debated the danger to their rights from a tyrannical national government, and they sought secession, a legal means, in response to the tyranny. Outside the capitol, anxious Tallahasseans gathered to watch the proceedings. Arguing the opposition, but overwhelmed, former territorial Governor Richard Keith Call did his best.

Meanwhile, the January 5th issue of the *Family Friend* reported that southern states continued to take federal facilities throughout the south, especially along its coastlines. Local state militia took Fort Pulaski near Savannah, and they captured a US revenue cutter. In Chattahoochee, Florida, at the Mount Vernon Arsenal, also known as the Chattahoochee Arsenal, the Quincy Guards (the local militia) took control on Saturday, January 5th. At about the same time, elsewhere, local militia quickly seized Fort Marion (now Castillo de San Marcos) in St. Augustine and Fort Clinch on Amelia Island.

In the interval, Washington waited for the inauguration of its new president, which wouldn't take place until March 4th. People expected the forts at Pensacola to fall any day now, and the Carolinians surrounded Fort Sumter, another battle expected any hour.

In Monticello, everyone grieved the loss of Henry Walker

with services held more than a week after he died. The service at the First Baptist Church in Monticello was held on January 5th. That morning, a notice appeared: "*Services at the Baptist Church at 11 o'clock. By order of W. M. H. Berry, Sec'y Dated January 5th, 1861.*

On Saturday, William escorted Mary and their family to the wooden church down the hill south of the courthouse. There was a crowd there, inside and out. Thankfully, he and Mary would each have a seat reserved inside for the family. They would take Joseph and Laura inside with them, but the rest of their children would have to fill in wherever they could find a place. Florrie held Henry tightly by his little hand. The service went quickly.

First Baptist Church, built in 1845

Henry also had a masonic burial. A notice in the January 10th paper noted: "Masonic Burial To Officers and Members of Hiram Lodge No. 5: BRETHREN—You are hereby requested to meet at your Lodge Room, on Sunday, the 13th instant, for the purpose of performing the Funeral Ceremonies of our late worthy brother HENRY WALKER. Brethren of neighboring Lodges are respectfully invited to attend our occasion." The lodge was located in the school building on the second floor.

Mary would never forget the holidays of 1860 as a sad time for her family. They missed Julia Ann during the holidays, sparse as they were with the nonstop talk about secession. Henry died a short time afterward. At the funeral, her father looked stricken and withering. It happened so suddenly; the deaths came in waves, one after the other.

The family indeed received solace from these elegant tributes (see Appendix 5). Also, the town certainly embraced them, showing their love and respect, as Monticello continues to do for its bereaved families.

Because of a receipt dated April 22nd, 1861, we know the mills were still in operation months later. It read, *"Received of Mrs. E. Forest $57.71 for five thousand and seven hundred @ 71 ft lumber sawed at H & JJ Walker Mills. This April 22nd, 1861."* Signed Joshua Taylor. The mills kept the same names, though Henry had died months earlier.

His recent bride's name, Julia V. Walker, was found in the letters of administration in the estate of her husband. They required a bond of ten thousand dollars. It mentions the appraisal and value of his estate, including slaves. His father may have frowned upon owning slaves, but Henry did not follow his lead. The bond, dated January 10th, 1863, shows

Julia still has not remarried two years later.

Because the 1860 census, dated August 8th, shows him still a bachelor living with his brothers J.J., George, Archibald, and David L., it appears Henry married Julia after August 8th but before the accident. On December 29, one tribute read, *"That we do deeply sympathize with his bereaved companion, who so soon has been called to mourn his untimely death."* They were newlyweds.

From the paper, we know Henry's injuries, and we know from the 1860 census that in the south, almost 5.5% of deaths were from burns and scalds. Within these deaths, females exceeded males by 37%. Female dresses took fire quickly and were not quickly extinguished. Scalds were more common among children who frequently were in their mother's kitchens.

Within four days of its beginning on January 7th, Florida's convention voted to draft a secession ordinance. Meanwhile, on the 8th, while all eyes remained on Tallahassee, in Monticello, the Jefferson Rifles celebrated the Battle of New Orleans with a parade at the parade ground in Monticello. Mary and William took the younger children and stood in the shade near the back door of the two-story school. The older ones had left earlier with their friends.

That Saturday evening, William read to her from the *Family Friend*, January 8th edition. *"Tribute of Respect, Rendezvous, Jefferson Rifle Company, January 8, 1861. Whereas, Our ranks have been invaded by the ruthless hand of death, and we are called upon to pay a tribute of love and respect to the memory of our deceased brother, private HENRY WALKER, who we trust God has enrolled among his hosts above, therefore be it—Resolved, That in the death of Brother Walker, this Company has lost a valuable and efficient member of society, a worthy friend, and the State a citizen . . ."* When he finished, her lack of tears and silence worried him.

The next day, Mississippi seceded. State after state showed they wouldn't abide by the rule of the northern Republican Party. Subsequently, northern citizens decided they would not stand for secession

Thereupon, Governor Perry continued to move ahead. He sent local militia units to seize control of the remaining Federal properties in the state, most captured without a single shot fired. During the noon hour on Thursday, January 10th, Florida's secession convention, with its ordinance in hand, voted. With the vote almost unanimous, sixty-two yeas and only seven nays, Florida crossed its Rubicon.

Later that afternoon, William came in from the railroad station with the news. He found Mary on the back steps, sitting with her red hen Brunetta. At her feet were nine little chicks, all Brunetta's progeny. He said, "Well, old girl, it's official. Right now, they're dancing in the streets of Tallahassee. We've seceded from the nation." But she noticed this time that his eyes didn't sparkle. He looked resigned and worried.

The papers reported the city went wild with excitement when Florida declared its independence. Leon Countians danced in the streets of Tallahassee along with the sounds of cannons and cheers from the enthusiastic crowds who mobbed its streets. They took down the American flag over the state capitol. Later, under a full moon, Tallahasseans held a grand illumination in honor of the event, a torch-light parade that streamed through the city. They chanted and shouted late into the night

Monticello did likewise. The *Family Friend* reported, *"Joyous shouts rent the air, rockets and guns were fired, bonfires lighted, and universal joy pervaded every heart. The Citizens repaired to the Court*

House to learn the particulars of the passage." William and Mary went to hear the speakers Colonel Blackburn, Colonel Dilworth, and the editor Fildes speak.

Later, William escorted Mary home and returned to the festivities, where he followed a crowd of men to Mr. Humphrey's hotel for "sparkling wine" to greet the new Republic of Florida.

The next morning, as a new day can often sober a mind, William nodded and looked at Mary, who sat in front of the fireplace darning socks. "They did it, Mary. Our leaders seceded from Washington, and we are going to war." He paced. Mary stopped and listened, but she heard little except that dreaded word, "war." All she could think about were her boys.

Young boys were so impressionable. Last evening she had overheard the young men talking about how this would be a historical second war for independence, and they peppered their conversations with words like self-sacrificing spirit, courage, gallantry, and the devotion of women. She realized John Slicer and her little brother George were so young yet old enough to go.

She hoped it would be over before James and Zech got old enough. Oh Lord, why do grown men wage war while their babies do the fighting? She didn't hear another word William said. She stared at the dying fire while he talked and paced.

Earlier, the town woke to a new flag flying over the cupola of the courthouse, a flag with a solitary star on a red background.

In Tallahassee, they held a public ceremony on the east steps of the capitol to sign the formal Ordinance of Secession. From a window above, Governor-Elect Milton unfurled a flag made by a group of women from Broward's Neck in Duval County. The flag's motto read, "The Rights of the South at All Hazards!"

Three stars represented the three seceded states. Later, the Broward's Neck flag hung above the speaker's desk in the House throughout the war. Florida was the third state to secede, joining South Carolina and Mississippi.

Only sixty-four of the sixty-nine delegates signed the ordinance during the ceremony. Regarded as one of the founding fathers of Florida, former territorial Governor Call, who spoke against seceding earlier, said he feared they had "*opened the gates of Hell.*"

Still, the state needed a statewide vote. So how did the vote go? One will never know, because it never went to an overall vote. Frankly, most Floridians now thought Florida was an independent country capable of making its laws. Many believed since they voted themselves into the Union, they had every right to vote themselves out. Few thought this might lead to a civil war, and many assumed it would be over quickly, with the South winning handily. Later, the convention formed a committee to draft a declaration of causes, but it never completed its task.

If they had held a statewide vote, only 12,800 men would have qualified, amounting to less than ten percent of Florida's total population of 140,000 people, of whom nearly half were slaves. Of the remaining 70,000 people, only a little less than 11% were adult, white male citizens eligible to vote.

Because of William's work on the census, he knew the numbers, and at breakfast one morning, he said to Mary, "I'm sure Governor Perry is, as we speak, mulling over the numbers. With only 13,000 men to fight and over a thousand miles of coastline to defend, it will be impossible." Lines of worry creased his forehead. He was right about Governor Perry but hadn't thought about the other inevitable problem, executing the forced expulsion of Federal troops from all of Florida's arsenals and forts.

The governor quickly appointed Joseph Finegan as director of state military affairs, a wealthy Irish Anglican who, at forty-five, was described as a jovial and hearty man. Subsequently, a call went forth to form state militia units to protect the state.

Meantime, more federal forts fell. More volunteers occupied Fort Clinch on Amelia Island and seized the arsenal at St. Augustine. They built defensive works on the St. Johns River. However, Forts Taylor, Jefferson, and Pickens continued under the stars and bars.

As planned, the general assembly returned from its thirty-seven-day recess. Because these were planters and businessmen, they felt the pull to get home to their plantations, businesses, and families; but there appeared to be no end to the work. With business from the Montgomery secession convention ongoing, they waited.

Within short order, in Pensacola, the first official act of war for Florida came on January 12th. With Florida and Alabama troops, Alabama's Colonel Tennant Lomax marched to the Pensacola Navy Yard and stopped at the east gate. There in the office of Commodore James Armstrong, they demanded in the name of Governor Perry the surrender of the Navy Yard and its stores to the Republic of Florida. Armstrong relinquished his authority, and they took down the stars and bars while they raised Florida's flag, again with no shots fired.

The following Sunday afternoon, the family gathered in the living room. William talked mainly to the boys, but Mary could stand it no longer. She quietly slipped from the room, moving down the hall away from the discussion. As often happened when she was upset, she retired to her kitchen, where she always had something to do.

She took some flour and plopped it into a wooden bowl. The silt filled the air, illuminated by a ray of sunlight through the window. With her little pitcher, she poured in buttermilk and began mixing the two with a wooden spoon. She kept wiping tears away, but every so often, one plopped into the flour. She knew they wouldn't hurt the cobbler she planned, but she kept dabbing her eyes on her sleeve. Mary, smeared with flour and buttermilk, heard the kitchen door open.

Florrie could only see her stepmother's back but noticed the telltale signs of her weeping. She hugged her, saying, "It'll be okay. Everyone says this won't last hardly any time, maybe even before the Florida boys get all the way north." Mary wasn't sure.

She and William decided against discussing their fears about the North's overall superiority in population and manufacturing in front of the family. It would not help for their sons to be sent North to fight, believing it doomed them from the beginning.

Florrie fetched two more logs for the cookstove. Inside, she opened the trap door and shoved them in, using a stick to stoke the fire so the older logs could get more air. On top was a big pot of soup Mary had made earlier. It smelled good and beefy.

Florrie watched her as she made the cornbread. How lucky they were that their dad found Mary. She couldn't remember her mother, but Mary talked about her occasionally. Mary felt it was her responsibility to help Elizabeth's children remember her. Still and all, though, the kids called Mary mother. After all, she had been their mother for over thirteen years.

Florrie peeked inside the pot of stew with its thick, brown gravy. They added potatoes, onions, and carrots, all winter root vegetables. She took a wooden spoon and stirred deep into the mixture to make sure nothing stuck to the bottom. She got another large pot and took it to the cistern for more water. Inside, she placed the pot on the stove and waited for it to boil. They would have rice with their stew tonight.

Florida Andrews, daughter of William & Elizabeth Andrews

Later, at dinner, in the yellow glow of the kerosene lamp which sat in the middle of the table, the children were full of questions. Zech asked, "How old do you have to be to join?"

William replied, "Eighteen, so none of you are old enough."

With a frown, James said, "What's the oldest they will take?"

Mary answered, "Forty-nine." The older kids all turned their heads toward their dad.

He stared, adding, "Well, they'll have to draft me first. They'll ask for volunteers before drafting."

Added James, "And we'll have whipped them by then, anyway." William and Mary bit their tongues—no need to upset the children with the facts until necessary.

When the Florida men voted for their secession delegates, there were men throughout the state who tried to hamper the undertaking, but the planters had the most to lose and were a solid and robust block. It also didn't help the disruptors when rumors circulated that Federal troops were coming to destroy the national arsenals in the state and reinforce federal forts.

Many thought Florida to be a solid plantation-slave state with solid secessionist leanings, and though mostly true, ambivalent were the thousands of settlers, farmers, and cattlemen who moved into the peninsula, lured by free lands through the Armed Occupation Act. In this new, next frontier, these settlers led a hardscrabble life, a hard day-to-day struggle to survive similar to Mary's family in their early days in Florida. Mostly subsistence farmers and ranchers, these new settlers traded their surplus locally. Most owned no slaves.

Most whites were subsistence farmers in the south. The Walkers came with cash and a foundation herd and were hardly poor, but even they were not slaveholders. All of

Florida was not against the Union, though the Walkers and many others would do their service for the Confederacy.

Florida was not united as a Confederate state. There were pockets of union sympathizers, with one of the largest located in East Florida. There were people there who moved from the north during the 1850s. Also, East Floridians still felt the need to rival the rest of the state, West and Middle Florida, as they had done since the statehood debate when they wanted to enter the union as a separate state. Other pockets of union sympathizers later developed in Taylor and Lafayette Counties, east of Jefferson County.

Unionists were also widespread throughout the rest of the Confederacy. They were especially prevalent in the Appalachians and substantial parts of Texas.

Still, the south produced two thirds of the world's cotton. It also supplied tobacco, sugar, and naval stores such as turpentine, all considered Florida crops, its chief economy. Even though Florida had bountiful ports, people outside the south controlled Florida's shipping. There was little manufacturing or mining in the south, especially in Florida. Ironically, Jefferson County, with its abundant streams and subsequent mills, led the state in manufacturing.

The principal source of wealth for the south was its 3 million enslaved people of color. Because of the widespread fear of revolt by the slaves, they assigned extra men to serve on the "home guard" to patrol the roads of their home counties. They kept militia units at home for protection.

White southerners feared a slave revolt because of an earlier one in Santo Domingo, today's Haiti. This revolt shocked and petrified slave owners throughout the world. Saint-Dominique, the home of coffee, cocoa, indigo, and sugar plantations, along with Jamaica, was the world's foremost supplier of sugar, an agricultural industry that depended on manual slave labor. Saint-Dominique, a French colony, was one of the most profitable European colonies in the world. On this island, African-born slaves outnumbered the white colonists and free persons of color ten to one. (Some of these free persons of color also owned slaves.)

In 1791, the slaves of Saint-Dominique rose against their masters, killing them and plunging the colony into a long civil war. They took control through rape, torture, mutilation, and death. They dragged masters and their mistresses from their beds, and the heads of their French children they placed on spikes before the rebel mobs. In their path, they burned plantations and cities and freed more slaves. Within weeks they killed 4,000 whites and burned or destroyed 180 plantations. The revolt would eventually lead to a free republic in 1804.

The south wasn't even a capitalist society. It did not have a free labor market. Industrial development probably did not grow in the south because of its top-heavy income distribution, held chiefly by the planters. Poorer whites and free people of color were subsistence producers, using what they made at home, so they did not generate the needed consumer demand to sustain a robust local manufacturing economy. With no competition, there was no growing middle class.

In addition, thirty percent of the south's population, its slaves, depended on others for their subsistence. There was no need to achieve maximum productivity with minimal wasted effort since the slaves would gain no assets or rise in class. In addition, slaves lacked the motivation to work harder to provide for their families because their masters separated the slaves from their parentage and their offspring. In that way, each plantation operated like a mini-socialist empire with their masters' families, a government providing for its workers' needs.

A few days later, Zech, with the family's horse and buggy and his father as a passenger, slowly pulled through a mist and a fog that had settled on the town the night before, the remnants of a stalled front. A shrouded mist enveloped the city's shapes, wrapped in an endless half-light from the almost full moon. Chilled and hardly speaking, they heard distant hooves falling softly on the dampened earth as shadows moved through the mist like ghosts. Everyone moved slowly in the limited visibility. They rode to the train station at 8:30 am on a Tuesday morning, the 15th of January.

The day before, William had accepted a temporary position in Tallahassee as sergeant of arms pro-temp for the House of Representatives when former Sergeant Kilby of Marianna asked to be granted a leave of absence from service for fifteen days. William looked forward to visiting old friends made when he and Elizabeth lived there fifteen years earlier, but as sergeant, they most likely required him to stay downtown in the Adelphi in a small room for $2.50 a night. He had to be near the capitol, especially as they waited for the frequent recesses, which sometimes lasted only for an hour or two, and he wondered if he would have time for anything else.

The train backed into the depot at Monticello with its bell clanging and steam hissing. Earlier, William and the youthful, slender, and well-dressed Burton W. Bellamy, a planter and one of the representatives from Monticello, passed the time as they talked in the depot's waiting room. They had known each other for quite some time, as his Bellamy cousins lived near

Mary's family.

Both men wore long coats pulled away from the front and long in the back half to their knees. With their tied ties and top hats, they heard the train approach and stepped onto the wooden platform, where they waited with several other passengers until the conductor dropped the steps for everyone to board.

Boarding the rail car, almost full with several representatives headed to Tallahassee, William followed Bellamy between the benches, greeting each individual as he passed. He sat near Dannitte Mays, the representative from Madison, Taylor, and Lafayette who was also going to Tallahassee for the session. They talked about the weather and about where each would stay in Tallahassee. When the train's shrill steam whistle announced its departure, the bells clanged, and with a pull and clank, each car pulled at its hinges as it moved away from the depot.

William loved this part of the rails, the rhythm of the engine's huff as the locomotive strained against its load. He and Mays stopped chatting and listened as the train increased in speed and the monotony of the metal wheels clacked over the joints. The whistle echoed through the woods and fields as it went south from Monticello, a quick ride to Walker Mills.

Later, past Bailey's Mills (now Lloyd), both men waited on the newsboy who worked his way down the center aisle of the long car. They had earlier watched him jump onto the train, where he sold his wares on the platform until the last minute as the train pulled away. They watched him calculate the exact speed at which to jump safely aboard.

These boys took chances, but neither man ever witnessed an

accident. Squinting his eyes, Mays said, "Maybe since the train only runs fifteen miles per hour."

Added William, "And it takes time before it reaches that speed." They both nodded. Usually, the newsboys also had a little food to sell, so when the boy came through, William gave him a coin for an apple and biscuit to add to his packed lunch. Mr. Mays bought a novel for twenty-five cents.

A chilled air stirred and lifted the fog. Leaves shivered, and William pulled his coat closer against his body. The cold numbed his hands, but a delegate from Columbia County joined them in conversation. Time flowed faster.

At Lloyd, there also boarded a lone traveler, a rustic type who had imbibed too much the night before. The rail car had nicely cushioned cross benches, where the man found a seat. Once seated, he turned sideways toward the aisle, slumped forward, and propped his booted feet on the edge of the cushion across the aisle. One representative looked at the boots beside him and looked at the stranger. But he was dozing.

Having done so, the stranger did not see the conductor enter the car or make a beeline to the legs which blocked the aisle. The conductor shook the stranger's shoulder and asked him to please remove his boots from the cushioned seat. But after he left the car, back up went the boots. A few minutes later, the conductor came through and brushed the man's boots off the cushion as he passed. This strongly-built big man scowled at the retreating official, and William worried for the conductor's safety, though any of the passengers would have intervened on the railroad official's behalf.

The uncouth man repeated his offense a third time, but this time, the conductor did not bother to do anything. He turned and left the car. Instead, a moment later, the train stopped. Everyone strained to see, and those near the windows tried to hang their heads out, looking in both directions. They soon learned the reason for the halt when the conductor and another railroad official entered the car and ordered the offender brusquely to remove himself from the train.

Weeks later, in Monticello, as William described the scene to his family, he added, "I wonder if he realized his predicament. He stood next to the departing train, miles away from anyone or any habitation. And the next train would not be along until the next morning."

Vollie said, "Did you see him again later in Tallahassee?"

"Nope," said William; "I never laid eyes on him again."

The train pulled into Tallahassee, circling the city's eastern side through the pines and hardwoods. After passing the Cascades, a small waterfall southeast of the capitol, they arrived at the depot station on the far southwestern edge of town. William disembarked with the rest of the passengers, and because the omnibus was full of representatives, he started the short walk to the hotel. He misjudged the hill and how quickly the day warmed after the fog lifted. Even January in Florida can become warm and muggy.

The two-mule-drawn omnibus and its driver knew William. When overcome by the returning empty wagon, William opted to take a ride instead, sitting up front with the driver. The two chatted to the depot and on the return to the Adelphi. They turned left, using a route due east until they came to Adam's Street. The mules plodded uphill to the higher ground behind the brick capitol where the hotel was located.

The Adelphi sat on the west side of Adams Street between

Pensacola and Lafayette, about where the Dolphin fountain now sits west of the western entrance of the new capitol. Built earlier of wood by Governor Thomas Brown, he named it Brown's Inn in 1834 (mentioned earlier when William and his first wife moved to Tallahassee). Its name changed many times thereafter. When he lived in Tallahassee, it became the City Hotel and was renovated extensively, becoming a brick building called the Adelphi when William's family moved from Tallahassee to Monticello. The large hotel sat on what they later called Waller Park, which existed until they built the new capitol in the latter 1970s.

The Adelphi (also known at different times as Pindar's Florida Hotel, Brown's Inn, and the Morgan Hotel, built in 1828 and burned in 1886)

The omnibus pulled to the front of the four-story, white wooden clapboard hotel, which had one story partially underground and a top story as part of its attic. Large, multi-paned windows allowed ample light and air to make its guests more comfortable. A row of dormer windows dotted the roofline, a columned wooden porch ran across its front with a long balcony above for the street's second-floor windows, and a wooden sidewalk below facing the back of the capitol.

William climbed from the omnibus and gave the old gentleman a few coins. With his valise, he crossed the wooden sidewalk and entered the lobby. Instantly, several acquaintances greeted him.

The Greek Revival capitol looked different from when William and Jesse came for the inauguration of Florida's first governor sixteen years earlier, the most significant difference of which was a roof. They inaugurated Moseley on the steps of a roofless capitol. The state had come a long way since. The economic boom of the 1850s helped Tallahassee grow from a rough-hewn frontier village into a handsome capital city.

Florida's State Capitol, before 1902, Florida Memory Collection

Later that afternoon, William met with the speaker per instructions from Russell. He learned they would swear him in the following morning in front of the assembly of representatives to discharge his duties faithfully and keep secret the proceedings of the House when sitting with closed doors. They gave him the responsibility of collecting any or all absent members, such as when they needed a quorum. He would also be responsible to see that all members received a copy of the Journal and Acts of the Assembly, as well as Thompson's Digest.

Florida's old capitol stood facing east, to new beginnings, but what is standing today is a capitol with wings added after the Civil War and a dome added in 1902. The 1845 building forms the heart of the structure at the end of a long incline, atop a hill from which the Apalachee Parkway sweeps to its entrance from below.

William stepped inside the second floor house chambers, with its walls covered with ornamental plaster painted a light blue with cornices stenciled in cornflower blue, a soft brown, and the new mauve so fashionable in its time. In addition, they painted the halls and the rotunda ceiling a light blue.

During the third week of January, Mary hosted a sewing circle with several ladies. The group was making blankets, as fighting could take place any day now. Sitting in a semicircle in front of the hearth with their wide skirts filling the space between their chairs, Ann Lightsey said, "I had hoped nothing would happen yet." She meant the incident in Charleston where the New York steamship Star of the West attempted to pass the southern-held battery of Morris Island. The battery opened fire, and the ship turned around, thus ending the north's first attempt to reprovision Fort Sumter.

Community-wide, the ladies met in an emergency meeting to

discuss the needs of their men and make plans. Added Mary, "Daddy is even raising more hogs than he normally does." Earlier, the newspaper suggested farmers plant more grain and raise more hogs.

They were right to be worried. Major James Patton Anderson, ordered to Pensacola, took command of the troops from Leon and Jefferson Counties, including the Jefferson Rifles. They left Monticello's depot the Tuesday before at 7:30 am with sixty men of all ages armed and equipped. They left amid cheers and shouts from a vast group—town dignitaries, women, children, and families.

In Tallahassee, the Jefferson County volunteers joined the Tallahassee Rifle Company at the depot. Both units were quickly sent by rail to St. Marks, arriving at noon, where they were to board a steamer bound for Pensacola. Thus, Jefferson County's first soldiers were engaged.

Still wearing all black, Mary thought about Henry, poor Henry who had been a Jefferson Rifle. Just a few weeks ago she and the older girls walked to the depot to watch the Rifles leave. She could not help noticing the long black ribbon attached to their flag, fluttering in the breeze. She stopped stitching, lost in thought, pondering an irony. Florrie noticed, and the others stopped talking.

Mary looked around teary-eyed and said, "If Henry were there, at least he would still be alive." Florrie reached to cup Mary's left hand, still holding a piece of fabric.

Mary added, "Oh, let's change the subject."

They all nodded, and Florrie said, "Did you read where our Uncle James grew a nine-pound turnip? They say it is not a record, but certainly it is close, don't you think?"

Still, the ladies, after a spell, returned to war talk. It began when Ann Lightsey added, "Mr. Palmer at the store asked his customers to pay off their notes for last year before he can provide credit again this year. He's never done it before. I guess he's worried about cash flow like all the rest of us."

Mary noticed the looks between the others, and several of the ladies fidgeted and looked away, so she added, "Now, all of you know Ann has had to take care of herself since Mr. Lightsey passed, and if our husbands leave, so will the rest of us. Don't act like talking money is beneath us."

The following Saturday, her son James read another tribute of respect for her brother Henry. It read, *"While the severance of the smallest and feeblest link which binds our Lodge together as a band of brothers, must be felt and deplored, yet in the death of brother HENRY WALKER, we feel that Hiram Lodge has suffered no ordinary loss."*

It still did her heart good to know he was not forgotten. All around town she noticed his Mason brothers wore a black ribbon on their lapels.

When Major Anderson and the companies from Jefferson and Leon Counties got to St. Marks, the steamer there refused to take Major Anderson's men to Pensacola because it was overloaded with cotton. So Anderson and his volunteers returned to Tallahassee. From there, because Tallahassee was the western terminal stop for the railroad, they traveled by wagons to Chattahoochee, waiting for further orders by telegraph from Montgomery.

However, Colonel Anderson, an older soldier and an experienced military man, heard nothing in reply. He waited and worried because his 180-man force only had six days of rations.

Meanwhile, the postmaster general in Washington instructed the Pensacola postmaster to forward all letters, arriving or being deposited, to the Dead Letter Office in Washington. The *Family Friend* called the act "petty spite." Postmasters in Montgomery and Milledgeville received similar dispatches.

The postmaster in Montgomery, though, relayed Pensacola's letters to the post office in Warrenton, Florida, a small town convenient to the forts there. Subsequently, the south scrambled and began its postal system.

The slated raid on Fort Pickens never happened. Florida's senators and leaders in Washington, including Senator Jefferson Davis, sent word to shed no blood. If not for this, the first shots of the war could have begun on Santa Rosa Island as early as mid-January.

Fort Pickens, Old Fort, FortWiki Historic US and Canadian Forts

The following Saturday, the governor disbanded the Jefferson and Leon Volunteers, and Sunday evening, the Jefferson Rifles reached home on a special train from Tallahassee. Mary and the kids, even though still in mourning, went to the depot to meet them as a sign of respect, and it surprised them how many other citizens were there too. The volunteers got a warm welcome.

The next day, most of the volunteers assembled on the courthouse square to be mustered out and then back into state service by Brigadier General Daniel B. Bird. The men gave three hearty cheers for both Bird and Anderson. They also heard Louisiana had joined the Confederacy, the sixth state to join.

The following Monday, the Southern Congress met in Montgomery. Soon after, though, Florida called the Rifles to the Mount Vernon Arsenal at Chattahoochee to become part of Florida's 1st Regiment.

William's letters were full of news about the state in the following weeks. Every few days they got a letter, and either James or Ellen usually did the honors of reading to the rest of the family, usually if warm enough late in the afternoon on the porch. It had been an uncommonly warm late winter. People wondered if the flowers would bloom too early and if a most expected frost would knock them back.

Friends stopped by to see what happened in Tallahassee. Because of the impending war, everyone was interested. James read from his father's latest letter. "They passed an act to create a county called Polk from the counties of Hillsborough and Brevard. Also, another exciting bill, destined to fail, provides payment to the Florida Volunteers, whom they haven't paid for services rendered in the last Seminole war."

Added William Cuthbert, who joined them and sat on the porch with the rest of the family because of the rain, "Well, you know why that bill is up? They'll have trouble drawing another army if they have not paid the last one." William was wrong about the bill. It did pass, but with many stipulations.

A few days later, another letter arrived, and James read again, but to a few more people who joined the family on the porch. It rained again. James read aloud, "New River County is to be split, and the northern portion will be Baker County. A bill changed a creek to a river and ruled the creek a navigable stream."

Interjected Mr. Chase, who, with Mr. Cuthbert, had joined them for the reading, "I wonder which creek he's talking about?"

James replied, "I'm not sure, as it doesn't say here." He continued reading, "Because of a split in voting, it took almost the entire session to elect an attorney general and comptroller for the state."

Mary thought, with the general assembly's business almost done, William might come home soon.

Uninterrupted, James resumed, "There was even a bill to re-survey the boundary line between Florida and Georgia," the area sometimes called "no-man's-land" because of the dispute between the two states. For years, men went to fight their duels there because neither state could claim jurisdiction.

James added, "Most distressing was a bill to move the capital from Tallahassee to Lake City, but most pleasing of all was Mr. Russell's bill to incorporate the town of Monticello. The former failed, but the latter passed."

Said Cuthbert as he leaned back in his chair and grabbed both his suspenders, "Well, it's about time."

Added Chase, "That's the best news of all."

It rained incessantly for days. Sick of the rain, Mary and the family stayed in the house all week. The older kids were away each day to school, leaving her with the younger ones. She found herself with a bit of cabin fever. Earlier, though, her father came. Sitting in her kitchen, he said, "All the streams are high. Fording them was a chore getting here."

Then their conversation took a turn when she said, "Remember when Henry crossed that stream on old Pet?"

He grinned, "Pet saw her chance and dumped him in the middle." They laughed and began telling stories about Henry. The memories did them both good. Her mama was right, as usual. She always told Mary to let the bad go and remember the good, especially the good memories.

William needed the letters from home. He seldom had time to think about anything but felt homesick for Mary and the children. Mostly, these letters were about what happened daily, about the kids' work in school or something that happened in town, but today he read a curious thing.

James wrote, "Dad, we have a recent development here at home. When we receive your letters, we usually read them on the porch before supper. But lately, others from town have joined us for the readings. John Cuthbert seldom misses, and Judge Chase occasionally joins us too. The other night we had half a dozen more people here. After everyone left, Mama said your letters are like reading the *Family Friend*, only people don't have to wait until Saturday."

One Friday evening, Mary received a quick note. William would not come home for the weekend as they only adjourned for the evening and would go into session the following morning. That night, she served her abundant dinner with one less person at her table. The following Friday, he still did not come home as the assembly met Saturday, January 26th, again.

Two weeks stretched to three, and each Friday came word they were still in session. James read to the crowd on the porch,

"Another bill, introduced by Mr. Russell, authorized the county commissioners of Jefferson County to sell their stock in the Pensacola and Georgia Railroad Company."

"Thank goodness," said Martin Palmer, "it's about time."

James added, "Yesterday, they introduced a bill to provide a flag and uniforms and another to incorporate the Pensacola Gas Light Company."

Said Cuthbert, "I tell you all, progress is coming fast to Florida." This letter William wrote to Mary. James read it and usually left out the more personal parts. Everyone grinned and discussed the new gas light technology and how before long, every house in Florida would have a gas light attached to its ceiling.

Disappointed, Mary received word through a letter on Thursday evening, January 31st, about his change of plans yet again. At supper, Florrie told her, "Mom, I know he would want to see you. He's been alone all this time."

Added James, "And we're doing well financially. He can afford the train trip for you."

Mary frowned, and shook her head. "We have money now, but there is a war coming. You do not know how hard it will get." Mary stayed and waited for his letters, which would become the norm for their household.

In Tallahassee, William ordered more cigars to be delivered on Thursday. At 3 pm, though, the House passed a resolution limiting the time for introducing local bills. After Saturday, February 2nd, no local bill could be introduced or entertained except by a unanimous vote of the House. He thought, "Good, another sign we might wrap this up soon."

William marveled at the rapid rate of bills processed through the legislative bodies. They quickly brought back and passed bills that earlier slowed. Second readings by title only, those bills rolled to their third and final reading the following day. He noticed one bill combined the offices of sheriff and tax assessor for Jefferson County, both offices he once held. Counties got ready for the absence of their male citizens.

William bought an ample supply of whiskey and cigars. One can find an invoice in his probate file. There exists only one document. There are no other papers or filings there. When beginning this research, it appeared based on this, William may have been a spendthrift and maybe had a problem with drinking. Upon more research, though, his employment for Florida's House of Representatives surfaced. He probably bought these for the legislators, and in the haste of war, they overlooked the invoice, which they never paid.

On February 4th, while Florida's general assembly worked on legislation and waited, the Southern Convention in Montgomery began their work to create a provisional government. Since Florida had seceded, four more states had followed—Alabama, Georgia, Louisiana, and Texas, in that order. There were seven states, leaving eight other slave states who had yet to secede. All seven of those who seceded sent delegates to the Montgomery Convention.

The state sent a three-man delegation, including James Patton Anderson of Monticello. Within a few short weeks, the delegates drafted a provisional Confederate Constitution, developed a provisional congress, and appointed its provisional leaders Jefferson Davis and Alexander Stephens.

In the meantime, Florida's general assembly kept meeting, and its governor continued to seize all federal property inside its boundaries. Three remained elusive—the forts in Key West, the Dry Tortugas, and Fort Pickens on Santa Rosa Island.

A few days later, on a Wednesday, the first week in February, James read to the crowd now spilling into the yard. People were even bringing chairs from home. Mr. Cuthbert left his chair on the porch full-time. Florrie joked, "Maybe we should start charging rent."

James read, "On Saturday, the House began with a new resolution. A committee of men carried the first announcement from the Senate. When there, they waited on the House for the return of the bill which provided for the Florida Volunteers' payment for their services during the last war."

"Ha," said Cuthbert, "they know the volunteers have them by the short hairs." A roar of laughter went up.

James glanced at his mother, who sitting behind Cuthbert, glared at the back of his head. She thought the remark crass and uncouth. James quickly read, "They plowed through all kinds of bills statewide in stature. Bills about divorces, trials of slaves, free persons of color, wharf-age in Florida's ports, and fees of port wardens. All to pass the time while they waited on the Montgomery Convention.

Though it appears they are getting a lot done, sometimes it is all a lot of talk. Remember the old maxim, when it is all said and done, more will be said than done. That is more true than not over here. A bill moves swiftly, and all of a sudden its wheels fall off. It stops and is left behind. I'm never sure if leadership decided it wasn't wanted or needed, if the person who needed it got in trouble with leadership, or if it just simply got lost in the crush of legislation. So many bills are left behind in committees or are never heard.

They passed a bill which required railroads to maintain

proper cattle guards and railroad crossings. Another passed which prevented someone from penning or detaining stock without the owner's consent. Mary, be sure to tell your dad about that one." James looked at his grandfather, who was grinning. Old Jesse was in town for the evening and joined the family for supper.

William heard them move that the "Sergeant of Arms have the leave of absence after 2 pm until Monday next at noon." It passed. With his valise packed and ready for his Friday afternoon train to Monticello, he planned to go home for the first time in many weeks.

There were several other motions for others to be granted leave. Before he left, though, the legislature took a motion to adjourn sine die on Friday, February 8th. He thought he might have good news for his family, but the assembly quickly postponed the motion until Wednesday next, the 13th. William knew this meant neither the leaders nor anyone else knew when they were going home.

On Friday the 8th, several more legislators requested leave on Saturday. The body worked on bills throughout the day, such as a bill to establish a new state mail service. From the Senate came a new bill to construct a railroad from St. Andrews to a point on the line of Georgia or Alabama. Because Savannah's port as well as Florida's always fought any connection between the two states by railroad, no railroads existed between Florida and Georgia. The ports in Florida feared such railroads would connect Middle Florida to the Georgia ports and vice versa. But now more pressing, authorities feared a northern blockade would surely cut off

Florida's ports.

That afternoon, another bill passed the Senate prescribing the form of an oath of allegiance. Later, he noticed a curious procedure regarding a bill to regulate the duties of registers and receivers of public lands in the state. It must have been an important bill because after being read a second time, they made a motion, and the House went into a committee of the whole for its consideration.

Every member of the House served on this committee. Upon action from this committee of the whole, the bill was reported back to the House as amended. No one left the floor for the entire procedure. The body concurred with the report of the committee of the whole.

They offered amendments, including one withdrawn, which said the registrars and receivers would continue in office until January 10th, 1862. Another adopted amendment changed the compensation from $2,000 to $600. They considered an amendment, which struck an entire section, but after much-heated debate, this amendment failed. Something or someone was being attacked. Somebody somewhere made someone here angry, thought William.

The amended bill rolled to a third reading for the next day. Again, the House recessed for lunch and came back at 3 pm. Sometimes, William could slip away and take a nap after lunch; today was one of those days. This waiting game with the Southern Convention became tiresome for all.

After the recess, a Senate bill relating to a new technology prevented breaches of trust by telegraph operators, but it failed to pass the House. A committee from the Senate requested all bills or resolutions pending in the House relating to military affairs. William realized he missed leaving on the Friday train for home.

The "Broward's Neck" flag with its three stars hung back of the speaker on the wall. William, lost in thought, pondered what the family was doing at home with so much indecision.

Saturday dawned with still no end in sight. The House went into recess for the rest of Saturday until 7 pm, when it resumed again; but they allowed William to go home. Homesick for the family, he took a quick train home for one evening, only to return the following day.

Unexpected, he knocked on his front door. Four-year-old Laura opened the door and squealed, "Daddy!" Everyone came running from all directions. Mary and Florrie in the kitchen came to investigate the commotion in the house. He met her halfway down the hall, his weeping Mary. He swept her into his arms and said, "Lord, Hon, I wouldn't have come home if I'd known it would make you cry."

Later, he walked through their home with its masculine smells of tobacco and oil. Mary kept a fine, gentle home. She had a way of making those around her feel easy and pleased with their lot in life. There was a simplicity in her kindness. He missed it.

By Monday in Tallahassee, he watched the legislature extend and listened with interest to a report about the revenue assessed and collected from the counties throughout the state. Wars cost money, and they worked on a budget. Leon County, with the most collected of any county last year, reported they gathered $16,000 in taxes, Jefferson second with a little over $10,000, and Jackson at almost $10,000. Gadsden and Alachua followed. Of the top six counties, Madison reported more than $7,000. None of the other thirty-one counties paid more than $5,000 into the state's coffers during the prior year. These were meager returns to finance a war.

That afternoon, they took up a bill to reorganize the state's military force and appoint a major general of the Army of Florida. Every step brought the state closer to war.

Later, Governor Perry charged the assembly with preparing for the state's defense. He said Florida was driven "*to the exercise of the right to re-assume to our State the powers delegated to the Federal Union of States.*" He described the federal government as "*like Egyptians of old, they are not willing we should depart in peace from our state of bondage.*"

He told them how President Buchanan expressed his lack of constitutional power to employ military or naval forces in any overt act of hostility against any of the states who seceded. Yet the president repeatedly reinforced forts and ordered men of war to hover on the south's coasts.

The governor pointed out: "*already our brethren of the Southern States are arming. . . . we too have made some preparation, but much remains done.*" The governor charged the assembly to "*swell a number of troops as may be equal to our defense.*" He also directed that they "*make special appropriations for the pay and maintenance of as many troops as possible.*" He requested munitions of war, transportation of troops, and other expenses incidental to the state's defenses. The governor ordered five hundred copies of his speech printed and distributed throughout the state.

On the same day the governor spoke, the Southern Convention met in Montgomery to provide a representative congress to meet for the Confederate States of America. Each state had one vote but had the same delegation size as it held in the US Congress. About forty-eight members attended. The men who led the south saw their move as a counter-revolution against changes *"away from their understanding of US founding documents."* They saw it as a transfer of rule, not an actual revolution. The Confederate Constitution allowed its president to subject a bill to a line-item veto. Davis's term was six years with no possibility of re-election.

Later, Florida's general assembly adopted a long-awaited resolution relative to the legislature's adjournment on Thursday next, the 14th of February. William almost sent home a telegraph but thought better of it. No use getting their hopes up if the legislature extended again.

The business of the House continued as they introduced a resolution to *"use all its constitutional power to aid the Governor to support the honor and safety of this State."* They immediately read it the first and second times, waived the rules, read it a third time, and adopted it. William got a cram course on how quickly they can make laws. After they recessed for the evening, he still ran high on energy. Where did it come from, this second wind? He sat for another hour in the hotel's lobby, drinking with the others.

The following day on the twelfth, the House made further preparations for war. They introduced a bill to raise two infantry regiments and one cavalry. They formed a select committee and referred an act to defend the port of Apalachicola. In other business, they decided no officer would receive pay for any servant, whether or not on duty, but they could draw one ration for each servant in actual service.

All day, they waited to pass the treasury note, bond, and military bills. They could not go home without them. They heard another bill granting land warrants to Florida volunteers and providing for the payment for lost horses while in public service.

The legislature provided for half a million dollars in treasury notes and another equal amount in bonds backed by the sale of public lands, with payment to be made in gold, silver, or the paper of solvent banks. However, hardly anyone had these forms of currency, and in time, the state sold no lands or raised any money.

Later in the day, the speaker read a letter from the governor, who had received a telegram from Montgomery. They would soon organize a permanent government. The governor called for electing Confederate senators at once before the legislature adjourned sine die. The dispatch also said a permanent constitution would be ready in ten days. They needed these elected Florida senators to vote on the new Confederate constitution.

By Wednesday morning, the 13th, they were preparing to sine die. A resolution passed. "*Hereafter*" they would allow no member to speak over five minutes on any bill or allow any other subject of discussion without the consent of two-thirds of the members present.

A bill followed regarding the mail and maintained the mail must be moved regardless of whether the Southern Congress or the state pays. It decided the mail must run tri-weekly from Savannah by steamer to Palatka, by routes from that port, and by steamer on the Apalachicola to routes around that river.

Another bill allowed the issuance of bonds for one million dollars. Still another provided for the issue of treasury notes and a permanent circulating medium. The latter was withdrawn.

In Monticello, when James read the latter, the crowd grew silent. Somehow, this last bit of news brought home how imminent this act of war had become. Changing the subject, James continued the letter, "It says here, 'in the middle of all this flurry of activity, they introduced a bill to amend the act of 1851, which earlier provided for the establishment of two seminaries of learning.'"

Said Cuthbert, "I wonder if they are readying their cadets for the war?" Several boys from Monticello were in Tallahassee or Ocala, where the second seminary existed.

James continued, "They voted on several acts to improve navigation of several rivers and to approve new railroad companies."

Meanwhile, in Tallahassee, during the lulls in activity, William noticed more local bills brought up unanimously and voted upon. With a hodge-podge of messages and bills, they introduced a bill to provide for the security of Florida's citizens transacting business with foreign corporations. Another bill came from the Senate to form a government of the state's military forces.

In the first business on the following day, February 14th, they adopted a motion to adjourn sine die at midnight. Bills moved even quicker than William thought possible. Because a committee of three house members repeatedly hand-carried each passed bill to the Senate and vice versa, he constantly opened and closed the chamber door. The Senate sent several bills, including more Confederacy bills, such as a bill to prevent citizens of any state which passed bank suspensions and stay laws, from collecting debts in Florida.

Most interesting, a telegraphic dispatch arrived from the Florida delegation at the Montgomery Southern Convention. The provisional government was no longer in operation, and there were no longer senators. A permanent government would supersede. It suggested that the assembly elect senators to congress in case a permanent government of the Confederate States of America came to pass. It would save an extra session of the legislature.

On the special order calendar arrived the bill they had all been waiting for, a representation of Florida in the Southern Confederacy. Thereupon, the legislature elected three permanent senators from Florida, and later in 1862, these men would sign the new Confederate State Constitution. One would be J. Patton Anderson of Jefferson County.

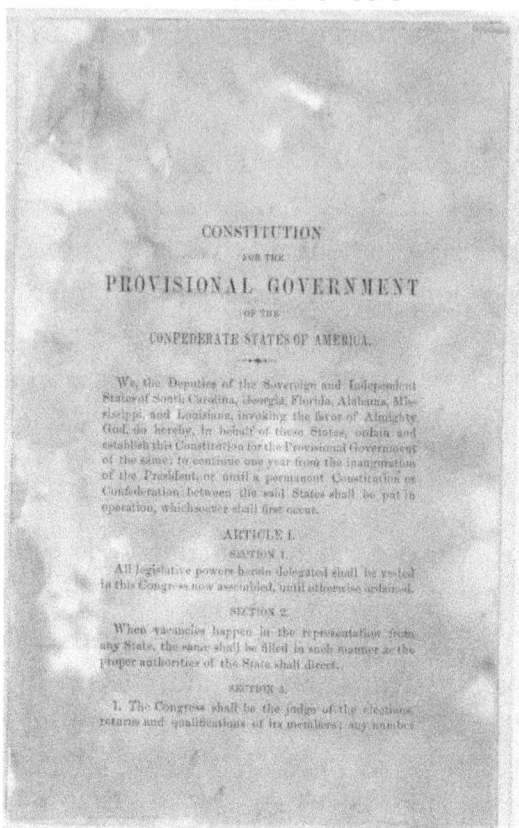
Library of Congress

They immediately moved many of the bills that failed for reconsideration. They failed again, but they agreed upon a new bill to provide safeguards for persons and property upon the state's railroads.

As the year's session ended, William could not help gathering his thoughts about what he had witnessed. During this session, significant events transpired in Florida's history. The union to which Florida belonged dissolved, and Florida resumed its sovereignty, vindicating her rights and honor. It amazed him how harmoniously the men worked together, including the other house. They were indeed one people with less sectional hostilities than he expected.

Because the House's work was ahead of the Senate, the House took a recess before lunch and planned to come back at 3 pm to resume. Meanwhile, members saw for the first time the provisional Confederate State Constitution. William noticed it replicated the US Constitution verbatim, except it had several protections for the institution of slavery, keeping it in any territory of the Confederacy. In addition, it kept in place the US ban on international slave trading. It maintained the existing internal trade of slaves among the slave-holding states.

It gave extraordinary powers to the state while curtailing the powers of its central government, and it gave each state the ability to act in its sovereign and independent character. It incorporated all twelve of the US constitutional amendments ratified to this point. Unlike the US Constitution, though, the Confederate Constitution asked for God's blessing.

When they resumed at 3 pm as expected, a message from the Senate said they concurred with the House amendments to the Senate Treasury bill. Later, a legislator asked for a leave of absence for the rest of the session. They approved it, and William thought maybe this meant they were getting ready to wrap it up.

Another message announced the Senate passed a resolution heralding the selection of the Convention at Montgomery of the Honorable Jefferson Davis and Alexander H. Stephens as president and vice president of the southern confederation. The House recessed again until 9 pm. William used the time to pack for home.

At 9 pm, they received a communication from the governor. He approved and signed several bills and resolutions, including an act making appropriations for the expenses for the fiscal year 1861. It discouraged the members that the governor had nothing further to communicate. Having no further business and having conferred with the Senate, the two bodies adjourned sine die at midnight.

William waited for everyone to clear the chambers before closing for the evening. He walked to the Adelphi, where several men collected for a nightcap. He pulled up a chair and joined the Jefferson and Madison Counties' delegations. It had been a long day, but too stirred to sleep, they talked long into the night, mostly about the news from Montgomery, the war, and their towns' roles to play. Glad no one asked him what he thought about the coming days, he mostly listened.

After checking out and ensuring the House offices and chamber were secure on Friday morning, William bid farewell and caught a ride to the train station. He had had all day to take care of his business in Tallahassee. The train left at 4 pm, and the town expected it in Monticello by 6:15 pm. Excellent; it only took over two hours to go from Tallahassee to Monticello. By horseback, it took 4-5 hours on a good day. When he left Mary on January 14th, he told her he would be gone for fifteen days. It had been a month.

At home, he knocked on the front door again like a stranger, and again, little Laura answered. She squealed loud enough to wake the dead. The house erupted. He swept Mary in his arms, and their children hugged the two of them—a scene that would happen again years later and of which his namesake Henry would fondly remember for the rest of his long life.

#

Chapter 10
Seizing Forts and Raising Militias, February to August, 1861

The women grew weary of hearing their men's war talk, which was all they heard after the Confederate States of America formed in February. Their men itched to go, but William felt differently. He had been there and knew the North had more resources. The South, not equally equipped, had fewer people and factories. The outcome worried him.

One Saturday, while Mary made breakfast biscuits, they talked in her kitchen, the one place they could talk privately. He said, "Nature has been good to our southland. With our climate, we have a long growing season. Our people are hardier and more loyal. That's probably because of the climate and the hardships of living here." Standing over the table, Mary rolled out her dough.

He picked up the latest newspaper. "I think I should read this away from the children. Listen to what they're saying in Virginia." Virginia had still not seceded.

"They entitle this *'The Signs of the Times. Since the developments made by the Harper's Ferry affair, the Press of the entire South has been flooded with column after column, giving expression to the popular sentiment of the masses.'*" Of course, they meant John Brown's raid on the US arsenal at Harper's Ferry in Virginia two years earlier. Brown meant to arm rebellious slaves in Virginia and move the rebellion south, arming slaves through Tennessee and into Alabama. There were rumors some of the US senators had known about Brown's plans.

William continued, "*That sentiment is that the people have at last been convinced of the utter impossibility of the Slave-holding portion of the Confederacy, to remain in the Union, without a ruthless sacrifice of honor—and we can safely say that—seven eights of the Southern people now favor a dissolution. Blood has been shed upon Southern soil, by commissioned agents of the north."* He looked at Mary, and she saw his concern. William continued, *"This is the first fracas of the 'irrepressible conflict'—it foreshadows what is to follow."* He stopped again and cleared his throat. *"The hot Southern blood is aroused, and it demands a severance of all connection with the Northern murderer."*

Arriving at the inopportune moment, four-year-old Laura slipped into the kitchen with her light-brown hair hanging in loose sausage-sized curls that reached halfway down her back. Wearing a deep blue calico dress, she crawled up on a chair to watch her mama cut lard into the flour with two knives. William sighed and stopped reading.

He added, "In short, it says that they expect our southern congressmen to walk out on the session any day now." They exchanged glances, and Mary sighed. She looked at Laura, whose tiny fingers were rolling a little biscuit with the dough.

Laura loved to help with the biscuits. At first, she liked to play with the dough, and Mary allowed it; but lately, Laura wanted to learn how to make biscuits herself. William continued to chat, but part of Mary's attention turned to their child.

"Your biscuits will be only as good as the flour you use, so make sure you use good, soft flour." Mary continued to pinch the cold lard into the flour using her hands. She added, "Some only use butter, but sometimes I like to use lard."

Mary broke the lard into small pieces and added, "You don't want to hold the lard in your fingers too long, because you don't want it to melt. You want it to stay in small pieces, about half a pea in size. Now you try to pinch lard into the flour."

Laura, kneeling on a chair at the end of the table, leaned over the big shallow wooden bowl and started fingering the lard, breaking it between her tiny fingers. Mary pulled her hair back and tied it with a strip of fabric from a group of strips she kept for this purpose. In the morning, even Mary herself left her hair long, and it often got in the way.

Mary watched and tried not to interfere. "In the summer, I usually cut the lard with two knives because the lard melts too fast."

William watched silently. He thought about having to leave them and travel who knows where. William knew the boys were old enough to take care of themselves, and Mary herself was quite capable. He sighed, and Mary looked his way.

Their eyes locked. He saw the worry there deep in her eyes.

When Mary and Laura finished cutting the lard into the flour, Mary showed how to make a small shallow hole in the flour, a hole about fist-sized. She took a salt-glazed clay stoneware jug, decorated with incised and in-filled cobalt flowers, and poured milk into the hole.

Mary said, "See this? It's Grandmother Wilson's milk jug that my mama used to keep milk handy in her kitchen. She said your Granddaddy Wilson got it on a business trip to Charleston. A potter in the Edgewater District made it." She showed Laura how to knead the dough.

Mary added, "But only knead it for a minute. Flour your hands and begin pulling out about a handful of dough like this." Mary rolled the dough between her hands until it made a biscuit about an inch high and about as big around as a cat's head. "Now, make your biscuits." Laura grinned as she made each biscuit, though they were not the size of her mama's.

Mary had a pan nearby that she wiped with lard. She showed Laura how to place each biscuit in the pan, one by one. "Make sure each touches the other. That way, they will rise more and be fluffier."

William watched the two as Mary instructed their youngest daughter. He loved that she taught each girl from a young age how to prepare meals and care for their home. His mind wandered. Sadly, with their nation on the verge of war, Laura's life and the lives of all their children would change, and probably not for the better.

"Mary, there are lots more people, many times more there than we have here. They've got big factories and plenty of them." Both silent, they locked eyes again, and she observed something she seldom saw—unbridled worry.

He added, "I fear that if we go there, all we have is loyalty, boys with big hearts, plentiful food crops, and an indomitable spirit." William stopped talking, and silence filled the space between them. She had heard it all before. He looked away and gazed out the window behind her. "But worst of all, I'm not even sure we have God on our side."

Several days later, with the older children at a party and the younger in bed, William and Mary sat on the porch. It had warmed nicely during the day, and the late February humid air probably meant a front was approaching, with more frigid air behind it. In the quiet, the boards squeaked as they rocked. William said, "Well, it's no surprise that Jeff Davis called all those men. The north will retaliate soon, especially since we seized all their federal properties. I guess they are waiting to inaugurate Lincoln."

Mary had heard it several times before that day from others. It was all anyone talked about at the stores, on the streets, or over dinner. The whole south was on edge. The crickets sang in the woods nearby, and William added, "There's also talk about moving the capital to Richmond."

Mary rocked silently, lost in her thoughts about her brothers who were of age to fight. William reached and took her hand. "I'm of age, so they'll likely get me, and they'll get John. At least we'll be in different units, but thankfully, James remains too young. Maybe it will be over by the time he reaches majority." She looked at his hand and into his eyes.

Mary had nothing to add, and she returned to her own thoughts. What if William didn't return? What would she do? Move to Elizabeth? Maybe she should do that anyway while William was gone, but what about schooling and the children? So many questions. She pushed the thoughts into the recesses of her mind, where her questions with no answers hid behind the shadows, sometimes never coming into the light of day. It would do no good to contemplate further, certainly not now. She felt numb and turned to look into the dark street.

William added, "I'm also worried about my years as sheriff. Like any lawman, I have enemies. If I join, I'll go early before they draft and place me where they wish. I'll join a unit out of the county. If I die, it won't be from a shot in my back."

The following day, Mary made lists in her head. She felt she needed a plan. She had tossed and turned all night, thinking about the Indian War and how her mother had prepared for leaner times ahead. They smoked extra meat, stored extra grain, and prepared the cabin for an attack. She needed a plan too.

She thought to herself, I might try the hermetically sealed goods at John Palmer's store. Tomatoes or lima beans might be something to keep on hand.

Palmer's hermetically sealed goods did not sell well, and he offered them cheaply. In the meantime, she planned to do canning herself. Vinegared, cucumbered pickles, onions, and cabbage would be good to keep, as well as brandied fruits. All of this plus the extra smoked meats and stored corn. She would also put in extra potatoes this year and dry fruit.

In February, when the southern convention formed the new Confederate government, the North considered it illegal. Both Jefferson Davis and Alexander Stephens wrote arguments about the legality of secession.

As soon as the South formed its provisional government, on February 22nd, they inaugurated former US Senator Jefferson Davis, president of the newly formed Confederate States of America, for a term of six years. During the recent US election in November, Florida had voted for presidential candidate John C. Breckinridge, a southern Democrat from Kentucky. He lost, and President Davis appointed him to his cabinet as the Confederacy's Secretary of War. Shortly thereafter, acting president Jefferson Davis called for 100,000 men to defend the Confederacy.

There were only two functioning bodies of government in the new confederation—an executive branch of Davis's administration and a legislative branch of the Confederate congress. The Confederate provisional congress, a unicameral body, would later become a permanent bicameral congress. The Confederate Constitution outlined a third judicial branch, but its creation and seating never occurred. State courts filled the void.

By March, William, Mary, and their family were glued to the news, mainly by word of mouth, because the *Family Friend* came weekly on Saturdays. People discussed what they heard and knew about the oncoming war, a topic of conversation everywhere from storefronts to porches, from offices to fields.

The first Saturday in March, the family and the whole county went to the courthouse to review a fine new company of recruits. This group of young men, actually schoolboys, lined up at the foot of the courthouse steps. Named the "Jefferson Guards," they would stay behind to guard the town and county. They were proud to be Monticello's only line of defense should the war venture this far south.

James and Vollie looked soldierly, standing at attention in their lines. Mary and the girls had made their uniforms earlier. Standing next to William in a full-skirted black dress that billowed in the wind, Mary hoped they would never use the uniforms outside the county. She felt an icy chill overtake her, and she trembled. The thought of her babies going off to war terrified her. William noticed her shiver, and he drew her closer to him for warmth.

William Denham, Florida Memory Collection. There were two William Denhams who were first cousins. One was sixteen at the beginning of the war and was the son of Andrew Denham of Tallahassee. The other was twelve at the beginning of the war and was the son of William Denham of Denham & Palmer Mercantile. Both probably served in their home guards.

Behind the school, the Monticello men and boys drilled on the parade ground throughout March. They practiced cavalry maneuvers, held shooting contests, and kicked up much dust, yelling until they were hoarse. You could hear them throughout the town, their voices rising from the town's southern border. Also, on calm days, dust hung in the air.

With Monticello full of revelry and militia drills, the city's girls and ladies frequently came to watch. Some girls practiced the art of coquetry. Mary noticed the sidelong glances, the swaying of hips accentuated by their bell-shaped gowns, and the laughter, flattery, half smiles, and cut of eyes toward her sons. None of this went unnoticed by either James or Vollie. She talked to William about it and encouraged him to speak to the boys.

The next evening, James, William, and Vollie sat around William's table in the parlor, using saddle soap and saddle oil to clean and treat their boots. Said William, "Boys, your boots are an absolute necessity. Take good care of them, and they will take good care of you. Keep your socks as dry as possible. Try to keep three pairs at all times."

Vollie replied, "The sergeant said the same thing."

Said James, "Well, between the extra socks and these heavy boots, I'll weigh a ton trying to march all day." Their father had taken all three pairs of their best boots and got them resoled with heavier soles. They added longer tops.

On Saturday, William walked to the schoolhouse to watch them drill, and later that evening, after the kids were in bed or visiting, he and Mary rocked on the porch. He said, "The worst part is the June bugs who don't know their rights from their lefts, clumsily running into anything in their way. James is right. That unit needs much more drilling than every Saturday."

Before long, they added practice on Thursdays too. The stores closed to give the men and boys the afternoon off, something done as late as a few years ago in Monticello to give the merchants and clerks time off because they work on Saturdays.

From the old timers, the men and boys listened to instructions about fighting with their swords and sabers. They had recently brought their sabers from their cabins, and some were as old as the seventy-five-year-old Revolutionary stories heard around the fireplaces of the county. Only three generations had passed since the Revolution.

The men fell into formation with squirrel guns, muzzleloaders from the Indian wars, horse pistols used under Andrew Jackson himself, and a few derringers. There were even dueling pistols along with a couple of handsome flintlock rifles with metal inlays. The sophistication of the few latter may be why they named themselves the Jefferson Rifles. Probably no one suggested they call themselves the Jefferson Squirrel Guns.

After drilling each Saturday, the same rhetoric continued in the town's saloons, whereupon general brawling frequently occurred. William always went home early to Mary, relieved to be no longer young or the sheriff.

While the South readied itself, on March 4th, the North inaugurated President Lincoln. Throughout the south, newspapers published his inaugural address word for word.

Sitting on the porch on a pleasant spring evening, William read Lincoln's address by the kerosene lamp on the little table underneath the parlor window. The lamp was something they had added when the family's young people began courting on the porch.

With his glasses on his nose, William's voice carried above the crickets and other night sounds. *"Apprehension seems to exist among the people of the Southern States that by the accession of a Republican Administration, their property and their peace and personal security are to be endangered."*

Said James, "You bet, old man." Mary winced at her son's disrespect for the president but held her tongue.

William continued because Lincoln meant this for the people of the South. "*I have no purpose, directly or indirectly, to interfere with the institution of slavery in the states where it exists. I believe I have no lawful right to do so, and I have no inclination to do so. There has been no reasonable cause for such apprehension.*"

William took a deep breath and added his thoughts, "That the north wants to change our economic structure overnight certainly causes apprehension."

William looked at Mary, and he could see the questions on her face. He said, "I'm not sure this will be enough. In the North, others voted for him who did not feel the same way. Many men feel they elected him to do away with slavery, and the South believes his electors will hold him to it."

William read on. "*There is much controversy about the delivering up of fugitives from service or labor. The clause I now read is as plainly written in our Constitution as any other of its provisions: No person held to service or labor in one State, under the laws thereof, escaping into another, shall in consequence of any law or regulation be discharged from such service or labor, but shall be delivered up on claim of the party to whom such service or labor may be due.*"

Asked Florrie, "Is that what they use to reclaim runaway slaves that flee to the northern states?"

"Yes," replied Mary, "if they can find them. Many disappear."

Added William, "It puts the Negro at a disadvantage wherever they go. There are always people there who will take advantage of another person, and a person running from the law becomes vulnerable—the reason we were so worried about John. If the wrong person found him, they could use this information to make him do whatever they wished. So many young men flee and grapple with trouble in their wake."

William began again and got to the meat of what Lincoln tried to relate regarding the fugitive slaves. He read, *"I do suggest that it will be much safer for all, both in official and private stations, to conform to and abide by all those acts which stand unrepealed than to violate any of them trusting to find impunity in having them held to be unconstitutional."*

Vollie frowned, and twelve-year-old Zech questioned, "What does that mean?"

William replied, "As long as the laws stand on our books, we must enforce them. The fugitive laws are still laws, and the North should return the runaway slaves until the laws change."

Added Florrie, "Poor things. I guess that's why some of them go to Canada."

William read Lincoln's truly historical words, *"The Union is much older than the Constitution. It was formed, in fact, by the Articles of Association in 1774. It was matured and continued by the Declaration of Independence in 1776. It was further matured, and the faith of all the then thirteen states expressly plighted and engaged that it should be perpetual, by the Articles of Confederation in 1778. And finally, in 1787, one of the declared objects for ordaining and establishing the Constitution was 'to form a more perfect Union.' But if destruction of the Union by one or by a part only of the states be lawfully possible, the Union is less perfect than before the Constitution, having lost the vital element of perpetuity. It follows from these views that no state upon its own mere motion can lawfully get out of the Union."*

That instigated more conversation, but the best occurred at the railroad station the following day. Men collected there and informally discussed Lincoln's address. The pros and cons of secession and its legality dominated their conversation. Said Andrew Denham, "The Constitution stayed mum on secession. Our founders wrote nothing about dissolving the union."

Added Shehee, "But the northerners must have thought it could be done. The New England Anti-Slavery Convention tried to get them to sever their ties with us years ago."

Added Judge Chase, "It all does not matter, though, because sovereignty stands de facto."

William observed frowns until Cuthbert said, "Speak English, Judge. We don't know what you mean."

"It means," said Chase, "that if we win, any illegality under US law would be irrelevant, much like the undisputed illegality of our American rebellion under British law. The new laws of America rendered the illegality of the American Revolution irrelevant."

The crowd chewed on that momentarily until James Walker added, "To the winner go the spoils." There were knowing nods all around.

Two days later, in retaliation for Lincoln's inaugural address, the Confederate Congress called for 100,000 southern volunteers for twelve months of service.

Days later, at dinner, William said, "Texas seceded. We're seven now." Texas left with a list of causes, including the fact that twelve northern states had violated the fugitive slave clause of the Federal Constitution. Texas felt this nullified a material provision of the compact.

Like Texas, four of the other seceding states listed their grievances. Like Louisiana, though, Florida's ordinance of secession did not state why it seceded, only that it simply declared its severing of ties with the Federal Union.

Later that month, Mary and William were early in the kitchen on a Saturday, letting the kids sleep in and enjoying the solitude. William read to her from a copy of the *Family Friend*. "Mary, it says here that the southern part of the New Mexico Territory formed a secession convention and voted to join the Confederacy. They call it the Confederate Arizona Territory. More than half of the American Indian troops have joined the Confederacy."

He raised his right brow, and she replied, "Goodness, now we're fighting together." Later, during the war, the five civilized tribes, including the Creeks, sent representatives to sit on the Confederate Congress.

After a spell, he added, "Well, they're complaining about the blacksmith's shop again. Listen to this." He read, "*There is one portion of our town that is really in a dangerous position, and we will not be surprised if, at any moment of the night, we hear the startling cry of 'fire, fire!' resounding through our streets; and we will know at once, as which point to hurry to witness the conflagration. We refer to the Blacksmith shop in the rear of our office. It is situated right in the heart of town, surrounded by a number of wooden buildings, and every night until 10 or 11 o'clock, huge volumes of sparks may be seen flying from its chimney.*"

Mary said, "You know they're right, but if the town wants the blacksmith's shop moved, they need to raise the money." William thought to himself, Mary is one of the best reasons for women's suffrage. His mother had been another.

Meanwhile, the South continued its war plans. In Montgomery, they appointed diplomatic agents to go abroad to keep trade open and solicit funds. The foreign governments, though, never officially recognized any of these men.

Meanwhile, Washington waited for any foreign government to waver to send a sharp warning to those who did.

By the end of March, instead of abandoning Fort Sumter in Charleston, Lincoln reinforced it with Federal arms and troops. The northern news appalled the people in Florida. Floridians flocked to join their local militias. War bonds began selling locally. Andrew Denham, William Bailey, and John Beard were the Confederate agents in charge of selling Confederate bonds for all of Florida except Pensacola. Both Denham and Bailey were from Jefferson County.

The turmoil for Mary and her family began in late March when local leaders raised companies for the state's quota of the Confederacy. The earlier local militias were a good start, but the existing independent militias merged, forming state infantry regiments to serve in the Confederate army.

Governor Perry ordered Colonel John W. Eppes of Tallahassee to organize a company of volunteers in reply to a requisition from President Jefferson Davis for five hundred troops from Florida. Eppes called for the 10th (Jefferson) Regiment to assemble in Monticello on March 28th. Men throughout the county came to the courthouse that morning, and the family went there to watch the regiment form at noon.

First, there were speeches by Colonel E. E. Blackburn, Dr. T. B. Lamar, and Colonel James Patton Anderson from above on the courthouse steps. They requested volunteers, and seventy-two men answered the call, including her cousins Jesse Allen (Jess), Joel E., and William J., all sons of her Uncle Littleberry Walker. People still talked about her Uncle Littleberry and the blockhouse siege on the Withlacoochee

River during the Indian War. Following family tradition, his sons were among the first to enlist for the Confederacy. Mary's baby brother Joseph also stepped forward.

    The volunteers elected J. Patton Anderson as their captain. Anderson and his volunteers were told to report to the depot at Station 3 (Walker Mills). At 8 am on Tuesday, a train of cars would carry them to Tallahassee, from which they would march to the Chattahoochee River (about 40 miles). From there, they would travel by boat to Pensacola. On their way to Pensacola, other Florida companies from Franklin, Jackson, Gadsden, Madison, Alachua, and Santa Rosa Counties would join them. That was the plan.

    Mary watched the group of men standing at attention in front of the courthouse that breezy March morning. Her dark indigo skirts billowed in the wind as she tucked loose tendrils of hair behind her ears. From the steps of the courthouse, the speaker's words carried on the breeze, *"Ladies, we need your prayers and words of cheer, and with those, we can be invincible . . . until the last armed foe is expelled from our soil and an honorable peace is secured."*

    She realized how hectic the past month had been as the nation prepared for civil war, each from its side. Mary also admitted that she might never see her brother or cousins again. She studied each of their tanned faces, watching the wind blow through their dark hair. Standing erect in their uniforms, they were handsome to her, as the Walker men always were.

    Mary's three first cousins and twenty-five-year-old brother left by train on the 4th of April for the Chattahoochee Arsenal with their destination, Pensacola. The company had planned to take the train only as far as Tallahassee and join there, but it didn't happen exactly that way.

Joining them from Jefferson County were an L. B. Walker, parents unknown, and an M. W. Walker, the latter believed to be Michael, the son of Mary's distant cousin David and Rebecca Walker. All expected six days of travel and to serve under General Braxton Bragg.

All signed for twelve months. At the Mount Vernon Arsenal they would become Company I of the 1st Florida Regiment, also known as the Magnolia Regiment. The 1st's members were from Leon, Jefferson, Madison, Gadsden, Franklin, Jackson, Alachua, and Escambia Counties. They were led by their first colonel, J. Patton Anderson of Jefferson County.

With Colonel Anderson and the rest of the Jefferson Rifles on their way to Pensacola, or so everyone thought, the remaining Rifles met in Monticello. They re-elected a new captain, William O. Girardeau, the schoolmaster at Jefferson Academy.

Elizabeth's and Aucilla's men did their part. In the Jefferson Rifles alone were A. J. Walker (Albert J.), son of James Sanders Walker; G. W. (George W.), son of Jesse Walker (Mary's brother); George, son of James Sims Walker; Jesse, son of James W. Walker; William B., son of Jesse (Mary's brother); and A. W. Walker (Alfred W.), son of David M. Walker.

Others, whose families were close, included Berry and A. D. Sledge, William H. M. Scruggs, T. J. Chase Jr., and two Palmer boys. As Rifles officers, there were two more Walkers, William Allen, son of Jesse (another brother of Mary), and Michael, as well as the well-known Samuel Pasco, voted 5th Sergeant. The company that Saturday voted to tender their service for active duty in the Confederate Army. This group would later become Company H of the 3rd Florida Infantry.

Meanwhile, several days later, Monticello received word that four hundred southerners were on board the Brooklyn outside of Fort Pickens under the command of General Bragg. Still, no one knew if Captain Anderson and the Rifles were there. Messages were meager and unreliable since there was no rail service to Pensacola or telegraph either.

Almost every conversation during these otherwise pleasant days in early April centered on Fort Pickens or Fort Sumter. All eyes were on both strongholds, surrounded by Confederate armies and awaiting orders to storm their ramparts. Monticello's face, though, looked west toward Pensacola because they thought their native sons were there.

A week later, Sarah left the house in her lavender frock with its ruffled boat neck that framed her face. She spent an hour with two friends, fixing each other's hair in cascades of curls. They headed for the parade ground behind Jefferson Academy. A battalion of cavalry from Hamilton, Madison, and Jefferson Counties under Colonel G. T. Ward assembled there to drill and for review. Sarah and her friends dressed well for the occasion and sashayed by to watch the men practice.

The men from the 1st Florida reached the Pensacola Navy Yard by Saturday, April 13th. Because there were no railroad or telegraph lines between Pensacola and Tallahassee, Monticello heard no information for three weeks. Finally, the county received word—the Jefferson Volunteers were all well and in excellent spirits. Captain Anderson prepared them with drilling and maneuvers.

In New York, rumors leaked. Several steamers loaded with horses, foraging carts, boats for surf landing, carbines, cannons, tent poles, and ammunition were heading south to ports unknown. Thus, the Charleston volunteers waited on the rumored war fleet ordered from Washington.

People speculated Sumter, Pickens, or even ports as far west as Texas would receive the steamers from New York. In a mere happenstance, Governor Sam Houston asked troops to repel Indians in Texas during the same month.

By the second week of April, the newspapers reported that outside the walls of Fort Pickens, over 3,000 men from Florida, Mississippi, New Orleans, and Alabama were encamped. Impatient for a fight, Bragg and his troops were eager to begin, but the warring began first in Charleston.

Why Charleston? April 1861

After seceding in December, South Carolina demanded the US Army abandon Fort Sumter and other facilities in Charleston Harbor. In reply, the Federal Army covertly moved all it had from Fort Moultrie to Fort Sumter, much like they did at Fort Pickens in Pensacola.

Meanwhile, adding to South Carolina's demands, each southern state seceded and ordered all United States property surrendered to them, including military property. One by one, the state's militias took control of these properties within their boundaries except for key properties like Sumter, Jefferson in the Tortugas, Taylor at Key West, and Pickens.

Recently inaugurated, President Lincoln did not want to provoke the states into conflict, but he refused to surrender any Federal installations still held by the north. His and the north's stated aim was merely to restore the South to the union, but the devil is always in the details.

Lincoln tried to resupply Fort Sumter in Charleston Harbor

until the South Carolina militia opened fire on Friday, April 12th, at 4:30 a.m. The battle lasted thirty-two hours until Fort Sumter surrendered on Saturday afternoon. They evacuated the fort without deaths, but the American Civil War had begun. (Actually, one Union gunner died in an explosion that occurred as the defeated Union troops fired volleys in honor of the Union flag being lowered.)

In reply, a Pensacola reporter reported that within forty-eight hours of the fall of Fort Sumter, 3,500 more men were on the march to Pensacola with equipment commandeered from Fort Sumter. The effort to take Fort Pickens had begun.

When the Civil War began in the spring of 1861, Mary, thirty-nine, had borne ten children. Together, she and William, forty-nine, had supported and raised thirteen children in all.

With only 140,000 people in Florida, Jefferson County, the third most populated county, had 9,800. The most numerous were Leon (Tallahassee) and Jackson (Marianna), but most people in these top three counties were slaves.

Of the total population of Florida, 78,000 were free, and the rest (61,000) were slaves, 44% of the population. Thirty-four percent of the families living in Florida owned at least one slave. In comparison, only 8% of the families living in the US did likewise, but this statistic included the non-slaveholding states.

The news about Fort Sumter probably reached Monticello the same day by telegraph at the depot. William may have been one of the first men in the county to receive the news. Places like Ocala, without telegraph or rail connections, would only learn about the beginning of the war two or more days later.

Most likely, William and Mary sat on the porch to consider what lay ahead.

Later, she dreamed about the Indians in her family's cabin again but remained acutely aware of her dream-like state. After she awoke, she lay there listening to the night sounds outside. She could not sleep and wrapped herself around her husband's back side. He must have been awake because he took her arms and held them within his own, next to his heart.

Businesses in Monticello prepared for the economic difficulties of war. The *Family Friend* carried several notices asking store's customers to please settle their accounts, probably a universal plea for money throughout the county, if not throughout the south. Several threatened to no longer extend future credit if people did not fully pay their debts.

Also, in April, a grand jury met to examine the public buildings in Jefferson County. Unfortunately, the courthouse leaked severely, the steps to the back entrance were unusable, the inside walls were defaced, and the railing around the upper portico was missing. They found the jail roof and fencing dilapidated. The report to the county commissioners omitted any recommendations for future repairs.

Meanwhile, General Bird formed another company of volunteers. The following Saturday, the 2nd Squadron of the First Regiment of the Florida Cavalry held their first parade in Monticello; the regiment included Mary's brother J.J. Under the command of Captain Livingston, one unit came from Waukeenah and another from the Jefferson Guards, which included both James and Valentine.

Speeches followed, and Mary noticed the rest of her boys hung on every word. She had to admit the men in full uniform made a handsome show. She looked at Sarah with her friends and saw the girls in full uniform themselves with their flounces and bell skirts swaying in the wind.

Strangely, Mary realized her giddiness about the impending war. It reminded her of their emotions before a storm—the excitement as it approached, the wind thrashing the trees amid the rumbles and lightning, and a fear of what it might bring.

After the firing on Sumter and still no formal declaration of war by the US government, President Lincoln signed an official presidential proclamation dated April 15, 1861 which called for the recapture of forts and suppressing the rebellion in the south.

Outside Fort Pickens on Santa Rosa Island near Pensacola, a rumored 8,000 Confederates led by General Bragg awaited orders. Inside the fortification, there were 4,000 Federals. The men outside the fort worked on constructing sand batteries and evacuated all the citizens in the nearby town of Warrenton. Both the men inside the fort and those outside expected a hard fight. Bragg asked for more men.

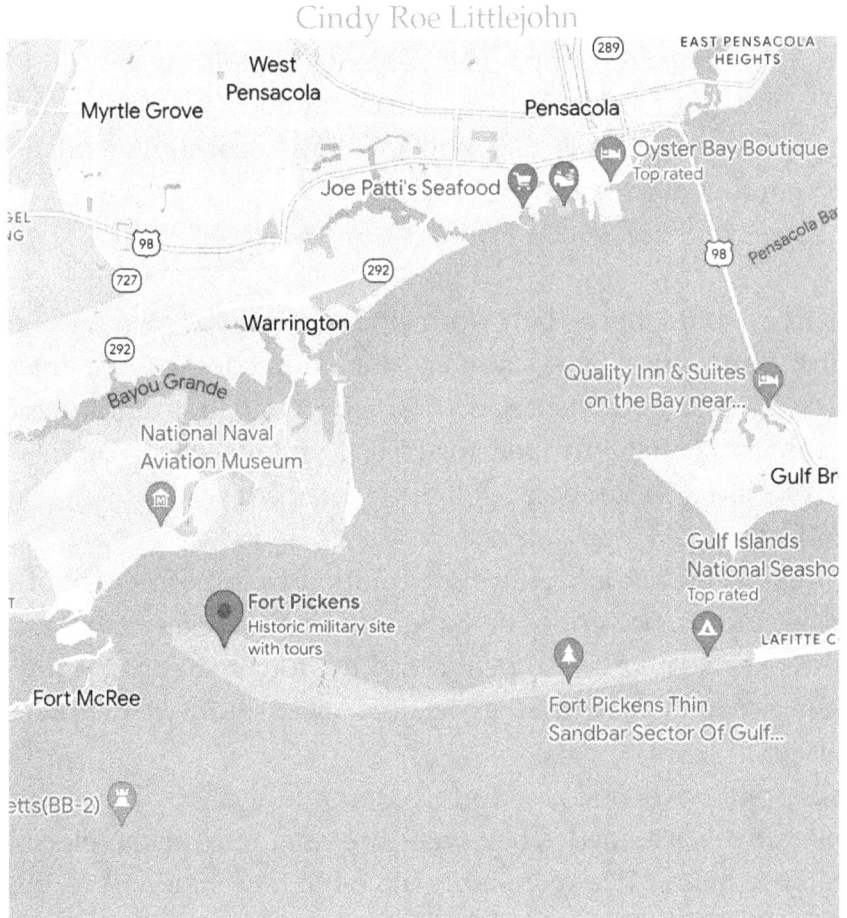

Map Showing Location of Fort Pickens, Warrenton, & Pensacola, Google Maps

In Pensacola, the reporters painted a scene of *"thousands of soldiers and every means of transportation were rushing back and forth carrying balls, shells, cannon, sandbags, lumber and much more. Far into the pines, back from the beach, stand long lines of tents lit by thousands of campfires sparkling through the woods. From those woods, one can hear singing, fiddling, and general joviality. Nine o-clock's retreat is sounded by hundreds of drums, and stillness falls throughout the woods as fires are put out and darkness and silence descends. Only the lanterns of the relief guards flicker through the trees like fireflies."*

The Confederacy appointed Colonel Patton Anderson to command the Florida Regiment. He resigned his seat in the Montgomery Congress, and William again went to the polls to elect another delegate from Florida.

There would never be a formal declaration of war by the North, but after Fort Sumter, the Confederate Congress proclaimed the existence of war. In retaliation, President Lincoln immediately called for 75,000 volunteers to suppress the rebellion and reoccupy the US properties taken by the south.

This resulted in a firestorm of emotion from both the South and the North. Both sides demanded war. Young men from the South and North rushed to join, and the four remaining states, when asked to raise militias against their southern brethren, refused.

Virginia, Arkansas, North Carolina, and Tennessee consecutively seceded. They were the final four of the eleven seceding states. The remaining slave-holding states were the border states of Delaware, Maryland, Kentucky, and Missouri, which never seceded.

Maryland tried, but President Lincoln did not let it happen because of the locality of the nation's capital, even breaking Federal law to do so when he sent Federal troops into Maryland to keep their legislature from meeting and seceding.

Maryland even showed sympathy for the Confederacy when a mob of southern sympathizers stoned train cars with Federal troops as they passed through on their way to Washington, DC. The New York soldiers didn't return fire, but the Massachusetts ones did, killing several Baltimore citizens. Kentucky declared its neutrality, but Delaware and Missouri remained silent.

With the bombing of Fort Sumter, Mary worried about her relatives in South Carolina and her cousins in Pensacola. She told William about her fears as they lay in bed. Neither could sleep. She said, "I guess Marse Lincoln will take Charleston, if nothing else, to seek revenge."

"I don't know," said William. "If he's smart, he's looking for the best place to begin, and Charleston or Pensacola may not be it. If I were him, I would strike Richmond and remove our ability to make munitions. It would strike an arrow through the heart of Dixie."

Meanwhile, in Monticello, the town made further preparations for war. A request in the *Family Friend* in late April called for all men who had volunteered to receive a vaccination for smallpox. It warned: "*Smallpox flourishes and prevails when men congregate and subject themselves to privations and hardship.*" Even though they did not expect their two older boys to go off to war soon, William probably took both James and Vollie to Dr. Palmer's, where all three got their vaccinations.

By May 1861, the Confederacy moved their capital from Montgomery to Richmond because it had to be held at all costs. Richmond's critical infrastructure, resources, and supplies were needed to sustain the war. Said Mary, "I can't understand why they moved the capital so close to the northern boundary."

Added William, "I think because the ironworks are there. They have to keep it operating, and having the capital within the same area will make sure they always protect it. The south does not need two distant major areas to protect at all costs. It will be easier to protect one than two. This probably means most battles will be in Virginia. That's good for Florida. Maybe it gives fewer reasons for fighting here."

Meanwhile, Tallahassee sent Robert Gamble and his company of eighty men to the newly-constructed Fort Williams at the St. Marks Lighthouse, a fort of logs and sand with two 32-pound guns. Within a week, they sighted the first Federal blockading ship, which scuttled and sank a Confederate sloop in the channel to the river, an act in retaliation for the sinking of a barge nearby to keep Union boats out.

Armies, local militias, and other units continued to form throughout the state. Officers were either appointed by the governor or elected by their units. The South's officers came from slave-holding and non-slave-holding families, and the ranks elected their junior and field-grade officers. Meanwhile, unknown to the Confederate army regulars, General Bragg received a request to forward any men he could spare to defend Virginia.

Men throughout Monticello and the county discussed the type of state militia unit they would join. William, forty-nine, one of the best riders in the county and known for having a cool head, signed immediately. Most of the men who joined were much younger and, unlike him, most were second-generation Floridians. All of Mary and William's children were of this generation.

With little class consciousness, almost everyone's fathers and grandfathers had worked hard to exist in the wilderness of Florida. By this time, most of Jefferson County's genuine aristocrats had passed away, bottomed out, or moved on.

The county's men discussed in the stores, at the livery stables, and at the bank those who were kind, illiterate, and even the best shot in the county at seventy-five yards. Who was best at living outdoors? Who could build a fire in the rain or wind or both? So and so could track food on foot, while illiterate John from the flatwoods could always find water. Many had learned their proficiencies from the Indians.

The recruits were not only the sons of planters but also the sons of merchants. Some were cow hunters, like the Walkers. Others were small farmers and swamp hunters. Full gentlemen by Virginia standards in Florida were rare. The recruits had all kinds of abilities which didn't necessarily come from the sons of the wealthy.

Cow hunters like the Walkers were landed and had mules and horses, but many of the county's men did not. Many lived hand to mouth on the game they harvested and using their bounty for barter. They had neither horses nor mules.

Small farmers had no horses, but they had their mules, animals of abstract intelligence though unusable for riding in battle because, unlike a teachable horse, a mule will always balk if it thinks its life is threatened. Plus, the farms couldn't do without their mules, anyway. They usually only had one, which their wives and children needed to sustain themselves. Uniforms were out of reach for many. A lot of men lived a hard life with hardly a pot to piss in.

James noticed this while in camp. The Jefferson Rifles spent two weeks practicing camp life on the Wacissa River. Days later, at dinner, he said, "The planter's sons thought the whole camping thing hard and weary. They were exhausted, many too fatigued even for supper. But the poorer boys thought it a holiday, they being used to working before dawn and till after dusk. They thought reveille at dawn meant sleeping in."

He added, "By the week's end, with everyone better conditioned, the camaraderie around the campfires grew interesting, if not captivating. Rich or poor, they had more things in common and formed new friendships."

With a gleam in his eyes, James added, "Daddy, I'm making $11 a month as a private." He thought it an outstanding salary, but William knew for himself it would be a terrible cut in pay. He and Mary had been frugal and saved, so he thought they would be fine economically for a while.

William added, "I noticed this too during the Indian Wars. Probably it is why your grandfather and I became close friends even though we both came from unique backgrounds."

He smiled at Mary and added, looking around the table at his children, "And it might be why all of you are here today." Mary blushed, and the kids cackled. Little Laura looked around and laughed because all the others did.

William initially joined the unit William O. Girardeau raised from the rest of the Jefferson Rifles Company. Mary's brothers Archibald and George did too. This might have also been Henry's regiment had he not become a casualty. It would later become the unit for her Uncle James's sons Jesse, twenty-two, Joel P., twenty-nine, and another of her brothers, William Berry, twenty-one.

William and Mary's sons James and Vollie were also in this unit, though their part would be to protect the local area. This group of volunteers would join the 3rd Florida Regiment.

Daniel Bird raised a company from the Jefferson Beauregards. The men in this company mainly came from below Walker

Mills, and Florida sent them to patrol the Indian River region on the eastern coast of Florida.

Though they initially would stay in Florida, unit after unit marched away from the county amongst much fanfare and well-wishes. Their women sewed flags with slogans and held parades in their honor. Two of the county's commissioners marched away with them. Still, three remained on the commission throughout the war—James S. Walker, a distant cousin of Mary's, Calvin Davis, and George Taylor.

William read a letter from his brother Jesse who lived in Tennessee. Jesse's son Samuel had enlisted in the Confederacy in Smith County, where they lived.

Meanwhile, downtown, Mr. Fleming's Theatrical Corps performed for three nights straight to meager crowds. The Andrews probably stayed home and saved their cash. People remembered how inadequate their means were during the Seminole Indian Wars.

A problem was when the men and boys left behind the wives and children, the real sufferers of the hardship caused by absent husbands and fathers. In time, they lacked cash for food, clothing, and other necessities not grown on the farm.

As an answer, the Florida general assembly enacted a law designed to allow counties to raise property taxes to relieve these soon-to-be indigent families. They levied and distributed the monies locally.

The town and county raised money for uniforms and guns. Those who could afford it paid for theirs and someone else's. Because of people's pride in not accepting charity, the women and benefactors kept to themselves who were given uniforms and who had to buy their own; the extra was hidden in the bolts of fabric ordered and purchased as a whole. In sewing circles throughout the county, the ladies made the uniforms.

In one such circle, at Mary's sister-in-law's home, Betsy Walker cut the fabric at a large table in her parlor when her scissors dropped to the floor, sticking into the wood. Said her Aunt Ann Lightsey, "Well, someone's coming."

Mary laughed and added, "Maybe fate is confused. More like someone's going!"

Added Betsy as she bit her lower lip and frowned, "More like everyone's going." All the men were leaving for war.

In the interim, the local militia continued meeting to drill and practice. Local units elsewhere also met similarly, such as Aucilla and Waukeenah.

William read on the porch from the *Family Friend*, "*A stagecoach now running from Madison to Valdosta connects our railroad to the Savannah, Albany & Gulf. One can leave the Tallahassee Depot at 3 pm and reach Savannah the next day at 12:55 pm.*" He looked up from the paper. "I guess the stage travels all night between Madison and Valdosta."

For Monticello, the best and most direct route to Savannah was provided by a first-class six-horse coach. One could leave at 7 pm and reach Savannah by 1 pm the following day. Railroad and stage competitions had come to the area. Both routes would carry local soldiers north to the war.

By early summer, Mary's Uncle David, her closest living playmate from South Carolina, enlisted in the state militia, the 5th Florida Infantry, Company G, at Camp Leon. He signed on for three years. David and little George worried her the most. David, more like a brother than an uncle, had been there before her brothers were old enough to play; and she always felt like George was her child since her mother needed so much help and had so little time for him.

Mary felt close to tears the day she learned about David. She walked around in a fog. After losing Henry and Joel, she felt her world spinning out of control. She remembered something her mother had told her: control was only an illusion. She could hear her voice, "Mary, only God has control, so you need to hand it to Him. Let Him do the worrying, because you have no control yourself."

She needed to let go as much as possible. Alone in her kitchen, she pushed the thoughts far back into her mind and tried to smile for the first time all day, though she had nothing or no one for which to smile. She took a moment to take it to prayer. Sitting at the kitchen table, she folded her hands and leaned forward, propping her elbows on the table and her forehead on her hands.

The new Confederacy and its seceded states were only sometimes in agreement. Florida's new governor, John Milton, a lawyer from Jackson County and relative to the famed English poet of the same name, feared a provisional army that was answerable only to the Confederacy. He was more concerned with raising a strong state army for Florida's self-defense. The state would need all its male citizens to defend its 1,197 miles of coastline.

Not alone, all the other southern states' local political machines feared the Confederate government's encroachment on their rights and individual freedoms. Conscription was on the horizon, along with collecting taxes. One man at Palmer's said, "*Next thing we know, they'll requisition our crops and impress our slaves."* Many of the state's leaders debated whether the state should cede power to this new government in Richmond.

Of course, the Confederacy disagreed and knew they needed complete control of the south's armies. They argued for the military necessity and the centralization of government.

Thus, at first, the Confederacy was at the mercy of the south's governors, who denied the new government their soldiers and treasuries. They pushed for the rights of their citizens, communities, and states.

Because of William's front-row seat to Florida's political theater, which made him a seasoned conversationalist, his family's political conversations were often complicated and complex. In time, their home became a gathering point for Jefferson County's who's who. Mary had learned long ago as a child how 'to be seen and not heard.' Now, as a woman, the advice remained equally important.

Around her sewing circle, though, she played a different role. As one who heard much, the women understood Mary had insights others didn't. Though her lady friends considered her a quiet woman, they knew that when she spoke, it contained information of inherent quality.

Unfortunately, though, Mary also had insights that distinctly worried her. Later, she woke screaming, and poor William didn't know what had happened. He put his arm around her. As she moved in closer, the two of them rocked gently. "What's wrong?" he asked.

She replied, "I had that terrible dream again. Lying on the bare floorboards underneath my bed, the Indians were there. I could see the stone hearth with its iron crane hanging over its flames. I was in my parent's cabin, though I hadn't a clue where they were or what happened to them." William pulled her close. She added, "Nothing ever happens, and I'm not sure why it still scares me."

Earlier, they had shared a cup in their room, now redolent of sassafras tea, a concoction brewed for its believed ability to thin the blood and help prepare for the heat of summer. The cup sat on a table near the fire with its dried leaves at its bottom. Moonlight from the window washed the room in a surreal glow.

They both lay there, drowsy and lulled by the soft hum of raindrops against the roof. Mary focused on the sound of the rain and the fragrance of the tea to help calm her mind. She murmured, "You would think I would get used to the dream and realize nothing ever happens." Hearing no answer, she listened to the rhythm of William's breathing. He had dropped off to sleep. Sleep for her, though, did not come easily.

To the west, near the Navy Yard in Pensacola, the 1st Florida, including her brother Joseph and cousins, continued to live in tents and wait for an opportunity to seize Fort Pickens from the Federals. Meanwhile, their general mulled over papers from his government asking him to send them to Virginia. Down the coast, they extinguished the St. Marks lighthouse light. It would remain dark for the rest of the war.

By mid-summer, the second regiment to be raised, the 4th Florida Infantry Regiment, was mustered into Confederate service in July. They raised the regiment in response to an increased quota assigned to Florida by the Confederate War Department, an overall request to raise 4,000 Florida men for Confederate service for one year. Florida now had the 1st, 2nd, and 4th Florida Infantry Regiments and the 1st Florida Cavalry Regiment.

The 4th included companies from Gadsden County, Franklin County's Beauregard Rifles, Madison County, Lafayette and Columbia Counties, Liberty and Washington Counties, and Jackson County's Dixie Boys.

The 1st Florida Cavalry, or Davis's Cavalry Battalion, was organized near Tallahassee in the same month and had eight companies. Mary's brother J.J. joined this battalion. All William and Mary's children especially thought their Uncle J.J. looked dashing in his uniform and sitting astride his sorrel mount. Instantly, Mary noticed the children's backyard games now included a cavalry officer.

The 2nd Florida, organized in Jacksonville on the 12th of July, marched through Monticello, numbering 940 men, en route to Virginia. Mary and the children made a point of seeing them as they marched through. Her sister's brother-in-law raised one company called Pillan's Company from Madison County. The other companies included Jackson, Leon, Hamilton, Alachua, Columbia, Nassau, Duval, Putnam, and Marion Counties.

They encamped near the depot, and the following day nine hundred plus men fell into line for the march to Groover's Station on the Savannah Railroad, a march of twenty-two miles. The county's citizens provided generous provisions for the men of the 2nd, including a fine supper and bountiful breakfast. They fed them another dinner in northern Jefferson County before they left the state.

No units from Jefferson County went with the 2nd Florida, but one of its most essential citizens did. Dr. Thomas Palmer left town as its regimental surgeon. Governor Perry had appointed Dr. Palmer, subject to approval by President Davis, and he mustered into service on July 13 in Jacksonville for twelve months. Dr. Palmer's departure with the 2nd worried Mary the most because he was her lifeline when the children were ill.

By mid-July, Tallahassee organized the 3rd Florida Regiment, including the Wakulla Guards, the Jefferson Beauregards, the Madison Grey Eagles, the Jefferson Rifles, and the Suwannee and Columbia Guards. The 3rd was placed under the command of Monticello's Colonel William S. Dilworth. Subsequently, Dilworth ordered Company H of the Florida 3rd under Captain Girardeau to Fernandina, but not before going into camps at Monticello on Monday, July 22nd. Also known locally as the Jefferson Rifles, the men were ordered to prepare to leave on Tuesday evening. Because the company was a little shy of the seventy-eight men needed, they called for more men.

Encouragement came through gentlemen officers and the best-equipped company in the state. They also told them this unit would stay in the state.

Since the Rifles encamped in town for two days, the citizens supplied them with all the necessities for their life there. The town came together and provided them with provisions and picnic baskets for the trip to Fernandina, plus cash for the expenses.

A sea of people gathered at the depot in the first week of August. William had been extra busy handling his side of the arrangements for the Jefferson Rifles to depart for Fernandina. Everyone waited on the train.

He listened all morning to fathers giving their sons manly words of encouragement, and he could not help thinking about

John Slicer, whom he felt sure would be drafted. In a letter to the *Family Friend*, one man described the sea of people as *"the bright eyes striving to smile amid their tears, and thus making our parting easier, the last words of caution and cheers from parents and friends. The last tokens of friendship and love are still fresh in our remembrance, and the whole scene is so daguerreotyped on our memories, that it can never fade away."*

Waiting for a train, Lloyd Depot, personal photo

The Rifles boarded and found the train crowded. The troops rode in boxcars, not in passenger cars, and because of the August heat, they kept the boxcar doors open. Outside the train it rained, and it was still raining when they stopped in Madison. Families in Monticello heard later that the men and boys appreciated the boxes of food the ladies made for the trip.

The rain pelted them all night long until they arrived in Fernandina the following morning at 8 am. The community did not welcome them since the people in Fernandina didn't know they were coming. Thankfully, they still had their boxes of food from home. They dined on these again for breakfast and dinner before they drew their first supplies from the commissary.

They marched four miles from the railroad to a town in Nassau County called Old Town, and the following day they witnessed two vessels, both of which made for the mouth of the harbor trying to run the Yankee blockade, a US frigate. The frigate captured one runner, but the other, a bark from Capetown, Africa, loaded with hides and wool, ran aground. Firing their big guns, the Rifles tried to aid them from the fort.

They eventually watched this vessel burn, but not before trying to help its crew escape with as much of their cargo as possible. Later, the company returned to its camp disappointed, fatigued, and hungry; but they were cheered to find their supper waiting, cooked for them by the ladies of Old Town. Old Town, also known as Old Fernandina, situated upon Amelia Island, had a full view of Fernandina, about a mile in the distance. They could also see the ocean and the town of St. Mary's in Georgia, about three miles away.

They split the Rifles into six companies on Amelia Island, three at Old Town, two at Fort Clinch, and one at the battery.

Mary joined the Jefferson Ladies' Soldiers' Aid Association in Monticello which met at the Jefferson Academy every Tuesday at 8 a.m. She, Florrie, and Ellen joined this group. They knitted socks and hand-stitched undershirts. Dozens of ladies labored each Tuesday until sundown, making shirts, drawers, undershirts, socks, and anything else their soldiers needed. Mrs. B. Bird served as their president and appointed committees for purchasing material and directing and inspecting the cutting and sewing.

About the same time, the Jefferson Beauregards, under Daniel Bird, joined the Florida 3rd Infantry Regiment as Company E. Underage boys begged their parents to allow them to join and began enlisting. The Confederacy's call for more men from Florida required its boys to join; there were not enough adult men to fill Florida's quota.

The Beauregards were at St. Francis Barracks in St. Augustine and remained under constant drill. They had yet to be tested in battle as had the Rifles. Mustered into the Confederate States service on August 5th, the Beauregards numbered eighty-six men, rank and file.

The ladies of St. Augustine formed a "Sewing Society" and tendered their services to the troops there. The unit had reported one death since they left Monticello. The wife of one of their members died on August 9th.

The Barracks today serves as the Florida State Arsenal, headquarters for the Florida National Guard, constructed by 1755. The historic structure made of coquina stone stands on Marine Street.

The first night, after the rumors began, James wasted no time. Supper became a battleground around the dinner table, with James on one side and Mary on the other. "You're too young, James. Your good sense hasn't even fully developed yet. You still think like a boy. War is man's work. You have no business being there," she told him.

James glared at her and looked to his father for help, but

William met his gaze for only a moment and looked from each of his children to his wife. He had a habit of never arguing with his wife in front of the children.

James replied, "Mama, all the parents are letting their sons go. They understand the South cannot win without all its men."

Mary, with her eyes narrowed into two slits, said, "Yes, it needs its men, but not its boys." She rose from the table, slammed her napkin, and added, "yet." Standing with her shoulders squared and both hands on her hips, Mary became an imposing woman when riled.

James pushed himself from the table, and his chair in its inertia fell backward. So mad that one of his boots got caught in his chair, he stumbled from the room. Sitting next to him, Val leaned over so far to avoid the ruckus he almost pushed Florida from her chair.

William, who had dropped his napkin by his plate, went after him. Frowning, though, Mary shook her head no to reinforce her sentiments to her retreating husband.

#

Chapter 11
Defending Florida's Coasts, August to December, 1861

In July 1861, when the 2nd Florida Regiment went from Fernandina to Virginia, the Confederate authorities mustered more men into the 3rd Florida Infantry near Pensacola. They sent them to Fort Clinch on Amelia Island north of Jacksonville to assist the 4th Infantry.

Before leaving Pensacola, though, they lost J. P. Sealley and William J. Moore, twenty-six, who died of typhoid fever. Most men in Pensacola suffered considerable sickness but were in better health when they left for Fernandina, where they saw little active service during their first year. They did a great deal of hard work, though, building sand batteries.

Sand Batteries, Pensacola, 1861, Florida Memory Collection

Company H of the 3rd Infantry, from Jefferson County (formerly the Jefferson Rifles), had 132 men and boys led by Captain William Girardeau, headmaster of Jefferson Academy. Within its ranks were people closest to Mary's heart—William A., Archibald, George W., and W. Berry Walker, her brothers; Jesse W. and Joel P., her first cousins from Uncle James's family; and two distant cousins, Alfred W. and Michael.

They remained on the east coast with companies stationed on the Atlantic at St. Augustine on a bluff of the St. Johns near the river's mouth, and at Fort Clinch, where they stationed men from Jefferson County.

Meanwhile, Captain George W. Parkhill called for volunteers to serve in Virginia. By August 7th, several men and boys from Jefferson County reported to camp in Tallahassee and joined the Governor's Guards. They became the Howell Guards and eventually a part of the 2nd Florida Infantry as Company M—a result of President Davis's War Department requisition—an increased demand for one thousand Floridians.

Elsewhere, Captain Daniel B. Bird raised his Company E, and they sent them to St. Augustine. All this took place within six weeks. Monticello grew void of its menfolk.

In the heavy humidity of the second Saturday evening in August, Mary and William sat outside on opposite ends of the porch with their family. It had not rained yet, though the skies darkened. Mary wiped her forehead and bosom several times with a rag from the kitchen. She had recently doffed her heavier mourning clothes, but her thin cotton chemise and pink floral bodice stuck to her skin. Every once in a while, she re-fanned her skirts around her chair, making an air current, but it was never enough.

At the table under the lamplight, William read from the *Family Friend,* "This one's entitled *'Col. Finnegan's Legion. We had the pleasure of meeting with Col. Joseph Finnegan, of Fernandina, in our town last Sunday. He was direct from Richmond, and informs us the War Department authorized him to raise immediately a Legion of Floridians, for service in Virginia.'"

Vollie interrupted, "Who is he?"

Replied William, "I think he has a sawmill near Jacksonville, but I've heard he is also David Yulee's business partner on the railroad between Fernandina and Cedar Keys."

Added Mary, "His wife is the sister of Governor Reid's wife, and his primary residence is in Fernandina." His illiterate Mary always amazed him with her knowledge and memory.

Several days later, all morning long, Mary wept; but she did it quietly, trying to keep anyone from seeing. In fact, mad, she could hardly look at her husband. Though it was still early in the day, it was already hot and sticky outside as the humidity level rose as darkened blue-gray clouds formed. Well into the dog days of summer, it would rain early today instead of the usual 4 pm deluge.

Mary, working since the first light to take advantage of a cooler kitchen, prepared their daily meals. Mostly, though, she didn't want to face William. The sight of him made her stomach churn.

Fifteen-year-old James walked into her kitchen. His gray eyes sparkled and reminded her so much of her brother Henry's eyes when he got excited. James, a handsome boy, had jet-black hair from her side of the family and a dark complexion. He would be sixteen in December, five months away.

He said, "Mama, can I get a couple of biscuits and ham to

take with me? The boys will go to the diner, but I want to save money for a new rifle."

Headed to the parade ground for drilling, the boys and men would be there all day. She could hear shouting and shooting throughout the city. Of course, he wanted to stay with his buddies rather than return for dinner at midday with the rest of the family.

A few days earlier, James had enlisted in the Third Florida Infantry, Company H; and William must have signed for him. She was furious and had been ever since.

The morning James left, she finished quickly in the kitchen. Outside, the wind swirled to gale force, and her dress wrapped around her. The winds were a welcomed relief when they whipped through her cotton skirts. Lightning popped, and the thunder rolled within seconds behind it. She rushed through the dogtrot into the house.

A light blue, beige, and green plaid frock hung to dry in her bedroom. She wanted to brush its hem to remove the dried soil left from a downpour day before yesterday.

A Short Dogtrot, Florida Pioneer Village, Silver Springs State Park, personal photo

She pushed in through the back door. In the hall, she saw William coming in the front. The back door slammed behind her as she quickly ducked into their bedroom.

Outside, the lightning and resulting thunderclaps came quicker. With speech almost impossible, William followed her and yelled. "Hon, do you know where James is?"

In their bedroom, with her back to him, her head high and shoulders squared, she squatted to look at the hemline of her dress. Frowning, he stood slightly slumped with his hands by his sides, waiting, but she ignored him. It had been this way for days.

He reached down and pulled her up, turning her around.

Looking her square in the eyes, he spoke loudly, "Hon, you know all of Florida's younger boys are on our coasts to protect our ports. They've hardly fired a shot. He's more likely to get shot in a hunting accident." But she knew things were heating in Virginia and Tennessee. When would they send other units north?

She pulled free and took the dress down, holding it by the hanger and draping its skirts across her other arm. She turned, looked past him, and disappeared into the hall.

He watched her leave and followed her, but as soon as he stepped into the hall, she rehung the dress and breezed past him again, headed toward the front porch where the wind and rain from the storm were blocked. He yelled after her, "The general orders say they will not move his regiment from the coasts, and they only raised it to support the regiments there." She disappeared out the front door.

He slumped, walked into the parlor, and plopped into his desk chair. She hadn't talked to him in days, and she kept her back to him at night. He thought, "It might be August, but everywhere that woman goes, it's as cold as January."

Before now, bit by the spirit of adventure, fifteen-year-old James Jefferson Andrews and his friends had dreamed about going to Texas to kill buffalo and Indians. Instead, they joined the military in the summer of 1861 to kill Yankees. They were not alone in thinking that the Yankees had a feeble constitution and were timid with no enthusiasm. They believed, as the newspapers told them, the northern boys were weak and would quickly perish in the sultry southern sun.

Of William and Mary's children still home, only James was

barely old enough to fight.

William watched as Mary drilled James on what to remember. On him, like dots on dice, she told James to keep her informed when and where they sent him. She said, "A mother invariably wants to know where her children live, so I expect you to write often."

William said, "My Lord, Mary, the boy won't have time for soldiering." She ignored him.

But William had instructions of his own. He had taken James aside yesterday and discussed sending letters home and how he could write any news he liked but to not cry and whine about the service. He would only upset his mother when there was nothing she or anyone else could do.

William explained that James belonged to the army now, and their word was law. No letters from home could help him. "You are theirs, son, lock, stock, and barrel. You were theirs when you signed your name to their papers. Your contract is between you and them, not us."

He added, "The military has to have total loyalty, and you must follow orders and do whatever your officer tells you. It is the only way things work in the military. The army has an overall goal or job it must do, and if everyone did whatever they wanted, they would never meet the goal. You must follow their orders. Keep your head down and protect yourself the best you can."

William wished he had sent James into one of the cavalry units, but Jesse could not do without the horses he had left. The army begged for more beef.

James, an excellent rider, had worked cattle since old enough to sit on a horse. William also wondered if a cavalryman would have a better chance of surviving. But there was no use now.

The Confederacy needed their horses, as their horses gained value. James would be in the infantry.

Washington Mackey Ives of Lake City, Florida, 4th Florida Infantry (taken in Chattanooga, TN, August, 1862) Florida Memory Collection

All the men in Mary's family would be mortified if they knew about her earlier visit with Colonel Dilworth, but James was her baby, a fifteen-year-old. She impressed upon the colonel, whom she had known since childhood, that James was only a boy—her boy she now placed in his hands. She asked him to please keep an eye on him.

Colonel Dilworth, about the same age as Mary, had moved to Monticello as a child when his father died. His mother moved there so her brother James Scott and his family could help raise her four children. Dilworth may have been one of the children Mary and Henry first met when they moved to the county. The colonel took Mary's hands in his, looked her in the eyes, and said he would monitor James. She felt better but still wouldn't look her husband in the eye.

She didn't stop with the colonel. She also conversed with others in James's unit. Anyone she saw on the streets, she stopped to chat with and always asked for their help in monitoring her boy, including J. A. Cuthbert, whose son also joined. In addition, she chatted with George Hartsfield, Joel Kinsey, and several Walkers, both cousins and especially her brothers George, William, and Berry, all of whom were in the 3rd in Company H. James would have lots of eyes on him, compliments of his mother.

James enlisted in the service on July 23rd, 1861. Captain Stockton mustered him in on August 10 in Fernandina. His schoolmaster William O. Girardeau of Monticello led his company.

Since Manassas, a dearth of war news followed as both armies retreated behind their lines. William told Mary, "A wise commander keeps his own counsel. General Beauregard probably surveyed what he saw during and after the battle but kept it to himself."

William Scott Dilworth rose quickly in the Confederate Army. Earlier in the month, he had joined as a private in the ranks of the Jefferson Beauregards, but because he had represented his county in the legislature, had served as a member of the late constitutional convention, and served as a soldier during the Indian Wars, he had a record. His colleagues and officers said he was one of the most *"orderly, sober, and unobtrusive soldiers."* The home he built in Monticello still stands on the south side of East Washington Street, three blocks east of the courthouse.

Since James was underage, someone had to sign for him. In this story, the someone was his father William. If so, his mother may have disapproved. It is uncertain, but this story shows a mother's anguish, and women all over the south and north most likely suffered these consequences.

Now, did Mary really act this way? I would have, especially in a town where everyone is so close. James joined with one of the Cuthbert boys, who was also underage, and one of the Palmers. Samuel Pasco, the headmaster at Waukeenah Academy, joined along with two of the Scruggs boys.

These regimental companies had names like the St. Augustine Blues, the Hernando (Wild Cats) Guards, the Wakulla Guards, the Duval Cow Boys, the Madison Grey Eagles, the Dixie Stars from Columbia County, and the Suwannee Guards.

James's military records described him as seventeen, having a dark complexion, gray eyes, and black hair. At 5' 11", almost six feet tall, they listed James's profession as a student. However, according to his earlier records, they sent him to Fort Clinch at fifteen. His first letter may have gone like this:

> *Dearest Mother and Father,*
> *We are here, and now I have seen the Atlantic Ocean. It is nothing like the Gulf at the St. Marks Lighthouse. Mother, enormous rolling waves of water crash upon a shore of white sand. It is beautiful, as is the island.*
> *The tenor here is anything but pleasant, though. First, there*

are no women at the fort. Maybe there are in Fernandina, but we wouldn't know because we've been here ever since. The bodily privations are of the worst kind. We've had nothing to eat but salt pork, ham, hog, and bacon. Our beverages consist of lousy whiskey and, even worse, water.

There are rattlesnakes as I've never seen, plentiful all around. Saltwater, sand gnats, sharks surround us, not to mention the volumes of sand we shovel daily. We expect the Federals any day, so we toil in anticipation.

Because of the beating sun, no shade, foul water, and the effort in building sand batteries, I expect to return home nothing more than a husk, dried and withered to the bone. Eight of our men deserted. You may soon read about them in the Family Friend.

At night, though, our time around the campfire is fun. I am surrounded by a great group that tells hundreds of stories. However, we're also surrounded by sand gnats and mosquitoes. Daddy, the sand gnats will be your worst enemy when you get to where you're going. Those things are maddening.

Tell everyone hello, and I love them.
Your loving son,
James

On the porch, William looked up from the letter and said, "I hear they're like our summer gnats, but they bite."

(James's letter was gleaned from other wartime letters written from Amelia Island.)

At Fort Clinch, James and his fellow soldiers practiced drilling and built batteries of sand. Earlier, the men had elected by ballot their own company and regimental officers, both commissioned and non-commissioned. He admired the democratic nature of the regiment and the ability to elect their leaders.

One night around a fire, he listened to the other boys his age as they bantered. One said, "No doubt in my mind; one of us is worth ten of them." He meant Yankees, and it was a common sentiment in the south.

There was always lots of talk, especially bragging rights. Another boy added, "I bet it'll all be over in ten months."

"Hah!" said another, who upped the ante. "It'll only take six months at the most."

But the conversation turned more serious, significantly, when James added, "My mama was much aggrieved. I tried to tell her everyone was doing it, but she told me I had to wait until I was sixteen. I'm only fifteen, so she's still mad at my dad."

Camp life excited James at first. Living outdoors and sleeping on the ground was all the adventure he imagined, but the drilling, sand gnats, and sergeants he had not. One night a month later, lying in his bedroll, damp and itching, he thought about his mama. He realized he had traded her for a sergeant.

Pensacola, 1861, 9th Mississippi, Florida Memory Collection

Because Florida exhausted its treasury notes, the Confederate Congress passed an act to reimburse Florida for the money it spent arming, equipping, and maintaining troops. Arms were challenging to get, even if one had money. The central government refused to accept unarmed Florida troops into service.

William first enlisted in the state's militia on May 11th, 1861, but this may have been a simple militia unit that stayed around Monticello. Some records reflect this service with Florida's 1st. Later, though, he joined the Florida 4th Infantry Regiment, earlier organized at Jacksonville, Florida that summer. Conflicting records show William enlisted in the 4th Florida as early as August 29th and as late as September 5th.

Mary tried to push back any thoughts about what could happen with James gone and William soon to follow. Lately, she couldn't get the latter off her mind. William might never return home, and little Joseph, Henry, and Laura probably would not remember their father. Her nightmare returned.

   William knelt on their bedroom floor to assemble last-minute items for his haversack. Mary walked into the room and laid two folded blankets on the floor. There would be one to lie upon and another underneath for warmth. Though still hot as Hades in Florida, an occasional cold front crept south in September. He hoped this year it would be sooner than later. Earlier, she had given him cookies, jellies, spicy rum raisins, and a package of tea leaves made by her and their daughters.
   She placed his boots and freshly pressed uniform on a chair in the corner near the window. When he finished packing his haversack and left the room, Mary slipped into it two little gifts—in his Bible, she placed a picture of herself and tied with a pale blue ribbon a lock of her auburn-tinged, dark brown hair.
   She changed into her best nightgown as he walked into the room. Mary brushed her hair, but William said, "May I?" She handed him the brush, and he brushed her long wavy hair, stroking it repeatedly while she sat. It felt wonderful, and though she was still worried, it relaxed her. They had sent all the kids to bed earlier. With the house quiet and the bedroom bathed in the soft glow of candles, he took her hand. She stood, and they blew out the candles one by one. They planned to go to bed early.

   At the first sign of daybreak, she awakened and wondered at the miracle of a good night's sleep. Mary found William shaving on the back porch. She hurried to the kitchen to fix breakfast, and Florrie joined her a few minutes later.

He looked pleasant, jovial. She knew how men loved adventure. Her father and brothers taught her that. From her mother, though, she had learned her part in these adventures. Her role was to stay behind and keep the home fires burning. But lately, she felt more like an appendage.

William entered the kitchen, buttoning the last buttons on his fresh white shirt. With his boots and tucked shirt, he made a handsome figure. At forty-nine, he wore it well. He smiled his contagious smile, and Mary said, "Lordy sakes, you're always happiest when going somewhere." He grinned.

True, he felt a touch of excitement, but sadness set in later at breakfast with his wife and children. This could be his last meal here. He maintained a pleasant face, but one look at Mary and he knew she knew.

Mary and William sat side by side in the buggy. It had been a hectic August morning of tearful farewells from neighbors and family. William looked dashing in his gray uniform and matching homespun shirt over blue britches. He left behind his excellent wool coat since it was still summer and his unit would remain in Florida.

Their younger sons ran ahead to the train station while their daughters walked alongside the buggy. Mary held two-year-old Joseph in her lap. Laura sat between her parents.

The entourage descended on tree-lined Dogwood Street, past the handsome Presbyterian Church. Mary said, "Why are we going this way?"

He sighed and said, "I guess I want to remember all this." Overhead, the moss dripped from the oaks in the canopy of limbs and leaves. Monticello had become a pretty town thirty years after she first saw it.

This morning, she put on her best day dress, the navy blue calico with its modest V neckline and matching V waistline. Its full sleeves added an hourglass appearance, especially when she added an extra crinoline to give the full skirt a bell shape. She wanted William to remember her at her best.

Florrie and Sarah made sure the kids dressed well too. William had to notice his fine family.

Mary and William heard a roar of voices. Buggies, buckboards, and families surrounded the depot to say goodbyes to their menfolk. He ushered her and the kids through the crowd and into the waiting room packed with people.

Then he guided her into his office. He had probably taken a leave of absence, but perhaps the railroad had hired no new agent yet since so many men had left the county. The clerk waved them in to wait for the train.

William sat with his back to his desk and the children gathered around him. Standing back, Mary, with her handkerchief, forced back tears and gave them time alone. She had said her goodbyes the night before and earlier that morning.

She entered the packed waiting room, then moved on to the platform. Her father and Uncle James arrived and hugged her. Jesse said, "How're ya holding up, hon?"

She got all misty-eyed again and replied, "As well as expected, Daddy. William will be pleased to see the both of you." She hugged her Uncle James and ushered both into the office.

The waiting room, partitioned by a tall wall which rose short of the ceiling, gave everyone an unobstructed view of the oncoming train through its gabled end with two windows.

Inside at the ticket window, men stood in a line taking care of last-minute business. People occupied every seat around the room's perimeter, and children sat on the floor or stood listening to their parents talk. With standing room only, the voices, footsteps, and creaking boards led to a roar.

On the other side of the ticket window, in the office that paralleled the waiting room and where her family waited, the clerk took telegraph messages and packages to be shipped to men at war. Inside the office, the noise lessened.

Mary went outside again to find her Uncle Littleberry somewhere in this crowd. She noticed to the left of the stove hanging on the wall, the board said: "Arrival of Train," and the clerk posted a paper showing 10 am. Mary hoped today, of all days, the train would be extra late, giving them more precious time. She stepped outside onto the platform where the benches were full of waiting men and their tearful families. Mary shook her head and thought, "These are sad, sad times."

They heard the far-off whistle. She quickly went back inside the office, finding her sister Jane and Dr. Carroll. They too came to bid William farewell.

In the old days of Indian fighting, the men wore dark blue or gray to attract less attention. Since the north's colors were dark blue, the south chose gray.

News from the War looked promising. The first Battle of Manassas (or Bull Run) in mid-summer made everyone insane with joy. Their side won and did it within twenty-five miles of Washington, DC. There were rumors about the Northern forces and civilians who watched the battle and skedaddled back to the city.

Almost overnight, the South had its first big hero, a relatively unknown brigadier general from the Virginia Military Institute named Thomas J. Jackson who had stood his ground with his Virginia brigade. By August, they called him "Stonewall" Jackson. William had heard earlier at Palmer's, "They should have pushed on and captured Washington and subsequently moved the capital and admitted Maryland."

For the South's leaders, though, the victory highlighted the many casualties, problems, and deficiencies. They could not employ their force effectively. Instead of using their army of 32,000 men, they had used only 18,000. The battle showed them they were ill-prepared to take Washington, DC.

Before Manassas, both sides thought the war would be over soon and victorious with one great battle, but the struggle made both realize the war might be longer-lasting and bloodier than expected. Thus, each side grew more cautious.

They sent William and his unit to rally with the 4th Florida Infantry, commissioned to protect and secure Florida's shoreline. His first assignment was St. Vincent's Island, a barrier island near Apalachicola. Though glad their assignment took place so far from the front in Virginia, Mary still couldn't understand why he felt he had to go.

William joined anyway at forty-nine, beyond the legal conscript age of forty-five. Times were so harsh they called the older men to go, though the conscript did not include men William's age. He probably felt young and robust and thought it his duty to do his part. "Mary, if my son has to go, I must too," he told her. No matter how she tried to wrap her mind around it, it made no sense. Now the family had two of their men to worry about. Plus, with James gone, Val itched to go.

As each unit left the county, much excitement, well-wishing, and fanfare followed. The town's ladies sewed flags with slogans appropriate to each unit, but William's company was from Quincy. The ladies there would sew his flag.

By September, four companies of the 4th Florida Regiment, one of which was Company A, were sent to St. Vincent's Island as there were rumors of a supposed federal attack.

William enlisted on St. Vincent Island. The unit he joined, the Quincy Guards, carried smooth-bore percussion muskets. In contrast, their friends in the Lion Artillery of Tallahassee and the Jefferson Rifles of Monticello had old flintlocks. William Trimmer of the 1st Infantry from Apalachicola said in early 1862 that they turned their guns in and received smooth-bore Springfield muskets.

The 4th's men came from Marion, Levy, Columbia, Lafayette, Madison and New River (now Bradford County), Jackson, Gadsden, Washington, Liberty, Franklin, and Hillsborough.

The 4th's ten companies of about one hundred men dispersed to various coastal inlets and towns to discourage raiding parties. Companies D, E and K encamped around Tampa. Companies B, C, and I spent the fall near St. Marks (one at St. Marks and the others at the lighthouse). Company F defended the island of Cedar Keys, and H and G were stationed at Fernandina. The rest, A and F companies, were at St. Vincent's Island. Company F came from Bradford County.

They sent William's company to St. Vincent Island to protect Apalachee Bay at the mouth of the Apalachicola River (an area called West Pass) and its seaport, Apalachicola. He arrived there on August 25th, 1861. William had enlisted for twelve months.

The South's governors worried about protecting their borders, especially their shorelines, and at first, the Confederacy's defensive strategy was specifically generated to ease those fears. With Florida's coastline almost 1,200 miles long, the governor and its people worried about a Yankee invasion along this sparsely populated coastline. Initially, governors fought to keep their militias at home to protect the home front. During the first year of 1861, most of Florida's men stayed in the state, protecting its ports and forts.

Everyone still felt the South would win the war quickly, though it was well into its first year. Because of what William told Mary about the north, though, she was less sure.

Several days after William left, Mary sat in Ann Lightsey's living room with her sister Jane, her Aunt Mary Jane Lightsey, Mary Jane's daughter-in-law Amanda Sledge Lightsey, Ann's twenty-four-year-old daughter Clara, and Ann's other daughter Mary, the wife of Frank Johnson. Ann Lightsey's home at the corner of West Dogwood Street and North Olive Street near the first Methodist Church (currently near the Old Jail) provided a nice yard for her grandchildren, whose father Henry served in the military.

Ann and Clara held this sewing circle meeting at home since they were busy watching Henry's children. Ann's daughter-in-law Mary Howell Lightsey, also Betsy Howell Walker's sister, had died two years earlier while giving birth to a daughter who survived, leaving Henry Lightsey with four children, including the daughter, now two.

Mary noticed nine-year-old George Henry, home from school

today, diligently watched over his little sister and all the younger children, including her four, Henrietta, Henry, Laura, and Joseph. Henry idolized George Henry, following him everywhere. They played outdoors in Ann's fenced yard.

Inside, talking over the children's voices heard through the open windows, the ladies sat in their sewing circle, their long skirts draped on the floor around their chairs. Today, they were making gray cotton shirts for the local boys. It would be hot for another two to three months, and shirts didn't last long, whether building breastworks or fighting battles. William didn't need the extra shirts, but others in their county left with only one to their name. They would need more.

Said Mary's Aunt Mary Jane, "Mary, how is William doing? I hear St. Vincent Island, though pretty on the surface, is quite harsh."

Mary pushed her needle through the fabric until it touched her thimble, saying, "He says that the island has more mouths to feed than all the rest of Florida." The ladies looked confused. She grinned and added, "He means there are all kinds of varmints and insects waiting to take a bite of anybody that passes by or sits too still."

Group Posing on St. Vincent Island (August, 1900), Florida Memory Collection

"Sounds like Florida to me," said Amanda. The other ladies nodded and chuckled in agreement, but Mary followed, "No, he says it's ten times worse than what we have here. They have sand gnats. When the sun goes down, they come in droves with their thousands of little stinging bites. And he says the biggest problem is you can't see them."

"Well, I've heard of them," said Ann. "When we first got here, George used to go near the mouth of the Econfina for salt. He said the mosquitoes were bad enough, but the little biters you couldn't see were maddening. The only things that help are wind and cold weather."

Of average height and build, wearing a cotton calico dress of a muted green and fitted at the waist, Amanda walked to the window to check on the kids. She had four, ages seven to two. Mary asked, "Are they alright?"

"Yes. Ann, George Henry is so good with children."

Ann added, "He and Caroline did their part after their mama died. Caroline might have only been thirteen, but she mothered

Baby Mary like a full-grown woman. Henry and Martha raised good children."

Ann patted her damp forehead with her handkerchief and added, "We're all worried about Henry. None of us could believe they would draft him, especially with a three-year-old and no mother to care for his children."

Mary placed her hand on Ann's and replied, "We know this burdens you and Clara. It surprised all of us he did not remarry."

Mary's candidness surprised the girls, but not Ann or her Aunt Mary Jane. The Walker women were honest to a fault with their feelings.

Ann said, "We were too. We thought he would quickly remedy the situation as so many men do, but I guess Martha was his soulmate. So many babies were lost between their four. They wanted children so badly, and I believe Henry still blames himself for her death, no matter how often we tell him God has His plans and His will." They all nodded and stitched in silence, listening to the children outdoors.

The Lightseys had so much sadness. With her husband's death at the height of the Indian Wars in 1838 and because there were no doctor bills in his probate file signaling an illness, George Lightsey may have been killed during the Second Seminole Indian War. Ann and her younger children probably moved into Monticello for their safety, and she never remarried. Henry may have followed his mother's lead.

Aunt Mary Jane broke the silence. "At least none of our boys are in Virginia yet."

Everyone nodded, and Clara added, "There are so many Madison boys there, though. Mary, I heard Susan's husband has kin there." Susan was Mary's other sister. The Madison

Rangers and another company, mostly made of Tallahassee boys, were with the Florida 2nd Infantry, the first Florida regiment sent north to Virginia in mid-July. Mary spoke, "Well, with all these boys leaving, we sure are having a lot of weddings. Betsy and Joel are worried about Sarah."

Said Ann, "We heard all about it through Henry. We're all shocked."

Mary replied, "Well, it did us too. John Kinsey swept her up this summer, and they got married with hardly a courtship. He's a good-looking twenty-seven-year-old, but Sarah's only sixteen."

A week later, Mary hosted the week's sewing circle at her home, and Ann brought Pamelia Williams, who had news about the good doctor. Sitting in Mary's parlor with borrowed chairs from Ann, the ladies sitting in a circle were a mixture of cotton skirts of faded calicoes and a couple of simple broadcloths. Today, they worked on making woolen scarves for their town's soldiers. Pamelia read a letter from her brother, Dr. Palmer. The letter had taken weeks to arrive.

"Richmond, Virginia
August 21st, 1861

Dearest Sister,
I am now far north, seven hundred miles from you and the family. We got into Richmond yesterday evening, but I haven't gotten to see much of the city yet, as we came directly to camp outside the city. So many of our men were sick with dysentery, over a hundred, so I've been busy. They got it from the immense amount of fruit they ate en route. Sister, I think

every depot on our northward journey supplied us with food, especially fruit. Most of these boys are not used to such a delicacy. It was so bad that we found one soldier dead in his tent this morning.

Also, the trip here was not without accident. I am still attending to Mr. Russell, who was injured with a strike to his head. We initially thought him dead, but now we believe he will recover.

The regimental men spent the day drilling while I spent my first full day setting up the regimental hospital tents. Already, I've seen a day's worth of cuts, scrapes, and dysentery.

On the way north, we ate breakfast in Augusta on Monday last, and the entire city turned out to greet us. There were all kinds of ladies and fellas everywhere cheering us on. It made us proud to be Confederate soldiers and boosted morale.

Augusta, now a major industrial city, has many mills and cotton stores down near the river.

Our railroad passed through plantations both south and north of the city, as well as rich farms. We crossed over the Savannah River on a railway trestle. Augusta also has a brand new gunpowder and explosives factory in operation called the Confederate Powderworks. Our train stopped to add cars filled with ammunition going north.

Well, there's taps, and I need to close. Tell everyone you see, both family and patients, that I miss them every day. I think of them and all of you often.

*Your loving brother,
 Thomas"*

Meanwhile, far to the southwest on St. Vincent Island, William and Florida's 4th Infantry fought mosquitoes, sand gnats, and rattlesnakes. One wonders why William joined the 4th and even more why Company A, primarily men from Gadsden County. One reason might be the other two Andrews men in the same company—Elisha and Owen E. Andrews. Elisha Andrews lived in Tallahassee while William lived there with his first wife, Elizabeth. Still, the research found no connection between William and this Elisha, though it appears he came from Kentucky. Or maybe having been the sheriff, William, as mentioned earlier worried about a shot in the back.

Several of William's mother's brothers moved to Kentucky, and his father's kin may have moved there too. We do not know because resources do not show the connections.

St. Vincent's Island, a barrier island off the coast of Florida in the Gulf, guards the western entrance to Apalachicola Bay. Florida shores were lined with these small low islands, separated from each other and the mainland by their shallow and narrow inlets. These islands provided outposts during the war. St. Vincent on the Gulf and Amelia Island on the Atlantic coast are barrier islands.

St. Vincent's 12,300 acres, with fourteen miles of beaches on its eastern and southern shores, sits between St. George Island and Cape San Blas to the west. Indian Pass separates the island from the mainland. West Pass is a critical inlet for commercial traffic, and Apalachicola's port is crucial for cotton trading for North Florida, Southwest Georgia, and Alabama.

Map Showing St. Vincent Island in relation to Apalachicola, Google Maps

Apalachicola, a river port, offered not only three access points to the Gulf but also an entrance to the three-river system of the Apalachicola, Flint, and Chattahoochee Rivers. The Apalachicola River extends north to the Chattahoochee River, and the Chattahoochee is navigable below Columbus, Georgia and its fall line. This provided deep access to the interior of Florida, Alabama, and Georgia.

Apalachicola was an isolated river town. Traveling by water was the only way in and out. There were no connecting roads in the 1860s, so we know William arrived by ship.

On the second Tuesday night in September, Mary, Ann Lightsey, and Florrie walked to the Masonic Hall on the second floor of the Jefferson Academy. With the summer's humidity abated, it was a pleasant walk. Mary, wearing her indigo floral dress, entered the east door and climbed the stairs to the second floor. Beside her, animated Florrie told them stories about her days at the school. Upstairs, inside the hall, a crowd gathered with much mirth, though their sons, husbands, and brothers were away somewhere on a tented field.

Jefferson Academy, stairs leading to 2nd floor (west), 1959 Jeffecello, Annual for Jefferson County High School

An evening to raise money for their soldiers' fabric, Mary, sitting in one of the chairs placed throughout the hall, listened to several vocal and instrumental arrangements. Afterward, the ladies retired to the other Oddfellow's hall. The three in her party quickly took their places behind the General Beauregard table, which displayed the many handmade dainties for sale. The following week, the *Family Friend* reported the event raised somewhere between two and three hundred dollars for the soldier's relief.

HIGH AND GRAMMAR SCHOOL, MONTICELLO, FLA.

The school in 1920, showing the front and east entrances. Keystone Genealogical Library

In the same paper was a distressing report from Dr. Palmer of the 2nd Florida Regiment. *"Encamped near Yorktown, Virginia, the number of those sick in the regiment, since its inception, now totaled 1,792 with 44 dead, (22 of which died of typhoid, 10 from pneumonia; 5 of measles, 2 from dysentery, and 1 each from diarrhea, consumption, congestion of stomach, congestion of the brain, and an accident on the railroad)."* It was a sobering account for the wives, mothers, and sisters left behind.

At the same time, the newspaper reported Colonel John M. Raysor sent from his plantation a stalk containing several bolls of open cotton, evidence of an advanced crop. He planned to pick in a couple of days. The paper believed Jefferson would be the first Confederate county to forward a bale of cotton in the support of its army.

The editor also complained Monticello's people were not sufficiently vigilant in patrolling the countryside surrounding the city. Jefferson County's male population was now outside the county because of the formation of the three companies of volunteers. With the area less secure, people feared the Negroes might rebel.

Mary got a letter from William. Vollie read it that night on the porch.

September 25, 1861
St. Vincent Island, Florida

Dearest Mary and my children,
Life on this remote island is no picnic. It has been hot and humid the entire time, and I miss Monticello and all of you. I assume it is not cooler there, and you are sitting on the porch reading this.

Mary, you asked about camp life, so I will paint a picture of the boys and men here. We are a motley group.

So many of these boys came thin, scrawny, and frightened; but they held their heads high, and we heard hardly a complaint, especially from the boys raised in the sticks. I heard one boy, when asked if his new boots fit, say, "No sir; it's my feet that don't fit."

To many, especially the boys raised in finer homes, military discipline comes as a shock. They aren't used to being bossed; and it amazes me they didn't realize that in the infantry, you march and march and march. We are, after all, foot soldiers. Discipline comes when they forget to take care of their firearm. Misery follows when they don't take care of their boots, socks, and feet.

We march in the morning and practice artillery in the afternoon. We also practice bayoneting.

In addition, these thin boys have blossomed. They've put on muscle, grown taller, and stand more erect. Many are handsome, square-shouldered men, drilled and prodded so they're no longer afraid of anyone. They think they're ready for anything the Yankees can throw their way.

Tell everyone I miss them more than they can know. I miss all the stories and shenanigans the children bring to light daily and look forward to this war ending soon so I can return.

All my love,
Father

William's letter reflects others written from Florida's barrier islands during the war. We're not sure how Mary replied since she did not read or write. Her older children did, though; and with both Sarah and Vollie still at home, they probably read and wrote for Mary. Perhaps letters were read, answered, and posted immediately.

The *Family Friend* posted the mail schedule, showing northern mail sent every evening at 5 pm except Sunday. The letter probably went with the Florida mail, which the post office sent every morning at 7 am, except Sundays when the post office was closed. Any of their letters going to Virginia, though, went by stage directly to Quitman, where it traveled eastward on the Savannah main trunk railroad. Any mail going to her cousins in South Carolina also took this route.

Florida's four regiments were amateurs trained in these disease-ridden camps across Florida. A regiment, usually commanded by a colonel, comprised one to two thousand men in two or more battalions.

William's 4th Florida Infantry regiment, commanded by Colonel Edward Hopkins, guarded West Pass on the island, where they built a small fort called Fort Mallory. They built it on the beach side near the point opposite St. Vincent Point.

St. Vincent Island shoreline, Florida Memory Collection

William's company, in the middle of a controversy with Apalachicola, commandeered the seaport's only cannon and took it to St. Vincent because the soldiers there had two passes to guard. The inlet between St. Vincent and St. George Islands provided access to Apalachicola, but another pass existed between St. George and Dog Island. Col. Hopkins felt his men needed the cannon more because they had more territory to protect. Subsequently, there was no love lost between the port of Apalachicola and William's regiment.

On the island, William's officers organized Company A into a small militia-like unit. The job came easily to William as he committed to safeguarding his and other North Florida homes from Yankee intruders. He also knew there would be marauding deserters on both sides, operating in the swamps and deep forests of their homeland. Though glad Mary lived in Monticello, he worried about the safety of Mary's kin who lived in the woods and fields of Jefferson County.

In camp, they drilled and practiced between the trees and palmettos. One could hear the lieutenants barking orders through the pines. Since they were in the infantry, this meant they were trained to march and fight on foot. William, a foot soldier, appeared to be up to the challenge.

Interior Road on St. Vincent Island, Wikipedia

The officers immediately taught them to protect their battle flag, symbolizing their identity. The one William would fight under was made by the loving hands of the women from

Quincy, Florida.

It usually took years to train a private to obey their officers unquestioningly, but no one had years for such training. Plus, a few short weeks ago, these officers were their colleagues in business or their childhood friends. Sometimes, when someone felt put upon by their officer whom they had known their whole life, the two would go somewhere and duke it out privately. Overall, though, the officers did not tolerate independent resistance, and eventually, the privates learned all about extra duty and half rations.

Unexpected, though, were the countless commonplace duties of a soldier—camping for months without firing a gun or marching and countermarching sometimes to mislead an enemy. They did not foresee driving wagons and ambulances, building bridges, currying horses and mules, or the endless guard duties, an unfathomable list.

William was in the infantry, the ground arm of the army. The men had to understand the use of their weapons and have an elementary knowledge of camouflage and concealment, patrolling, recognition of the enemy and their own men, first aid, field sanitation, and maintenance of life and health out of doors over long periods and under conditions of extreme difficulty.

Back home, Mary worked with several friends and family through the Soldiers' Aid Association. She, Ellen, and Florrie made three pairs of pants, two undershirts, and several socks to donate. She and Ann Lightsey had formed another sewing circle for this purpose.

Later, at the circle in Mary's parlor, the ladies discussed the recent reports in the paper. Said Ann, "Well, of course, Mrs.

Finlayson donated all those pants, drawers, towels, shirts, and socks. She's got slaves to help her."

Women in the Civil War, by Winslow Homer, Harper's Weekly, September 6, 1862, Wikitree

Added Betsy Howell, "I heard Caroline Goodman say she didn't plan to individually donate anymore, because *who wants the paucity of their work to be compared in the newspaper to Mrs. Finlayson's abundance?*"

In October, the 2nd Florida Infantry remained in Virginia while Florida's other troops moved by the two railroads that crossed the state. The Florida Railroad ran from Fernandina to Cedar Keys, while the second road, now called the Florida Atlantic and Gulf, ran from Jacksonville to Tallahassee. The two railroads crossed at Baldwin.

Neither of the two lines connected to the rest of the Confederacy north of Florida. Whenever a unit went north, they either marched to the Georgia rail line, which went to Savannah, or took a ship. Once they reached Columbus on the Chattahoochee River, they boarded trains going north.

Near Pensacola at midnight on October 9th, two small steamers crossed from the mainland to Santa Rosa Island with a detachment of 180 men from all companies of the 1st Florida Regiment. After marching for three miles over the dark sand dunes of prickly pear cactuses and sand spurs, they surprised the Union forces encamped outside Fort Pickens. The rebels wore white strips of fabric around their left arms to distinguish themselves from their enemy.

Several of Mary's cousins were there, including Joel E., Jesse A., and William J. Walker, all of whom joined under Captain J. Patton Anderson at Camp Magnolia in 1861. Their attempt to capture the enemy position failed.

Battle of Santa Rosa Island, sketched by Charles F. Allgouer

Taking this Union encampment took time, and daybreak came before the objective was taken. With daybreak, they risked the fort firing upon the steamers, so Anderson abandoned his original plan and issued orders for a full and orderly retreat, though it was anything but orderly when the Union companies pursued them.

The Union reported 14 killed, 29 wounded, and 24 captured. The Confederate casualties, though, numbered 87, and a Union sniper severely wounded Brigadier General Richard H. Anderson. Thankfully, all three of her Uncle Littleberry's sons survived.

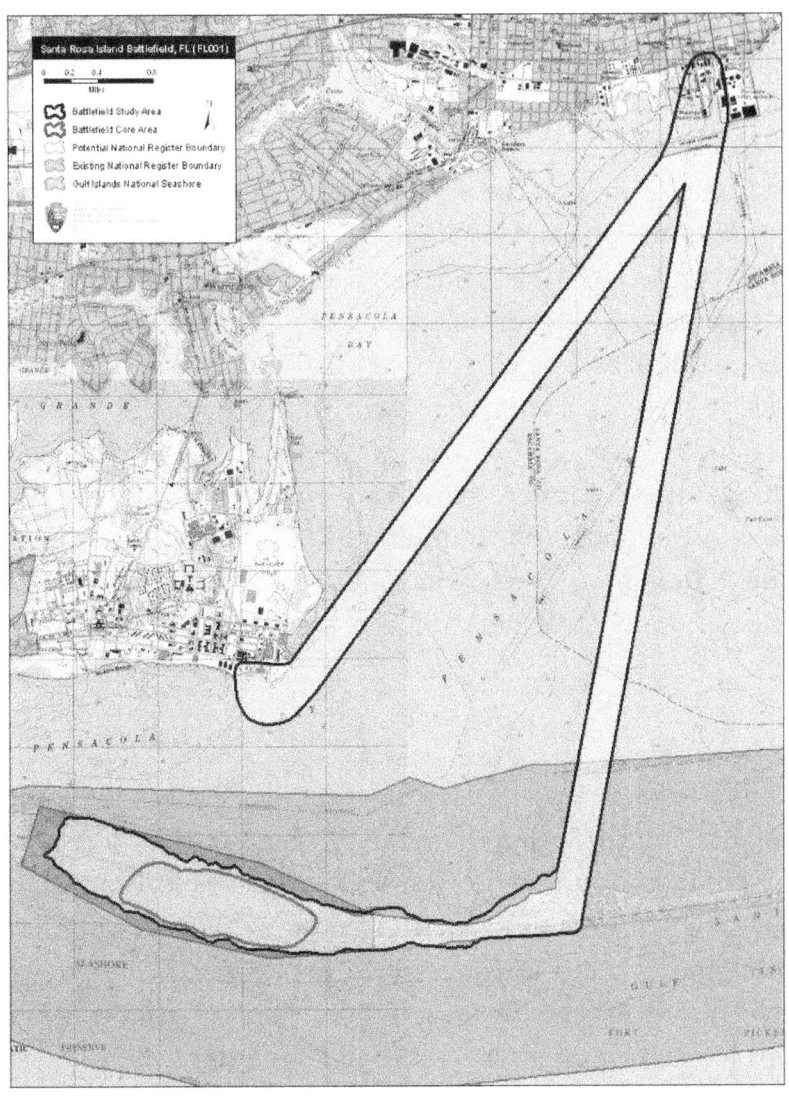

Santa Rosa Battlefield Map & Study Areas by the American Battlefield Protection Program, Wikipedia Commons

It emboldened people, though, because Anderson got within close range of the fort without being detected. They successfully scattered a Yankee regiment and destroyed their camp. From the Union's standpoint, they learned about their foe's vulnerabilities, and the Southerners lost the element of surprise. The Confederates camped in Pensacola would never again assault Fort Pickens.

At home, sitting on the porch, Vollie read the *Family Friend* to his mother and siblings. "Mama, this one's entitled '*How Shall we Pay our Taxes!*'" He said to no one in particular, "I guess they mean our Confederate war taxes?"

She nodded, and he continued, "*The above query is upon almost everybody's tongue, and it is one about as difficult to answer as to tell how long the war will continue.*" Vollie added, "People are running out of money. How can anybody pay these taxes, especially anybody gone to military service? Isn't it enough?"

Mary thought, "Such big questions for a boy of only fourteen." Lately, all her children seemed wise beyond their years.

Days later, Mary visited with her father. She needed a trip to Elizabeth, and the two rode to the oak hammock and cemetery. Their conversation ranged from Uncle Joel's insolvent estate to those indebted to the Elizabeth Auxiliary Soldiers' Aid Society. Besides the war, all anyone talked about was everyone's and every entity's indebtedness. Even the *Family Friend* could only afford to run two pages weekly, half its regular size.

He pondered as Mary talked. *How is it that even our women are discussing money and economies?*

As she knelt by her mama's grave, she placed a hand-picked bouquet of goldenrod at the base of the wooden cross her father made. She said, "Mr. Fildes cannot get people to pay their debts to the paper. He's not sure how much longer he can keep printing it."

Jesse stood watching his daughter and sighed. "Yes, Valentine Clem came by here yesterday. They plan to tax my lands and my livestock. He even asked me if I had any bank stock or other stock. They're taxing that, too."

Mary looked wide-eyed and added, "They even wanted to know if William's watch was gold. Thank goodness it is only silver. They would have taxed it too, and William on St. Vincent trying to defend our state while being eaten alive by its sand gnats and mosquitoes. It's lunacy."

Meanwhile, the mosquitoes and sand gnats remained fearsome on St. Vincent Island even in hot and humid October. It rained almost every day. Tent living made William lonesome for home. They issued him a variation of a tent which he pitched as a lean-to type of shelter. He placed it as closely as possible to a large pine tree, hoping to be inside its narrow drip line. Underneath, he placed a blanket of deep straw. When the sea breeze died, the air above the camp hung in a haze from the dozens of campfires.

Given an allowance to purchase clothing, William probably made at least one trip to nearby Apalachicola, a boom town, a prosperous cotton port, and one of the five largest towns in Florida.

Later, because it was growing cooler at night, he and some other men constructed a better hut, large enough to accommodate several men. They used the abundant palmetto fronds to build its roof.

Fisherman's Hut (made of palmetto fronds) on St. Vincent's Island, 1909, Florida Memory Collection

William, though, was only on St. Vincent for a short time. Almost as soon as they raised their palmetto hut, Governor John Milton ordered them off the island and all supplies and equipment removed. They dismantled Fort Mallory and deserted it by November. The federal blockaders took the island by December 1861.

There is no evidence of how William got to Amelia Island from St. Vincent. They probably transported the men by ship to Cedar Keys, the western terminus of the Florida Railroad. From there, the railroad took them directly to Fernandina on Amelia Island.

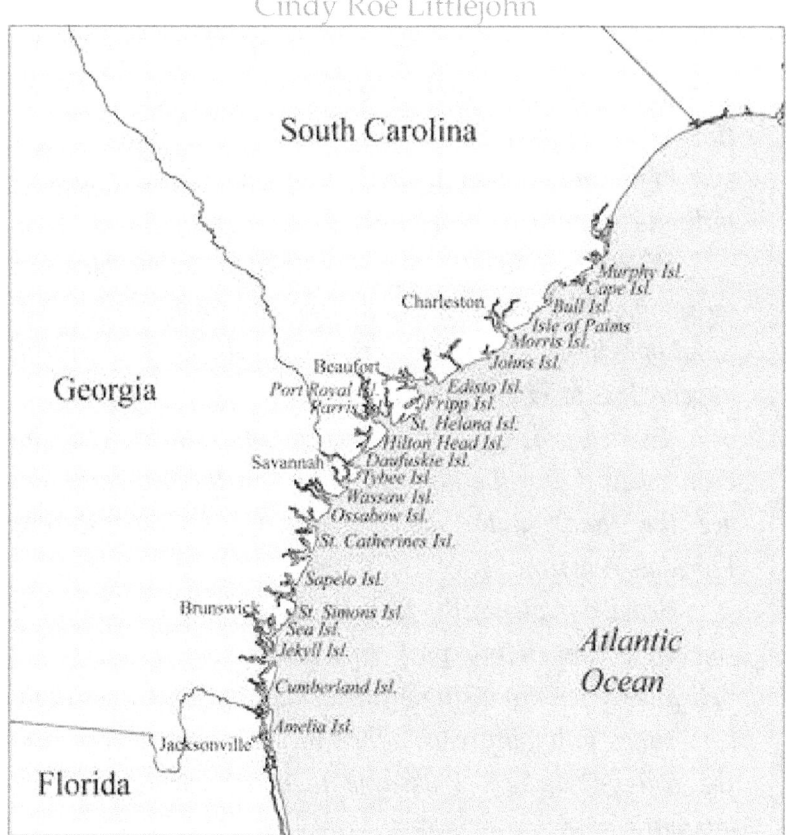

Amelia Island is the southernmost of the Sea Islands, Wikipedia

Mary received another letter in November from William.

>November 3, 1861
>Amelia Island, Florida
>
>Dearest Mary,
>   Oh, how I wish we had taken time to travel. Amelia Island is a place I want to share with you. As you can tell my heart grows fonder with every day I'm away. Oh, to have you here by my side.

Mary, you should see the Atlantic Ocean from Amelia Island. I have been on the ocean for travel, but I never spent time on a beach with a rolling sea. This morning, I saw the sun high enough that its reflection on the water looked like millions of shards of broken glass.

When the tide's in, one cannot see the submerged sand or oyster bars. When it goes out, the seascape totally changes. Sand bars, oyster bars, and the sea's millions of tiny creatures appear. It is fascinating.

There persists a gentle breeze, and it helps cool oneself even when doing the hardest labor. On the flip side, though, are the sand gnats, which I assume are everywhere on Florida's coastline.

Seabirds constantly look for food; and the seagulls call, sometimes quarreling with each other over a tidbit. Stately pelicans fly past in a single-file formation, sometimes high and sometimes following each other to slide low, hovering above the water's surface. I assume they are riding an invisible current.

On the bay side at the water's edge, the green reeds stand like short sentinels; and when the tide's out, betwixt and between are hundreds if not thousands of little transparent crabs. The locals call them ghost crabs because one can almost see right through them. They scurry along in front as you walk, and if one steps too quickly, one could crush dozens underfoot.

We are living high on the hog here, with lots of fish, crabs, and oysters to eat. I sent you a barrel of salted mullet on the last train. Make sure you share with all the others, especially your dad.

Well, time to end my missive. Kiss all our babies and tuck them in at night for their dear old dad.

Your loving husband,
William

Amelia Island Marshes, Wikipedia

A few days later, he wrote again.

> November 7, 1861
> Amelia Island, Florida

My Dearest Mary,

Here on Amelia Island, we continue to fortify against the enemy with mundane work, but it helps the time pass. Let me describe my compatriots. Most of them were once farmers and planters, and initially, they had trouble taking orders, especially from those younger than them. If you can imagine your father having to take orders from anyone, you can understand what I mean. They spent their days mostly alone except for family or slaves and took orders from no one.

Palmetto Pioneers

Initially here, this caused problems. Camp life, full of chores called fatigue duties, persists. It takes a lot to keep an Army working efficiently. They have assigned me all kinds of these duties.

Yesterday, my company built breastworks. Last week, I spent time in the mess peeling potatoes. When I get back, I hope I never eat potatoes again.

A few weeks ago, I polished the metal fittings for a young lieutenant, from his boots to his bridle to his spurs. I don't mind, though. It makes time go quickly.

By the way, I'm one of the few that can afford a railroad ticket home, so a furlough might be had soon. I can't wait to see the beautiful faces of all my family, but especially you, my dear.

As for free time, we have much here in camp, but not so much as I remember from my Indian War days when I first met your father as a much younger man. We spent many long hours talking.

The younger men here are impatient to get to the front, especially after part of our regiment in Tampa seized two sloops and two US flags. The boys here in Fernandina feel like they missed something big—they relish the thought of actively moving and fighting. The veterans don't revel in it because we know what comes with it. So many of these younger men do not know what may come.

I usually spend my free time reading and stay away from card games, though there are some where no money exchanges hands. Right now, a card game continues outside my tent, but I seldom win—maybe once in a blue moon. When we move, though, we have little time for anything except writing letters, cleaning uniforms, and sleeping.

Well, I must end as the bugle will sound any minute. Give all my love to our babies and tell your father it is lonely here in camp without him.

Your husband,

William

After drills and while on his way to camp, William thought it odd when he was approached by one of his lieutenants with a letter. This one they hand-delivered outside of the usual mail call. Like all his mail, they had opened and inspected it. The lieutenant waited while William read it. When he finished, he looked at the lieutenant and said, "It says the general assembly needs me in Tallahassee for another legislative session." First Lieutenant William Gorman agreed and added, "Captain Gee has written your leave for an indefinite period. You can leave the Thursday before the session begins the following Monday." William immediately went to his tent to write to the family. He was coming home for a weekend. He needed someone to meet him at the depot that Thursday afternoon, but he had second thoughts.

On a beautiful, warm, but humid November 14th afternoon, Mary, in the kitchen making supper, pushed back a wet tendril of hair that had escaped, curling it behind her ear. When she heard a creak behind her and steps on the stairs, she looked over her shoulder. There he stood—William was home.

She whirled around, and time stopped. He grinned and closed the space between them. Up to her elbows in flour, it couldn't have mattered less to either. He swept her into a big bear hug.

He had been gone almost two months but would be home for a weekend. That night, little Laura slept in her own bed.

While home, the town continued preparations for the growing war. There were several soirées held to raise money for the cause, like the one held the weekend before William went to Tallahassee. If in town, they expected William there with Mary at his side.

William and Mary walked in the twilight toward the courthouse, its windows glowing from the second floor. At the foot of its stairs, they may have greeted the Chases, and both couples took the long staircase to the second floor. Pine branches lined the banister. Carefully mounting each step, Mary held up the front of her indigo bell-shaped gown as William's right hand rested on the small of her back.

A cool evening, Mary wore a ball gown made of blue satin brocade. Though several years old, the dress was fashionable because it was in vogue to wear well-worn clothing, saving dollars for the cause. Its modest, wide neckline reached from shoulder to shoulder, and because she worried she would get chilled during the walk, over the gown she wore William's collared cape, which extended below her fingertips. Single-breasted, with a row of black velvet buttons down the front, its gray wool shell had a heavy black cotton lining.

The city's ladies decorated the courtroom with garlands of smilax and containers of goldenrod. Ivy decorated the tables. Above the judge's desk, someone hung a Confederate flag tacked at four corners and fully unfurled. William thought every candle and candlestick in Monticello was in the room. They gleamed in the light—brass, silver, and pewter. The windows were open, and a tiny breeze of night air added relief.

Mary unbuttoned the cape inside, and William removed it from her shoulders. He noticed looks of admiration from both men and women in the room. With Mary's hair loosely arranged, her dark cascading curls accented the deep blue brocade gown. He admired his stunning wife.

William wore his dress uniform, a knee-length gray wool coat belted with blue britches. The double-breasted jacket with gold buttons had a standing-band collar, to which Mary sewed the fabric to match his britches. She added the detail to his cuffs too. Instead of his Confederate cap with its flat circular top and peak or visor, he wore his broad gray felt hat to which Mary added a hat band of gold cord and a feather.

The next evening, because of the night's warmth, the family gathered on the porch to talk about the day's events like old times, but there were many questions about St. Vincent and Amelia Islands. At one point, Jessie questioned, "But Daddy, what is so important that someone has to protect an island none of us has ever heard of?"

William replied, "Well, the island isn't essential. Apalachicola's port and its river are. Through the port, they ship a lot of cotton. The river is used to transport cotton south to the Gulf of Mexico. Still, more importantly, the river could also be a way for the Yankees to invade north into Florida, Georgia, and Alabama.

"It is a similar situation at Amelia Island, which sits near the Port of Fernandina, the second busiest port in the nation. A natural deep-water port, its strategic location is closest to the rest of the other Atlantic states like Georgia, South Carolina, North Carolina, and Virginia."

Mary spoke during a lull in the conversation and added her news, "Guess what? Valentine Clem asked Daddy if he could use his home to collect war taxes. Daddy reluctantly agreed, so everybody in Elizabeth will take their tax returns there on November 26th."

Added William, "Well, ours have to be paid next Monday or Tuesday here in Monticello. We're lucky. We still have cash, but there are lots of the wealthier whose assets are in their land. They're hurting. They'll have to liquidate to pay their taxes. Mary, you'll need to take care of it for us on Monday."

By early morning Monday, November 18th, William caught the train to Tallahassee. Mary, up since daybreak, cooked breakfast and got ready herself. She wanted to look her best when he left. With the war raging, one didn't know when his unit might get called with little or no notice.

He got ready, dressed in his best frock coat and silk cravat, and entered the kitchen. "Can you help me with this tie?" He looked dashing with his broad shoulders which had widened as he approached middle age.

Mary thought, "Men get more manly and handsome as they age, while we get more weathered and rounder?" She decided it was all the babies and hard work, a cruel turn of nature.

She looked into his eyes and he into hers. In her thoughts, she wanted to hop back into bed with him. It amazed her how, after all these years, the spark there had grown more assertive lately. She stared at his back as he sat at his desk or watched him walk away when he left a room. Absence made her senses keener, as she had learned early in this sweet marriage.

She remembered last year's session and how she felt about his absence of so many weeks with no break, but this year affected her more acutely. He could die. She wanted to hold on to him, even if for only a few days, before letting him leave for Tallahassee. These were golden moments, and they squeezed every second from them.

By noon on Tuesday, the general assembly ordered William as sergeant-at-arms of the late House to notify any absent members in the city that their attendance in the House was requested to affect its organization. On foot and horseback, he searched the inns, saloons, and boarding houses. By 3 pm, they had their quorum. During this session, he knew where to find the members.

Tallahassee in 1885, Lafayette Street is now the Apalachee Parkway. The Adelphi is behind the Capitol. Florida Memory Collection

Later that afternoon, though, William watched a curious event. After they elected an enrolling clerk, a legislator asked whether *"the Sergeant-at-Arms of the last House, being an appointee of the Speaker thereof, to fill a vacancy occasioned therein, should remain."*

Subsequently, another member asked, *"Should the House proceed to an election to fill such a vacancy?"*

William was the choice of the last speaker, but he thought to himself, "Maybe I'm not the choice of the current speaker." He looked at the well where the current speaker stood.

The new speaker slammed his gavel and said, "*There being a vacancy in the House of Representatives, the House shall proceed with the election of a Sergeant of Arms.*" William watched with interest, wondering if the long train ride would be repeated the following day back to Monticello.

Quickly, though, Representative James S. Russell of Jefferson County appealed the decision of the speaker, and the House overruled the speaker's decision, declaring William under a resolution to be the sergeant-at-arms of the present House. They ran right over their new speaker, and William knew he would not have as easy a session as the last.

At home the same afternoon, Mary walked down to the courthouse with their tax return and the cash needed to pay their war taxes. She didn't take anyone with her. She trusted Mr. Clem.

During the cold winter and later that month, they read William's letters by the fireplace. From Tallahassee, he wrote every few days about the happenings in Florida. One letter said the legislature ruled to construct a dam on the Ochlockonee River to build a mill. Another said Columbia County got fifteen sections of land from the state to build a courthouse. Still another allowed Escambia County's leaders to borrow money to build a courthouse and jail, but they later amended it to change county to counties, including much more than Escambia. William wondered if these men realized how much money the War would suck from Florida's coffers.

While William served in Tallahassee, Mary's brothers Berry and George enlisted on November 28 under Captain William Bailey's Aucilla Guards. In the Aucilla Guards were several more Walkers, Kinseys, Hamricks, and Bishops. They sent the Guards to posts in St. Marks, New Port Leon, and Tallahassee to protect those cities. Later, they would dissolve this unit, and her brothers would re-enlist in Company G of the 5th Florida Infantry along with the former Aucilla Guards.

George was elected 1st Sergeant in the 5th Florida Infantry, Company G. Later, they promoted him to 1st Lieutenant. One wonders if the two brothers stopped in Tallahassee on their way to St. Marks by train to see their brother-in-law at the capitol.

Mary's brother Henry had been dead for almost a year. He remained on her mind because there appeared in the December 21st issue of the *Family Friend*, "*Steam Saw Mill, Near Station 4 on P. & G. R. R. Known as the Walker & Allmon Mill. All persons indebted to the above Mill are hereby notified against settling, either by Cash or Note, with S. C. Ward, for special reasons. T. J. Linton, December 21, 1862.*" Since this appeared in the December 21, 1861 issue, the 1862 date has to be a typo.

Who are Allmon, Ward, and Linton? In addition, this documents the first time Walker Mills appears by another name. They now refer to Walker Mills as Station #4 because it's the fourth station from the end of the rail line initially built.

By motion on Friday, November 29th, they granted William a leave of absence until Monday next at noon. While home, he said, "Mary, they'll probably meet on Saturdays until the end of the session. I'll try coming home on Sunday, but I'm unsure."

She hesitated and said, "Maybe you shouldn't try to come home every Sunday. You'll need your rest, and the trips cost money, which we'll need to save for later." He agreed.

Later, in Tallahassee at the Adelphi Hotel, William sat with a group of men in front of the fireplace. They were having a drink before retiring from another day of the session. The talk all day had centered on the fall of St. Vincent Island to the Union. Fifty Yankees landed on St. Vincent on December 4th, and the frantic people of Apalachicola, ten miles away, left in droves.

Russell raised his glass and offered a toast to the islands and Apalachicola. However, about St. Vincent, William thought to himself as he raised his glass, "Good riddance. They can have it with no regrets. Coastal duty was harder because we were on duty all the time. When the wind blew, sand got in your eyes, and when it stopped blowing, the gnats and flies ate you alive. Good riddance."

The session went as he described to Mary. By Thursday, December 12th, they were still in session at 7 pm. Whereas last year their business established a new government and seized federal property, this year their business had to do with armies and militias.

One evening in front of the hearth, with both William and James away, Vollie read a letter from James. "They sent us to New Smyrna to protect government stores brought from the Bahamas. Our job is to protect them and wait for more. We're dogged by the Federal blockading vessels, whose ships lay in wait continually off the coast. They haven't tried to come ashore yet."

"Yet," thought Mary. "Yet" haunted her. As well it should, because it wasn't long before the Federals attempted to land

and destroy the stores, though unsuccessfully, as James's letters later reflected.

Because of the telegraph, Monticello got war news from all over the country. One could walk down to the depot to receive it more timely. Still, each Saturday, the *Family Friend* carried a shortened version under a new column entitled "Telegraphic News" gleaned from their Savannah, Macon, Atlanta, and Charleston Exchanges.

Meanwhile, in Tallahassee, in a message from the Senate came an attempt to allow the city of Pensacola to issue change bills, a type of currency. The House adopted an amendment to insert "Tallahassee" after the words "city of Pensacola," and the bill upon its final passage failed, ten yeas and sixteen nays. They were meeting well into the evenings now.

On Saturday the 15th, William rolled from bed; though they were not going into session until 11 am, yet the assembly still had much to do. William, though weary, felt his adrenaline kick in later that afternoon, a good thing because they were still hard at it well into the night.

Sunday the 16th began at noon, but the trouble started after 3 pm when someone discovered a quorum not present. The speaker dispatched William to request the attendance of the assembly's absent members. He walked out the back door of the capitol, and fortunately he found most of them were at the Adelphi.

By Monday, William realized he had his second wind sometime later that morning. He felt almost giddy. The House moved through bills at a good clip, and by 3 pm, they took up the appropriations bill.

Under Florida's constitution, its general assembly has only one job to do when it meets in session. It must pass a budget.

Its constitution required a balanced budget. Good news indeed, they would adjourn sine die soon.

The body went into a joint session to elect two Confederate senators. Tuesday came and went late into the night. They clothed state troops, authorized the exchange of treasury notes for bonds, and in the end, Governor Milton signed an act relative to militia and volunteer elections.

At the hour of ten o'clock, at which they resolved to adjourn, they struck out the hour and inserted 12 o'clock instead, which they agreed upon. But on a motion, the speaker appointed a committee of three to wait upon the Senate and inform them of the Houses' action. The three men left the chambers but quickly returned.

They reported the Senate had adjourned and left the building. The speaker adjourned the House sine die. This time William didn't get to drop the ceremonial handkerchief, but he didn't care. He went home on the Wednesday train.

Research showed in the appendices, later added to the 1861 General Assembly Journal, the House went into Secret Session on two occasions while they were in Tallahassee — November 22nd and November 27th. The former provided supplies for Florida's army to prevent monopolies and other purposes. Said bill came from a joint committee, and a committee of the whole in the House heard it. The latter amended the act, but the procedure allowed them to hear and pass the bill through all three readings in one day. The assembly made up the committee of the whole.

That Christmas, Mary and the children may have spent the day with her father. They sat around the hearth which had been decorated by her and the children. Her sister Susan came by, and the family enjoyed each other's company. Said Jesse, "My hides are getting a paltry sum lately. I guess people need money, and the market must be flooded. Otherwise, I'm not sure why it is happening. I got less than six cents a pound last time."

Asked Mary, "How much money does the tanner get after he processes them?"

"Forty cents."

Susan said, "Well, there's something rotten outside Denmark."

Mary added, "Extortion is more like it, Daddy. What are you going to do?"

Jesse thought for a minute and said, "Sit on them. I'll not sell any more for six cents."

At the end of 1861, a stalemate occurred. Both armies used the winter to train for the following year. Soldiers in the southern army were mainly white males aged sixteen to twenty-eight. Half of its soldiers were twenty-three or older by the end of 1861. Mary's brother David L. Walker, nineteen, fits into this category. He enlisted on December 11th at 5' 10", fair complexion, grey eyes, and light hair, which he took after their mother. He would later be in the 5th Florida, Company A.

Why were so many young men eager to fight and die? Countless reasons include the firm belief of state's rights, the need to protect the institution of slavery, the importance of liberty, the defense of one's home and family, and the honor of brotherhood while fighting alongside others. Scores of Florida's youth fought for the latter.

Jefferson County had more than its fair share of officers in the war. With another state convention to be held on January

14th, 1862, the county worried. Its delegates were all in critical military positions—Colonel J. P. Anderson in Pensacola, Colonel W. S. Dilworth in Fernandina, Captain T. B. Lamar on the east coast, and Dr. T. M. Palmer in Virginia. The *Family Friend* worried the county would suffer the consequences.

Florida may have had great officers and leaders, but it lacked the men needed to fight. Because of Florida's sparse population, no Florida Division existed, but it had nearly a brigade of men (1,500 to 4,000 soldiers) in each of the two armies of the Confederacy. This is why some refer to Florida's men in the war as the Florida Brigade. A division holds between 10,000 to 18,000. Underneath a brigade, a battalion includes a combat unit of 500 to 800 men and a company of about 100 to 200.

Offensive measures were aggressive. The south thought its climate would assist it. Heat exhaustion, sunstroke, and endemic diseases can take its reckoning, but the south miscalculated the numbers of young men in the north by 4 to 1.

During the first year of the war, the Union Navy seized most of the Confederate coastline from Virginia to South Carolina. They also blockaded the major southern ports such as Apalachicola, but they still did not control all of Florida.

It's uncertain if William stayed home for Christmas before returning to his unit, but as 1861 faded, 1862 arrived and William was sent back to Amelia Island. Mary would be alone again with their children.

Fin

Appendix 1
Fort Brooke (Tampa Town)

In 1824, Colonel George Mercer Brooke and Colonel James Gadsden, who lived in Jefferson County, arrived to establish a military post initially named "Cantonment Brooke." They built it on the east bank of the Hillsborough River, which flowed into Hillsborough Bay (now Tampa Bay).

View of Fort Brooke during Seminole War in 1835, Gray & James, 1837, Library of Congress

The site now sits under the Tampa Convention Center. Fort Brooke became the US army headquarters during the Second Seminole War, and they later quartered soldiers there during the Third Seminole War.

During the Civil War, Confederate forces occupied it, but

Union forces captured it in 1864, only to be abandoned two days later. In 1883, it was decommissioned.

The site itself is marked with a historical marker. Two unmarked cannons on the University of Tampa campus are all that remain of the fort. "Tampa Town" was the small civilian community that grew up around the fort.

#

Appendix 2
1850 Census, Growth of the Town and County

Since the 1840 census, Jefferson County boomed, having grown 36% by 1850. It had a total population of 7,718. During this decade, 2,005 people moved into the county.

Below is a map of Monticello. The businesses and homes marked in maroon are those known to be added in the 1840s. The blue ones were added in the 1820s, and the green in the 1830s. (For a listing of the businesses and homes represented by the blue and green discs, see volume one of *Palmetto Pioneers*, pages 323-324.

1850 Monticello

Maroon Discs
1. Jail Complex, 1848
2. Cuthbert House, 1840

3. *Presbyterian Church, about 1842*
4. *Budd Mercantile, 1840s*
5. *Puleston Drug Store, early 1840s (underneath 3 & 4)*
6. *Episcopal Church, 1843*
7. *Methodist Church, 1844*
8. *Jefferson Academy, 1848*
9. *Thomas Palmer Physician's Office, 1844*
10. *Madden House, 1840s*
11. *Denham House, 1844*
12. *Waller Taylor House, 1842*
13. *Simkins & Manley Store, 1840s*
14. *Block of Log & Frame Stores*
15. *Baptist Church, 1846*
16. *Barrington Bar & Billiard Room*
17. *Smith Simkins House, 1844*
18. *Denham House, 1840s*
19. *Murdock House, 1844*

Additional Information on Buildings Built Between 1840 and 1850

1. Jail–built in 1848 at the corner of Cherry and Pearl Street. The brick building was 34' long and 40' high (two stories), with its walls two feet thick. It had three rooms below and three above with two fireplaces. An iron cage on the upper floor measured 10x10 feet square and 7 feet high. A stockade fence of logs surrounded the jail, standing end on end.

2. Cuthbert House–built in 1840 at 380 N. Jefferson St., the SE corner of Jefferson & High St., still standing; fanlight entrance, Classic Revival in style.

3. Presbyterian Church–built in late 1841 or early 1842 on Lot 55. Trustees were Graham, Johnson, and Denham. Tuggle,

Ramsey, McCants, Moore, Williams, Arledge, Graves, Parrish, and Scott were members. The church was a focal point for the community, where they held many public meetings. Greek Revival in design.

4. William Budd & Brother–opened in the 1840s. Later, Josiah Budd survived his brother and operated it under his name; it was still in business in 1860. The building later became a bank and is still standing today. It now serves as a coffee house.

5. Puleston Drug Store—opened in the early 1840s.

6. Episcopal Church–built in 1843 on a lot at the southwest corner of East Washington Street & Waukeenah Street, where an accounting office sits today. The church burned in 1884.

7. Methodist Church–built in 1844 on Lot 2 adjoining Academy Square, which was the parade grounds. A wooden church was built and occupied until 1887 when they constructed the current brick building.

8. Jefferson Academy–first school was built in 1848. It sat in the middle of West Washington Street at the western edge of town in front of the present-day Jefferson Arts building and county offices. They laid out four lots for the school on the south side of West Washington Street. This original wooden school building later became a teacher's home and boarding house in 1852.

9. Thomas Palmer Physician's Office–opened in May 1844, still standing.

10. Madden House–faced courthouse and sat where the Rev Café sits today—a wooden building of twenty rooms.

11. Denham House–built in 1844 on Palmer Mill, back of the parade ground, still standing, and today is a bed and breakfast.

12. Waller Taylor House–built in 1842 on West Washington, where the Sledges now live. It became the Dixie Hotel at the

turn of the century. No longer standing.

13. Simkins & Manley Store–started before the war. A livery stable was owned by T. B. Simkins in 1885 at the corner of West Washington and Olive (otherwise, location unknown).

14. Block of log and frame stores–Just before the Civil War, this block of stores burned. It occupied the lot at the corner of which the post office stood in 1935. One store that burned was Josiah T. Budd's first mercantile, built of pine lumber. He replaced it with a brick structure and remodeled it into a stucco building. It was later the Bank of Monticello (now a coffee house).

When the block burned, they built new buildings, one of which was a two-story brick structure on the lot which housed Milady's in 1935 (not where we remembered it in the 1960s). This two-story brick structure was owned and operated as a mercantile business by Samuel Puleston. The post office in 1935 was a one-story brick building, the first drug store of Monticello of B. W. Johnson and Tinnie Tuckers, Partners. Later, these brick stores burned. They erected one-story brick buildings in 1935 (when the Green Book was written by the WPA). This was believed to be the Braswell's/Bank building block, but they are unsure because the post office in the 1930s was also across the street on the northeast corner of the courthouse square.

15. Baptist Church–built in 1846. Set in the middle of S. Jefferson Street, up the hill from the current grocery store, Food Outlet.

16. Barrington Bar & Billiard Room–west side of the public square in Monticello. Not sure about the location, but it sounds as if it was where the Opera House is today.

17. Smith Simkins House–built 1844 on the northeast corner of

Waukeenah and E. Washington, Classic Revival Style, Saddlebag design with central chimney. Still standing.

18. Denham House–built before 1850 at 435 N. Jefferson Street. Still standing.

Location Unknown

1. Henry Wirt, Physician–next door to Edward Taylor's Apothecary. It opened in 1842.
2. Turner's Tavern –$12 per month for a room.
3. Banner House–built in 1847. They added a livery stable, but it closed in 1853. It was bought by Christian Bless later in 1853 and renamed the Florida Hotel. McKinney Russell painted portraits there for $50.
4. Gilbert & Folsom Store–operated during reconstruction.
5. Goodbreads Tavern and Hotel were listed years later as a brick hotel just south of the courthouse. (Could this have been the later Madden House? We're not sure since photos of the Madden House appear to show a wooden structure.) Blackburn bought it in 1853 and renamed it the Monticello Hotel.

#

Appendix 3
Who is Buried at the
Old Elizabeth Church Cemetery?

There are no records for the old church graveyard, but there is word of mouth in the Walker family. Several of the older members, still living in the 1960s, told several of their offspring that Joel and Elizabeth are buried there, as well as their oldest son Jesse and his Elizabeth.

There is no written proof, nor did anyone pass down information on William and Mary or their child Julia Ann. There are also no records of where Mary's Uncle Joel is buried.

The only marked graves are those of Mary's Uncle James and Elizabeth Padgett Walker, who lived long lives. Others include Jesse A. Walker and his wife, Mary Jane Hamrick Walker, William Berry Walker, Caroline Lightsey Walker, Harriett Walker, and Amanda Sledge Walker. Other families include Bell, Lamb, Lewis, Lightsey, Sledge, Sparks, Waters, and Whitaker.

Through older members of the family, there are descriptions of many unseen graves in the graveyard. Aunt Lizzie Walker Stanley, born in the 1880s and who lived into her nineties, on several occasions with several different people described the plethora of unseen graves. One person asked for a number, and Aunt Lizzie said she thought more than seventy unmarked graves lie in the cemetery. Another time, she spread her cane through the air over the ground. She said there were many graves here, more than she could remember. Aunt Lizzie was the granddaughter of Joel and Betsy Walker.

Personal Photo

Appendix 4
1860 Census, Growth of the Town and County

Between 1850 and 1860, the county grew twenty-eight percent. Monticello reflected this growth with many new stores and homes as seen below.

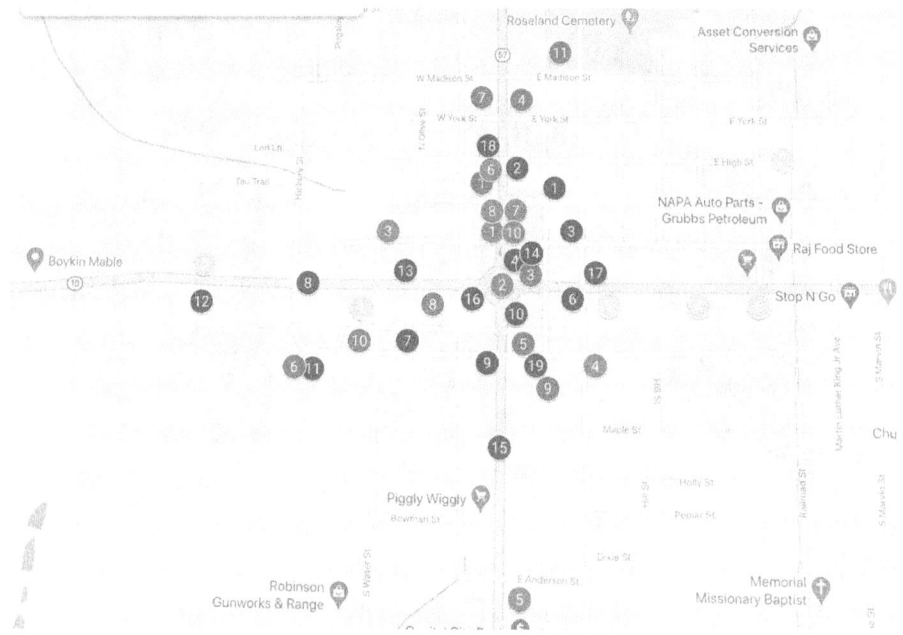

1860 Monticello

Yellow Discs
1. Jefferson Academy, 1852
2. Railroad Depot, before 1859
3. Dilworth House, 1853
4. Budd House, 1856
5. Pasco House, 1850s
6. Christian Bless House, 1855

In 1860, the population of Jefferson Count was 9,876. The county had grown by 2,158 people.

Buildings and Homes Built between 1850 and 1860
1. Jefferson Academy–built in 1852 at 430 W. Washington Street. Originally it did not have the wings, only the center building. Two stories, Colonial Revival Style. Built to house the school on the bottom floor and the Masonic and Oddfellows Lodges on the top. It still stands.
2. Railroad Depot—built by 1859, sat west of the railroad tracks, north of Pearl Street, east of Railroad Street, and south of York Street, almost at the dead end of High Street. Torn down many years ago. Today, a vacant wooded lot sits there.
3. William S. Dilworth Home–built 1853 at 345 East Washington Street on the south side of the street, one lot east of Waukeenah Street. Classic Revival in style. Dilworth was a prominent attorney who commanded Confederate troops in Middle and East Florida during the Civil War. It is still standing.
4. William Budd Home—built in 1856 at 555 E. Washington Street. Greek Revival in style. William Budd and his brother, both born in South Carolina, owned Budd Mercantile on the courthouse square. This home is still standing.
5. Samuel Pasco House—built in the 1850s at 710 W. Washington Street by an unknown person. Frame Vernacular in style. It is still standing. From Massachusetts and Harvard, Pasco served as Waukeenah Academy's principal. Later, he served as the county's clerk of the court and legislator. They named Pasco County for him.
6. Christian Bless House, built in 1855 at 695 E. Washington

Street as the Methodist Parsonage. Classic Revival in style with a Greek Revival influence. It is unusual for this type of home during this period. It is still standing.

7. Presbyterian Manse–built in 1853 at 420 East Washington Street.

Also built in the 1850s but the location is unknown
8. John S. Devine Store
9. Johnson Store
10. Bird & Company, dissolved during the 1860s after the war.
11. W. R. Roach & Company, and later as Lingo and Roach. Because of severe depression in 1873, it went bankrupt in 1874.
12. Cuthbert Brothers
13. Partridge & Randolph
14. W. P. Streety Store, closed in 1867
15. Stephen Ellenwood's Ice Cream Saloon
9.

#

Appendix 5
Henry Walker's Death Notices

A notice in the January 10th, 1861 *Family Friend* entitled:

"Masonic Burial To Officers and Members of Hiram Lodge No. 5

BRETHREN—*You are hereby requested to meet at your Lodge Room, on Sunday, the 13th instant, for the purpose of performing the Funeral Ceremonies of our late worthy brother HENRY WALKER. Brethren of neighboring Lodges are respectfully invited to attend our occasion."* The lodge was located in the school on the second floor.

In the *Family Friend* in the January 8th edition.

"Tribute of Respect, Rendezvous, Jefferson Rifle Company, January 8, 1861.

Whereas, Our ranks have been invaded by the ruthless hand of death, and we are called upon to pay a tribute of love and respect to the memory of our deceased brother, private HENRY WALKER, who we trust God has enrolled among his hosts above, therefore be it—Resolved, *That in the death of Brother Walker, this Company has lost a valuable and efficient member of society, a worthy friend, and the State a citizen whose place cannot be easily supplaced. Resolved, That we deeply sympathize with the bereaved wife and family of our brother, and do most cordially extend to her and to them a brother's love and sympathy. Resolved, That in expression of our respect, these resolutions be entered upon our minutes, and that our colors be clad* with the usual badge of mourning during sixty days. Resolved, That a copy of these resolutions be sent to the family of the deceased, and that a copy be published in the Family Friend. Signed A. C. McCANTS, M. H. STRAIN, THOS. L. SHEHEE Committee.

In the January 26th edition of the paper appeared this notice from the Masons of the Hiram Lodge:

"While the severance of the smallest and feeblest link which binds our Lodge together as a band of brothers, must be felt and deplored, yet in the death of brother HENRY WALKER, we feel that Hiram Lodge has suffered no ordinary loss. Possessing indomitable energy and prudent foresight of character, he had secured the confidence of all with whom he had business relations, while his generosity and native nobleness of heart endeared him to all who knew him. Thus surrounded by friends and a large family circle, that looked to him as their chief adviser and ablest counselor, he has been suddenly stricken down, in the very meridian of life and usefulness. While feeling that we must bow in meek submission to His will, "who doeth all things well," yet we feel that it is not only our duty, but privilege to pay some feeble tribute to his many virtues and excellencies. He was an earnest, consistent, and devoted member of Hiram Lodge, and constantly exemplified by his life and conduct those high virtues which masonry inculcates. To the tale of our sorrow or suffering, his generous heart was ever ready to respond, and the widow and the orphan never applied to him in vain for assistance; no brother ever sought his confidence without receiving sympathy and advice, feeling at the same time that his secrets were lodged in the safest depository—a brother's breast. Therefore—Resolved, 1st, That the members of Hiram Lodge wear the usual badge of mourning for thirty days, and our Lodge room be draped in mourning for the same time.

Resolved, 2nd. That we do deeply sympathize with his bereaved companion, who so soon has been called to mourn his untimely death. Resolved, 3rd, That a copy of these resolutions be sent to the bereaved widow, and the same be published in The Family Friend." Signed, W. O. GIRARDEAU, M. G. W. JORDAN, and T. J. CHACE Committee."

Dear Reader,

Thank you so much for reading *Palmetto Pioneers: From Harmony to Hostility*. I sincerely hope you enjoyed reading this book, as much as I enjoyed writing it.

The best way to thank an author for writing a book you enjoyed is to leave a honest review on Amazon, Goodreads, or your favorite book website.

Reviews are crucial for any author, even just a line or two can make a huge difference.

Cindy

<u>About the Author</u>

Cindy Roe Littlejohn was born February 10, 1954, in Thomasville, Georgia, at the nearest hospital to Monticello, Florida. Her parents brought her home to Monticello, two days after her birth.

With residences in Tallahassee and Wakulla County, Florida, she has mostly lived in Monticello where she is married to Chuck Littlejohn. They raised a son and two daughters.

<u>Also by Cindy Roe Littlejohn</u>
Palmetto Pioneers: The Emigrants,
the prequel to *Harmony and Hostility*

Cindy Roe Littlejohn
Book 1 -- Palmetto Pioneers: The Emigrants

Read an excerpt from the prequel to *From Harmony to Hostility*

A day later, while Jesse stayed with the wagons to help the kids gather firewood, storm clouds banked in the west, blocking the closing sunlight. The skies darkened.

The mixed pines and hardwoods shaded the light even more when Jesse reached into a pile of branches to pick up a small log. He felt a sting. Instinctively, he snatched his hand back. Hanging from his little finger was a ground rattler; its fang hung in his fingernail. He flung it off, and the pain intensified quickly. He stood there looking at his hand, instinctively flicking it, hoping to keep the poison down into his fingers, but he hardly saw the wound in the gathering dusk.

He must remain calm. He walked toward the camp as he sucked on the wound. With no cuts or sores in his mouth, he assumed this was safe until his tongue felt one of the snake's fangs buried in his fingernail. He grabbed ahold with his teeth and pulled it out. He continued sucking on the wound until he stepped out into the road amid more light, where he yelled for Elizabeth down at the camp, only a few hundred feet away.

He needed to wash the wound quickly, and Elizabeth jumped into action. She got a chair down from the side of the wagon, and he sat while the other Elizabeth brought a small table to rest his elbow. He kept his hand up because he felt lightheaded. His Elizabeth brought a pail of water and soap. She worked quickly because he needed to lie down before much longer. He grew pale, and she worried he would pass out before she finished.

His face was awash in his own sweat. She told Mary to prepare a place for him to lie down in one of the wagons, and the two of them helped him crawl up. Elizabeth crawled in behind him, holding a small bowl of oil with its lighted rag. She looked for a safe place to put it down. Mary handed her the pail of water. Elizabeth continued to wash the wound and suck on it. She also took a rag and used the cool water to cool Jesse's forehead. A fever was upon him.

Of all the times for this to happen, she thought. It would storm soon, and she was sure they wouldn't be able to get the fire going soon enough to cook. They would have to depend on the hardtack and cold coffee. Outside, she heard the other Elizabeth yell for the kids to come back in with any firewood they had. Her sister-in-law took over all the chores. Mary crawled into the wagon because she could do whatever Elizabeth needed done. By now, Jesse was unconscious.

Elizabeth kept thinking back to what the old-timers said about snake bites. It was fuzzy. Some died and some didn't, according to how healthy the victim was or what type of snake. Jesse said it was a ground rattler, one of the worst. "Come on, Jesse, honey," she said as she cupped his cheek in her palm, lightly kissing his forehead.

Find it on Amazon!

Author's Note

I'm frequently asked where I got my inspiration to write this series. My answer is from my family and my love for this part of Florida, my home.

My mother's family in this county reaches back many generations, and I was blessed to grow up listening to their lore. I was intrigued by their stories of hardship and their pride in survival and intended to tell their stories, adding the information gleaned from the documents, journals, newspapers, and diaries of frontier Florida.

I also wrote this because I love my state, and I'm concerned we're losing these stories.

I worked hard to keep the facts and circumstances as they happened-in Jefferson County, neighboring counties, and nationwide--bring empirical truths to light as much as possible.

--Cindy Roe Littlejohn, Monticello, Florida, February 27, 2023

No-Spam Newsletter
Palmetto Pioneers
Follow [Cindy Roe Littlejohn](#) on Bookbub

Bookbub has a New Release Alert. Not only can you check out the latest deals on books, but you can get an email when I release the third book in this series.

Follow me by clicking on my name above. Or you can find me at:

https://www.bookbub.com/profile/cindy-roe-littlejohn

Bibliography

Media

1st Florida Battle Flag. 1862. Unknown source.
https://commons.wikimedia.org/wiki/File:1FLAinf1.gif.
"Amelia Island Marshes." 2023. Wikipedia.
https://en.wikipedia.org/w/index.php?title=Amelia_Island&oldid=1153161521.
"Amelia Island, Southern Most Island in the Sea Islands." 2023. Wikipedia.
https://en.wikipedia.org/w/index.php?title=Sea_Islands&oldid=1154798837.
1863. *Riots: Southern Women Feeling the Effects of Rebellion, and Creating Bread Riots.* Frank Leslie's Illustrated Newspaper.
https://commons.wikimedia.org/wiki/File:Apr2_richmond_riot.jpg.
"Battle of Antietam." 2023. Wikipedia.
https://en.wikipedia.org/w/index.php?title=Battle_of_Antietam&oldid=1155686185.
"Battle of Mobile Bay." 2023. Wikipedia.
https://en.wikipedia.org/w/index.php?title=Battle_of_Mobile_Bay&oldid=1150866739.
Boetticher, Otto. n.d. *Civil War Prisoners at Play | Baseball as the National Game | Origins and Early Days | Explore | Baseball Americana | Exhibitions at the Library of Congress | Library of Congress.* Accessed May 30, 2023.
https://www.loc.gov/exhibitions/baseball-americana/about-this-exhibition/origins-and-early-days/baseball-as-the-national-game/civil-war-prisoners-at-play/.
Camp Chase, Columbus, Ohio—Prison of the Rebels Captured by U. S. Forces. Frank Leslie's Illustrated Newspaper. 1862.
Library of Congress Catalog: https://lccn.loc.gov/2007675765
Image download: https://cdn.loc.gov/service/pnp/ppmscd/00000/00001v.jpg
Original url: https://www.loc.gov/pictures/item/2007675765/.
https://commons.wikimedia.org/wiki/File:Camp_Chase,_Columbus,_Ohio._Prison_of_the_rebels_captured_by_U._S._forces._LCCN2007675765_(cropped).jpg.
"Constitution of the Confederate States of America. Djvu/3 - Wikisource, the Free Online Library." n.d. Wikipedia. Accessed May 25, 2023.
https://en.wikisource.org/wiki/Page:Constitution_of_the_Confederate_States_of_America.djvu/3.
"Dr. Thomas Martin Palmer (1821-1895) - Find a Grave," n.d. Accessed May 24, 2023. https://www.findagrave.com/memorial/44196837/thomas-martin-palmer.
"Field_hospital_after_the_battle_of_Savage_Station,_Va._June_27_LOC_cwpb.01063.jpg (953×682)." n.d. Accessed May 30, 2023.
https://upload.wikimedia.org/wikipedia/commons/b/b2/Savage_Station%2C_Va._Fie

ld_hospital_after_the_battle_of_June_27_LOC_cwpb.01063.jpg.

Florida, State Library and Archives of. n.d. "Budd & Son Dry Goods Store - Monticello, Florida." Florida Memory. Accessed May 24, 2023. https://www.floridamemory.com/items/show/33839.

———. n.d. "City Hotel on the West Side of Adams Street Looking North - Tallahassee, Florida." Florida Memory. Accessed May 25, 2023. https://www.floridamemory.com/items/show/27634.

———. n.d. "Dixie Hotel - Monticello, Florida." Florida Memory. Accessed May 24, 2023. https://www.floridamemory.com/items/show/33864.

———. n.d. "Dr. Thomas Martin Palmer from Jefferson County, Florida." Florida Memory. Accessed May 24, 2023. https://www.floridamemory.com/items/show/255328.

———. n.d. "Jefferson County Court House - Monticello." Florida Memory. Accessed May 23, 2023. https://www.floridamemory.com/items/show/144808.

———. n.d. "Jefferson County Court House - Monticello." Florida Memory. Accessed May 24, 2023. https://www.floridamemory.com/items/show/144808.

———. n.d. "Jefferson County High School - Monticello, Florida." Florida Memory. Accessed May 25, 2023. https://www.floridamemory.com/items/show/39851.

———. n.d. "J.T. Budd & Son General Merchandise Store - Monticello, Florida." Florida Memory. Accessed May 24, 2023h https://www.floridamemory.com/items/show/26782.

———. n.d. "Monticello after the Fire - Monticello, Florida." Florida Memory Collection. Accessed May 24, 2023. https://www.floridamemory.com/items/show/26053.

———. n.d. "Monticello High School - Monticello, Florida." Florida Memory. Accessed May 24, 2023. https://www.floridamemory.com/items/show/144832.

———. n.d. "Old Capitol before Addition of Dome - Tallahassee, Florida." Florida Memory Collection. Accessed May 25, 2023. https://www.floridamemory.com/items/show/33249.

———. n.d. "Old Capitol Looking across Dirt Road - View of West Front, Tallahassee, Florida." Florida Memory. Accessed May 25, 2023. https://www.floridamemory.com/items/show/25850.

———. n.d. "Pensacola, 9th Mississippi Unit during the Civil War - Pensacola, Florida." Florida Memory. Accessed May 25, 2023. https://www.floridamemory.com/items/show/26276.

———. n.d. "Pensacola Rebel Battery - Pensacola, Florida." Florida Memory. Accessed May 25, 2023. https://www.floridamemory.com/items/show/28286.

———. n.d. "St. Vincent Island Shoreline with Cabbage Palms, Florida." Florida Memory. Accessed May 25, 2023. https://www.floridamemory.com/items/show/40965.

———. n.d. "St. Vincent's Island Fisherman's Hut." Florida Memory. Accessed May 25, 2023. https://www.floridamemory.com/items/show/8166.

———. n.d. "St. Vincents Island. Group Posing." Florida Memory. Accessed May 25, 2023. https://www.floridamemory.com/items/show/259379.

———. n.d. "Tallahassee Illustration - Tallahassee, Florida." Florida Memory. Accessed May 25, 2023. https://www.floridamemory.com/items/show/24682.

———. n.d. "Wagons Unloading Cotton at the Seaboard Air Line Depot - Lloyd, Florida." Florida Memory. Accessed August 11, 2023. https://www.floridamemory.com/items/show/26673.

———. n.d. "Washington Mackey Ives from the 4th Florida Infantry in Chattanooga, Tennessee. Portrait." Florida Memory Collection. Accessed May 25, 2023. https://www.floridamemory.com/items/show/1659.

"Fort Pickens3 Old Fort - 06.jpg - FortWiki Historic U.S. and Canadian Forts." n.d. Accessed May 25, 2023. http://www.fortwiki.com/File:Fort_Pickens3_Old_Fort_-_06.jpg.

"Frontier Definition." n.d. https://www.google.com/search?q=frontier+definition&rlz=1C1GCEA_enUS1064US1064&oq=frontier+defin&gs_lcrp=EgZjaHJvbWUqDQgAEAAYgwEYsQMYgAQyDQgAEAAYgwEYsQMYgAQyBggBEEUYOTIHCAIQABiABDIHCAMQABiABDIHCAQQABiABDIHCAUQABiABDIHCAYQABiABDIHCAcQABiABDIKCAgQABiGAxiKBTIKCAkQABiGAxiKBdIBCDUyMDBqMGo5qAIAsAIA&sourceid=chrome&ie=UTF-8&bshm=rimc/1.

"Google Maps, 1850's Elizabeth Community." Google Maps. Accessed May 24, 2023.

"Google Maps, Apalachicola Bay & Saint Joseph Bay Area."

"Google Maps, Fort Pickens." Google Maps. Accessed May 25, 2023. https://www.google.com/maps/search/Museums/@30.3770658,-87.3475487,12z/data=!4m2!2m1!6e1?entry=ttu.

"Google Maps, Road Between Bellamy Plantation and the Salt Road." Google Maps. Accessed May 24, 2023.

Hal Jespersen. 2023. "Battle of Stones River, Night of December 30-31, 1862." Wikipedia. https://en.wikipedia.org/w/index.php?title=Battle_of_Stones_River&oldid=1156689583.

Hitching Post, Historic American Buildings Survey Alex Bush, Photographer, April 17, 1936 HITCHING POSTS ON NORTH SIDE OF HOME - Elmoreland, U.S. Highway 241, Glenville, Russell County, AL. n.d. https://www.loc.gov/pictures/item/al0711.photos.006566p/. Accessed June 16, 2023. https://commons.wikimedia.org/wiki/File:Historic_American_Buildings_Survey_Alex_Bush,_Photographer,_April_17,_1936_HITCHING_POSTS_ON_NORTH_SIDE_OF_HOME_-_Elmoreland,_U.S._Highway_241,_Glenville,_Russell_County,_AL_HABS_ALA,57-GLENV,1-28.tif.

"How to: From Genealogy to a Family Book." 2023. OLD AGE IS NOT FOR SISSIES. March 19, 2023.
http://oldageisnotforsissiesblog.com/how-to-from-genealogy-to-a-family-book/.
Jeffecello Academy, inside Looking West, 1959 Jeffecello Annual. n.d. Vol. 1859. Jefferson County High School Annuals.

Jespersen, Hal. 2010. *Battle of Stones River, January 2, 1863 (Later in the Day) Drawn in Adobe Illustrator CS6 by Hal Jespersen. Graphic Source File Is Available at Http://www.Cwmaps.com/Dansk: Slaget Ved Stones River, 2. January 1863 Kl. 16.45*. Own work (Original text: own work).
https://commons.wikimedia.org/w/index.php?curid=4540294.

"John Jumper (Seminole Assistant Chief)." 2023. Wikipedia.
https://en.wikipedia.org/w/index.php?title=John_Jumper_(Seminole_chief)&oldid=1156537452.

"Monticello First Baptist Church Photo." 1940. Keystone Genealogical Library, Monticello, Florida.

"Monticello High School, 1920, Front & East Entrance." Keystone Genealogical Library, Monticello, Florida.

"Monticello's Jail Built in 1846." Keystone Genealogy Library, Jefferson County, Florida Library.

"Old Capitol - Tallahassee, Florida. Lithograph, 1885." Florida Memory Collection. Accessed May 25, 2023. https://www.floridamemory.com/items/show/24592.

"Perryville, Western Theater of the American Civil War." 2023. Wikipedia.
https://en.wikipedia.org/w/index.php?title=Western_theater_of_the_American_Civil_War&oldid=1132531443.

Program, American Battlefield Protection. 2011. *Santa Rosa Battlefield, Map of Battlefield Core and Study Areas by the American Battlefield Protection Program*. National Park Service.
https://commons.wikimedia.org/wiki/File:Santa_Rosa_Island_Battlefield_Florida.jpg.

"Richmond 1862.jpg." 2017. Wikipedia.
https://en.wikipedia.org/w/index.php?title=File:Richmond_1862.jpg&oldid=807150529.

"St. Vincent National Wildlife Refuge Road." 2022. Wikipedia.
https://en.wikipedia.org/w/index.php?title=St._Vincent_National_Wildlife_Refuge&oldid=1119086702.

"Tallahassee, 1885, Aerial Map, Norris, Wellge & Co., Milwaukee Wisconsin." Florida Memory Collection. Accessed May 30, 2023.
https://www.floridamemory.com/items/show/323098.

"Tallahassee Depot Florida Memory Collection - Google Search." Accessed August 11, 2023.
https://www.google.com/search?q=tallahassee+depot+florida+memory+collection&rl

Palmetto Pioneers

z=1C1GCEA_enUS1064US1064&oq=Tallahas&gs_lcrp=EgZjaHJvbWUqBggAEEUYO
zIGCAAQRRg7Mg0IARAuGIMBGLEDGIAEMg0IAhAAGIMBGLEDGIAEMg0IAx
AuGIMBGLEDGIAEMhMIBBAuGIMBGMcBGLEDGNEDGIAEMhMIBRAuGIMBG
K8BGMcBGLEDGIAEMg0IBhAAGIMBGLEDGIAEMgYIBxBFGD3SAQgyOTE5ajBq
N6gCALACAA&sourceid=chrome&ie=UTF-8.

"The Battle of Santa Rosa, Sketched by Charles F. Allgauer." n.d.

"The West Point Atlas of the Civil War." n.d. Image. Library of Congress, Washington, D.C. 20540 USA. Accessed May 30, 2023. https://www.loc.gov/item/map62000023/.

"Trains, Riding on Top of Box Cars [Atlanta, Ga. Civilians Crowded on Tops of Boxcars at Railroad Depot as Soldiers Gather around an S.D. Goodale & Sons Stereoscopic Viewer next to Office of the Daily Intelligencer Newspaper]." n.d. Image. Library of Congress, Washington, D.C. 20540 USA. Accessed May 30, 2023. https://www.loc.gov/resource/cwpb.02216/.

"Ulmer's Mill." n.d. Keystone Genealogical Library, Monticello, Florida.

Waud, William. 1878. "Prisoners of War (Returned) Exchanging Their Rags for New Clothing on Board Flag of Truce Boat New York." Image. Library of Congress, Washington, D.C. 20540 USA. 1878. https://www.loc.gov/resource/ppmsca.21722/.

"Women in the Civil War." 2021. April 4, 2021. https://www.WikiTree.com/photo/jpg/Profiling_Civil_War_Nurses.

Life in Antebellum Florida

"1860 Agricultural Census, Jefferson County, Florida." Accessed April 14, 2019. http://files.usgwarchives.net/fl/jefferson/census/1860agri.txt.

"19th Century Fashion Trends, "Fashion Plate Collection" n.d. Accessed March 2, 2020. https://content.lib.washington.edu/costumehistweb/fashion-trends.html.

Akerman, Joe A. 1976. *Florida Cowman: A History of Florida Cattle Raising*. Kissimmee: Florida Cattlemen's Association.

Ancestry. 1860. "1860 United States Federal Census - Ancestry.com William H. Andrews & Family." September 5, 1860. http://search.ancestry.com/cgi-bin/sse.dll?db=1860usfedcenancestry&h=10615420&ti=0&indiv=try&gss=pt&ssrc=pt_t23894133_p1441729078_kpidz0q3d1441729078z0q6 pgz0q3d32768z0q26pgplz0q3dpid.

Baptist, Edward E. 2002. *Creating an Old South: Middle Florida's Plantation Frontier before the Civil War*. University of North Carolina Press. http://uncpress.unc.edu/browse/page/197.

"Clothing Of The 1830s." n.d. Accessed December 13, 2019. https://www.connerprairie.org/educate/indiana-history/clothing-in-the-1800s/.

Denham, James M. 1994. "The Florida Cracker before the Civil War as Seen through Travelers' Accounts." *The Florida Historical Quarterly* 72 (4): 453–68.

E. J. Vann. n.d. *Journal Kept by E. J. Vann from August 29, 1859 to September 28, 1859.*
"Early Railroad Schedule Tallahassee to Walker Mills Family Friend." 1859. FPK Yonge Library Newspaper Collection. March 29, 1859.
http://ufdc.ufl.edu/UF00079911/00006/3x?search=monticello.

Egerton, John. 1993. *Southern Food: At Home, on the Road, in History.* Chapel Hill: The University of North Carolina Press.

F. R. Fildes. n.d. *The Family Friend,* newspaper of Monticello, Florida. January 7, 1860. Accessed March 2, 2020.
https://ufdc.ufl.edu/UF00079911/00042?search=jefferson+=county+=florida.

F. R. Fildes, Editor. 1859. *Family Friend* newspaper. October 22, 1859.
http://ufdc.ufl.edu/UF00079911/00034/2x?search=jefferson+%3dcounty.

———F. R. Fildes,. n.d. *Family Friend.* March 9, 1861. Accessed April 23, 2020.
https://ufdc.ufl.edu/UF00079911/00100/2x?search=jefferson+%3dcounty+%3dflorida.

———. n.d. *Family Friend.* March 19, 1861. August 3, 1861. Accessed July 16, 2020.
https://ufdc.ufl.edu/UF00079911/00120/2x?search=jefferson+%3dcounty+%3dflorida.

———. n.d. *Family Friend.January 28, 1860.* Accessed March 5, 2020.
https://ufdc.ufl.edu/UF00079911/00045?search=jefferson+=county+=florida.

———. n.d. *Family Friend.* March 16, 1861. Accessed March 11, 2020.
https://ufdc.ufl.edu/UF00079911/00101?search=jefferson+=county+=florida.

———. n.d. *Family Friend.* March 17, 1860. Accessed March 12, 2020.
https://ufdc.ufl.edu/UF00079911/00052?search=jefferson+=county+=florida.

———. n.d. *Family Friend.* May 19, 1860. Accessed March 12, 2020.
https://ufdc.ufl.edu/UF00079911/00060/2x?search=jefferson+%3dcounty+%3dflorida.

———. n.d. *Family Friend.* November 5, 1859. Accessed March 12, 2020.
https://ufdc.ufl.edu/UF00079911/00035?search=jefferson+=county+=florida.

———. n.d. *Family Friend.* November 17, 1860. Accessed March 13, 2020.
https://ufdc.ufl.edu/UF00079911/00085/2j?search=jefferson+%3dcounty+%3dflorida.

———. n.d. *Family Friend.* November 17, 1860. Accessed March 13, 2020.
https://ufdc.ufl.edu/UF00079911/00085/2x?search=jefferson+%3dcounty+%3dflorida.

———. n.d. *Family Friend.* November 24, 1860. Accessed March 13, 2020.
https://ufdc.ufl.edu/UF00079911/00086/2j?search=jefferson+%3dcounty+%3dflorida.

———. n.d. *Family Friend.* December 1, 1860. Accessed March 13, 2020.
https://ufdc.ufl.edu/UF00079911/00087/2x?search=jefferson+%3dcounty+%3dflorida.

———. n.d. *Family Friend.* July 14, 1860. Accessed March 19, 2020.
https://ufdc.ufl.edu/UF00079911/00068/2x?search=jefferson+%3dcounty+%3dflorida.

———. n.d. *Family Friend.* July 21, 1860. Accessed March 19, 2020.
https://ufdc.ufl.edu/UF00079911/00069?search=jefferson+%3dcounty+%3dflorida.

———. n.d. *Family Friend.* December 1, 1860. Accessed March 20, 2020.
https://ufdc.ufl.edu/UF00079911/00087/2x?search=jefferson+%3dcounty+%3dflorida.

———. n.d. *Family Friend.* December 8, 1860. Accessed March 20, 2020.
https://ufdc.ufl.edu/UF00079911/00088/2x?search=jefferson+%3dcounty+%3dflorida.

———. n.d. *Family Friend*. December 15, 1860. Accessed March 20, 2020. https://ufdc.ufl.edu/UF00079911/00089/2x?search=jefferson+%3dcounty+%3dflorida.

———. n.d. *Family Friend*. January 5, 1861. Accessed March 27, 2020. https://ufdc.ufl.edu/UF00079911/00091/2x?search=jefferson+%3dcounty+%3dflorida.

———. n.d. *Family Friend*. January 12, 1861. Accessed March 27, 2020. https://ufdc.ufl.edu/UF00079911/00092/4x?search=jefferson+%3dcounty+%3dflorida.

———. n.d. *Family Friend*. January 12, 1861. Accessed March 31, 2020. https://ufdc.ufl.edu/UF00079911/00092/2x?search=jefferson+%3dcounty+%3dflorida.

———. n.d. *Family Friend*. January 19, 1861. Accessed March 31, 2020. https://ufdc.ufl.edu/UF00079911/00093/2x?search=jefferson+%3dcounty+%3dflorida.

———. n.d. *Family Friend*. January 26, 1861. Accessed April 1, 2020. https://ufdc.ufl.edu/UF00079911/00094/2x?search=jefferson+%3dcounty+%3dflorida.

———. n.d. *Family Friend*. February 2, 1861. Accessed April 1, 2020. https://ufdc.ufl.edu/UF00079911/00095/2x?search=jefferson+%3dcounty+%3dflorida.

———. n.d. *Family Friend*. March 17, 1860. Accessed April 28, 2020. https://ufdc.ufl.edu/UF00079911/00052?search=jefferson+%3dcounty+%3dflorida.

———. n.d. *Family Friend*. February 23, 1861. Accessed April 29, 2020. https://ufdc.ufl.edu/UF00079911/00098/2x?search=jefferson+%3dcounty+%3dflorida.

———. n.d. *Family Friend*. March 9, 1861. Accessed April 29, 2020. https://ufdc.ufl.edu/UF00079911/00100/3x?search=jefferson+%3dcounty+%3dflorida.

———. n.d. *Family Friend*. December 15, 1860. Accessed April 30, 2020. https://ufdc.ufl.edu/UF00079911/00089/2j?search=jefferson+%3dcounty+%3dflorida.

———. n.d. *Family Friend*. April 27, 1861. Accessed April 30, 2020. https://ufdc.ufl.edu/UF00079911/00107/3x?search=jefferson+%3dcounty+%3dflorida.

———. n.d. *Family Friend*. April 13, 1861. Accessed April 30, 2020. https://ufdc.ufl.edu/UF00079911/00105/3x?search=jefferson+%3dcounty+%3dflorida.

———. n.d. *Family Friend*. March 30, 1861. Accessed May 1, 2020. https://ufdc.ufl.edu/UF00079911/00103/6x?search=jefferson+%3dcounty%2cjefferson+%3dcounty.

———. n.d. *Family Friend*. April 6, 1861. Accessed May 1, 2020. https://ufdc.ufl.edu/UF00079911/00104?search=jefferson+%3dcounty+%3dflorida.

———. n.d. *Family Friend*. March 29, 1859. Accessed November 10, 2015. http://ufdc.ufl.edu/UF00079911/00006/3x?search=monticello.

———. n.d. *Family Friend*. November 30, 1861. Accessed July 9, 2020. https://ufdc.ufl.edu/UF00079911/00137/1x?search=jefferson+%3dcounty+%3dflorida.

———. n.d. *Family Friend*. "Elizabeth Walker Death Notice," March 22, 1859.

"Florida Census 1860." Exploring Florida. https://fcit.usf.edu/florida/docs/c/census/1860.htm.

Florida Department of Corrections. n.d. "Florida Corrections: Centuries of Progress." History. Accessed December 10, 2018. http://www.dc.state.fl.us/oth/timeline/1821-1845.html.

"Florida Memory - Interior View of H.G. Hires Store - Fenholloway, Florida 1910."

n.d. Florida Memory. Accessed April 10, 2015. https://floridamemory.com/items/show/37856.

"Florida Plantations Misc." n.d. Accessed April 7, 2020. http://www.dejaelaine.com/miscplantations2.html.

Florida, State Library and Archives of. n.d. "History of Jefferson County." Florida Memory. Accessed September 6, 2020. https://www.floridamemory.com/items/show/321121.

———. n.d. "Monticello Baptist Church." Florida Memory. Accessed September 6, 2020. https://www.floridamemory.com/items/show/249045.

———. n.d. "Monticello Baptist Church." Florida Memory. Accessed March 22, 2023. https://www.floridamemory.com/items/show/249045.

"Gamble Family. - Social Networks and Archival Context." n.d. Accessed January 24, 2023. https://snaccooperative.org/ark:/99166/w6231rkk.

"Great Philadelphia Wagon Road." n.d. Accessed November 10, 2020. http://mayfieldsofsc.tripod.com/great_philadelphia_wagon_road.htm.

Hartog, Hendrik A. n.d. "Marital Exits and Marital Expectations in Nineteenth Century America" 80: 36.

"History of Port at Fernandina." n.d. Ohpa. Accessed May 27, 2020. https://www.portoffernandina.org/history-of-port.

Houston, E. 1863. "President's Report, Pensacola & Georgia Railway 4/1/1863."

"Inaugural Addresses of the Presidents of the United States: from George Washington 1789 to George Bush 1989." n.d. Text. Washington, D.C. : U.S. G.P.O. : for sale by the Supt. of Docs., U.S. G.P.O., 1989. Accessed May 18, 2020. https://avalon.law.yale.edu/19th_century/lincoln1.asp.

"Indian Peace Treaty Concessions in Georgia Map." n.d. Accessed November 10, 2020. https://www.tngenweb.org/cessions/ilcmap15.jpg.

Jabour, Anya. 2022. "'The Privations & Hardships of a New Country': Southern Women and Southern Hospitality on the Florida Frontier." *Florida Historical Quarterly* 75 (3). https://stars.library.ucf.edu/fhq/vol75/iss3/3.

James M. Gould. n.d. "Florida Herald and Southern Democrat." Accessed May 23, 2021. https://ufdc.ufl.edu/UF00079918/00221/1x?search=1843.

"John Jumper (Seminole Chief)." 2023. Wikipedia. https://en.wikipedia.org/w/index.php?title=John_Jumper_(Seminole_chief)&oldid=1137029708.

MacLeod, Gordon, and R. Ken Murdock. 1994. *Florida's Railroads*. Dinky Line.

"Miscellaneous, Bellamy Family Genealogy." n.d. Accessed October 1, 2020. https://ufdc.ufl.edu/AA00017204/00005/57x.

"Monticello-FL-1885-SM.jpg (3000×2000)." n.d. Accessed November 10, 2020. https://www.knowol.com/wp-content/uploads/2019/04/Monticello-FL-1885-SM.jpg.

"Mourning." 2018. Wikipedia. https://en.wikipedia.org/w/index.php?title=Mourning&oldid=841285725.

Nancy Andrews Graham. n.d. *Lest We Forget, Dowling Family History*. Union County Times.

"Old City Cemetery, Monticello, Florida - Burial Records." n.d. Accessed July 31, 2020. http://www.interment.net/data/us/fl/jefferson/old-city-cemetery/index.htm.

"Pensacola & Georgia Railroad, Confederacy." n.d.

Rivers, Larry. 1983. "'Dignity and Importance:' Slavery in Jefferson County, Florida-1827 to 1860." *The Florida Historical Quarterly* 61 (4): 404–30.

Rogers, William Warren. 1963. *Ante-Bellum Thomas County, 1825-1861*. First edition. Florida State University.

"Sanborn Fire Insurance Map from Monticello, Jefferson County, Florida. 1884." Image. Library of Congress, Washington, D.C. 20540 USA. Accessed November 10, 2020. https://www.loc.gov/resource/g3934mm.g3934mm_g013121884/?sp=1.

"Sanborn Maps, Available Online, Florida, Monticello." n.d. Library of Congress, Washington, D.C. 20540 USA. Accessed November 10, 2020. https://www.loc.gov/collections/sanborn-maps/?fa=location:florida%7Clocation:monticello.

Scarborough, William Kauffman. 2006. *Masters of the Big House: Elite Slaveholders of the Mid-Nineteenth-Century South*. LSU Press.

Shofner, Jerrell H. 1976. *History of Jefferson County, Florida*. First edition. Sentry Press.

"Southern Recorder. (Milledgeville, Ga.) 1820-1872, October 15, 1834, Image 2 « Georgia Historic Newspapers." n.d. Accessed October 8, 2020. https://gahistoricnewspapers.galileo.usg.edu/lccn/sn82016415/1834-10-15/ed-1/seq-2/.

"Statistics on Slavery." n.d. Accessed June 29, 2021. https://faculty.weber.edu/kmackay/statistics_on_slavery.htm.

Swell, Barbara. 2001. *Secrets of the Great Old-Timey Cooks: Historic Recipes, Lore & Wisdom*. Asheville, N.C.: Native Ground Music.

The Daily Crescent. n.d. "Very Late from California: Gold! Gold! Gold!," Morning edition, sec. December 8, 1848. Library of Congress.

"The Declaration of Causes of Seceding States." 2008. American Battlefield Trust. December 15, 2008. https://www.battlefields.org/learn/primary-sources/declaration-causes-seceding-states.

"*The Enterprise*. (Thomasville, Ga.) 186?-1865, July 12, 1865, Image 3, Georgia Historic Newspapers." 1865. July 12, 1865. https://gahistoricnewspapers.galileo.usg.edu/lccn/sn88054093/1865-07-12/ed-1/seq-3/.

"*The Enterprise*. (Thomasville, Ga.) 186?-1865, July 19, 1865, Image 1, Georgia Historic Newspapers." Accessed January 17, 2019. https://gahistoricnewspapers.galileo.usg.edu/lccn/sn88054093/1865-07-19/ed-1/seq-1/.

"*The Enterprise*. (Thomasville, Ga.) 186?-1865, July 19, 1865, Image 2, Georgia Historic Newspapers." Accessed January 17, 2019. https://gahistoricnewspapers.galileo.usg.edu/lccn/sn88054093/1865-07-19/ed-1/seq-2/.

The Floridian. n.d. May 15, 1841. Accessed March 6, 2021. https://ufdc.ufl.edu/UF00079927/00403.

Turner, Gregg M. 2012. *A Journey into Florida Railroad History*. University Press of Florida.

Vann, Enoch Jasper. 1937. *Reminiscences of a Georgia-Florida-Pinewoods-Cracker Lawyer*. Florida State Library: s.n.

"Warranty Deed Dated December 1841, Deed Book D, Page 558-562." 1841. https://www.ancestry.com/mediaui-viewer/collection/1030/tree/23894133/person/1441730176/media/ba4224c2-99a7-43ad-acff-92ff1292da32?_phsrc=Eul8264&usePUBJs=true&galleryindex=15&sort=-created.

The War Between the States: 1861 to 1862

"2nd Battalion, Florida Infantry (Confederate) Genealogy - FamilySearch Wiki." n.d. Accessed July 9, 2019. https://www.familysearch.org/wiki/en/2nd_Battalion,_Florida_Infantry_(Confederate).

"4th Regiment Florida Infantry1." n.d. Accessed September 25, 2017. http://www.rootsweb.ancestry.com/~gatroup2/fl4threginfantry1.html.

"10th Florida Infantry Regiment." n.d. *The Civil War in the East* (blog). Accessed July 8, 2019. http://civilwarintheeast.com/confederate-regiments/florida/10th-florida-infantry-regiment/.

"11th Florida Infantry." 2018. Wikipedia. https://en.wikipedia.org/w/index.php?title=11th_Florida_Infantry&oldid=856031549.

"11th Regiment, Florida Infantry (Confederate)." n.d. FamilySearch Wiki. Accessed June 30, 2020. https://www.familysearch.org/wiki/en/11th_Regiment,_Florida_Infantry_(Confederate).

"ACWS - Gilhams Manual for Civil War Drill." n.d. Accessed August 11, 2020. https://acws.co.uk/gilhams/.

"Amelia Island." 2023. Wikipedia. https://en.wikipedia.org/w/index.php?title=Amelia_Island&oldid=1146035479.

"American Civil War Soldiers - Ancestry.com." n.d. Accessed April 5, 2021. https://search.ancestry.com/cgi-bin/sse.dll?indiv=1&dbid=3737&h=2933182&ssrc=pt&tid=23894133&pid=1441728990&usePUB=true.

"Ancestry.com - U.S., Civil War Prisoner of War Records, 1861-1865." n.d.

Accessed April 5, 2021. https://www.ancestry.com/imageviewer/collections/1124/images/M598_46-0227?pId=356557.

"Ancestry.com - U.S., Confederate Army Casualty Lists and Reports, 1861-1865." n.d. Accessed April 5, 2021. https://www.ancestry.com/imageviewer/collections/2401/images/33124_b042407-00631?pId=55455.

Anderson, James Patton. 1896. "Southern Historical Society Papers, Volume 24., Autobiography of James Patton Anderson, C. S. A." 1896. zotero://attachment/199/.

Andrews, W. H. 1992. *Footprints of a Regiment: A Recollection of the 1st Georgia Regulars, 1861-1865.* Taylor Trade Publishing.

"Battle of Fort Sumter Facts & Summary." 2010. American Battlefield Trust. December 2, 2010. https://www.battlefields.org/learn/civil-war/battles/fort-sumter.

"Battle of Stones River - Wikipedia, the Free Encyclopedia." n.d. Accessed March 8, 2015. http://en.wikipedia.org/wiki/Battle_of_Stones_River.

Blue & Gray Magazine. 2012. "The Battle of Stones River, Volume XXVIII, Issue #6." Blue & Gray. 2012. http://www.bluegraymagazine.com/stonesriver/sr1.html.

Charles, Harry K. 2016. "American Civil War Postage Due: North and South." http://stamps.org/userfiles/file/symposium/presentations/CharlesPaper.pdf.

"Civil War Service Records (CMSR) - Confederate - Florida." n.d. Fold3. Accessed December 29, 2021. http://www.fold3.com:9292/image/264682342?xid=1945&_ga=2.113464071.1055167981.1640803876-358856399.1639690271.

"Civil War Service Records Compiled (CMSR) - Confederate - Florida." n.d. Fold3. Accessed April 5, 2021. http://www.fold3.com:9292/image/110748004/?xid=1022.

"Confederate Dead and Hospitals (Randolph County)." n.d. *Georgia Historical Society* (blog). Accessed January 12, 2018. http://georgiahistory.com/ghmi_marker_updated/confederate-dead-and-hospitals-randolph/.

"Confederate States of America." 2019. Wikipedia. https://en.wikipedia.org/w/index.php?title=Confederate_States_of_America&oldid=888576529.

Confederate Veteran. 1912. 4th ed. Vol. 20.

F. R. Fildes, Editor. n.d. August 10, 1861. *Family Friend.* Accessed July 2, 2020. https://ufdc.ufl.edu/UF00079911/00121/1x?search=jefferson+%3dcounty+%3dflorida.

———. n.d. *Family Friend.* October 26, 1861. Accessed July 3, 2020. https://ufdc.ufl.edu/UF00079911/00132/4x?search=jefferson+%3dcounty+%3dflorida.

———. n.d. *Family Friend.* November 9, 1861. Accessed July 3, 2020. https://ufdc.ufl.edu/UF00079911/00134/4x?search=jefferson+%3dcounty+%3dflorida.

———. n.d. *Family Friend.* November 30, 1861. Accessed July 10, 2020. https://ufdc.ufl.edu/UF00079911/00137/1x?search=jefferson+%3dcounty+%3dflorida.

———. n.d. *Family Friend.* December 21, 1861. Accessed July 16, 2020.

Cindy Roe Littlejohn

https://ufdc.ufl.edu/UF00079911/00140/1x?search=jefferson+%3dcounty+%3dflorida.
———. n.d. *Family Friend.* November 3, 1860. Accessed July 31, 2020.
https://ufdc.ufl.edu/UF00079911/00083/2x?search=jefferson+%3dcounty+%3dflorida.
———. n.d. *Family Friend.* November 9, 1860. Accessed July 31, 2020.
https://ufdc.ufl.edu/UF00079911/00084/2x?search=jefferson+%3dcounty+%3dflorida.
———. n.d. *Family Friend.* August 17, 1861. Accessed August 6, 2020.
https://ufdc.ufl.edu/UF00079911/00122/1x?search=jefferson+%3dcounty+%3dflorida.
———. n.d. *Family Friend.* April 20, 1861. Accessed August 27, 2020.
https://ufdc.ufl.edu/UF00079911/00106?search=jefferson+=county+=florida.
———. n.d. *Family Friend.* April 20, 1861. Accessed May 1, 2020.
https://ufdc.ufl.edu/UF00079911/00106/3x?search=jefferson+%3dcounty+%3dflorida.
———. n.d. *Family Friend.* July 20, 1861. Accessed June 20, 2020.
https://ufdc.ufl.edu/UF00079911/00119/2x?search=jefferson+%3dcounty+%3dflorida.
———. n.d. *Family Friend.* July 13, 1861. Accessed June 21, 2020.
https://ufdc.ufl.edu/UF00079911/00118/2x?search=jefferson+%3dcounty+%3dflorida.
———. n.d. *Family Friend.*December 14, 1861. Accessed July 10, 2020.
https://ufdc.ufl.edu/UF00079911/00139/1x?search=jefferson+%3dcounty+%3dflorida.
"Edwin Francis Jemison." 2023. Wikipedia.
https://en.wikipedia.org/w/index.php?title=Edwin_Francis_Jemison&oldid=1153113514.
Family Search Wiki. n.d. "2nd Regiment, Florida Infantry (Confederate)." FamilySearch Wiki. Accessed July 14, 2020.
https://www.familysearch.org/wiki/en/2nd_Regiment,_Florida_Infantry_(Confederate).
———. n.d. "3rd Regiment, Florida Infantry (Confederate)." FamilySearch Wiki. Accessed July 14, 2020.
https://www.familysearch.org/wiki/en/3rd_Regiment,_Florida_Infantry_(Confederate).
———. n.d. "Florida Civil War Confederate Infantry Units." FamilySearch Wiki. Accessed July 14, 2020.
https://www.familysearch.org/wiki/en/Florida_Civil_War_Confederate_Infantry_Units.
Fildes, F. R., Editor. n.d. *Family Friend.* August 3, 1861. Accessed July 2, 2020.
https://ufdc.ufl.edu/UF00079911/00120/1x?search=jefferson+%3dcounty+%3dflorida.
———. n.d. *Family Friend.* June 2, 1860. Accessed January 17, 2022.
https://original-ufdc.uflib.ufl.edu/UF00079911/00062/2j?search=family+%3dfriend.
———. n.d. *Family Friend.* February 2, 1861. Accessed January 17, 2022.
https://original-ufdc.uflib.ufl.edu/UF00079911/00095/2x?search=family+%3dfriend.
"FL 4th Inf Co. H." n.d. Accessed June 12, 2020.
http://myweb.fsu.edu/rthompson2//cw/4-fl-inf/4-fl-inf-h.html.
Florida. Board of State Institutions, and Fred L. Robertson. 1903. *Soldiers of Florida*

in the Seminole Indian, Civil and Spanish-American Wars. Live Oak, Fla., Democrat print. http://archive.org/details/soldiersofflorid00flor.

Florida Genealogy Trails. n.d. "Civil War Florida Infantry Rosters." Accessed July 14, 2020. http://genealogytrails.com/fla/military/civilwar_infantry3.html.

Florida, State Library and Archives of. n.d. "Fisherman's Hut, St. Vincent Island." Florida Memory. Accessed March 29, 2023. https://www.floridamemory.com/items/show/8166.

— — —. n.d. "Portrait of William Denham - Monticello, Florida." Florida Memory. Accessed June 14, 2023. https://www.floridamemory.com/items/show/34033.

"Florida's Soldiers Beyond the Borders 1861-1865." 2012. *Department of Military Affairs* (blog). June 15, 2012. http://dma.myflorida.com/floridas-soldiers-beyond-the-borders-1861-1865/.

Futch, Ovid. 1964. "Florida during the Civil War. By John E. Johns. Gainesville: University of Florida Press, 1963." *Journal of American History* 51 (1): 107–8. https://doi.org/10.2307/1917949.

Gates, Paul Wallace. 1965. *Agriculture and the Civil War*. New York, NY: Knopf, Inc.

"Historic Battlefield Maps of Stones River National Battlefield - Photo Gallery (U.S. National Park Service)." n.d. National Park Service. Accessed September 25, 2017. https://www.nps.gov/media/photo/gallery.htm.

"How Captain Samuel L. Cowan Escaped From Camp Chase During The Civil War—Samuel L. Cowan—Luara Keeble (Kibby) Clayton." n.d. Accessed September 19, 2017. http://www.storyhouse.org/kibby.html.

Jonathan C. Sheppard. 2004. *Everyday Soldiers: The Florida Brigade of the West, 1861-1862*. Florida State University Libraries. http://diginole.lib.fsu.edu/islandora/object/fsu:176255/datastream/PDF/view.

Jordan, Robert Paul Robert Paul. 1982. *The Civil War*. Washington, D.C: The Society.

Kurz and Allison. 1891. *Battle of Stone River Painting*.

Lamers, William H. n.d. *The Edge of Glory: A Biography of General William S. Rosecrans*. Baton Rouge, Louisiana, USA: Louisiana State University Press.

Loderhose, Gary. 1999. *Far, Far from Home: The Ninth Florida Regiment in the Confederate Army*. 1st edition. Carmel, Ind.: Clerisy Pr.

Nulty, William H. n.d. "Confederate Florida - University of Alabama Press." Accessed June 8, 2020. http://www.uapress.ua.edu/product/Confederate-Florida,690.aspx.

Osborn, George. n.d. "A Confederate Prisoner at Camp Chase, Letters and a Diary of Private James W. Anderson through the Ohio History Connection." Ohio History Connection. Accessed September 19, 2017. http://resources.ohiohistory.org/ohj/browse/displaypages.php?display[]=0059&display[]=38&display[]=57.

"Page 1 Civil War Service Records (CMSR) - Confederate - Florida." n.d. Fold3. Accessed April 5, 2021. http://www.fold3.com:9292/image/110766705/?xid=1022.

"— — —." n.d. Fold3. Accessed April 5, 2021. http://www.fold3.com:9292/image/109144270/?xid=1022.
"— — —." n.d. Fold3. Accessed December 31, 2021. http://www.fold3.com:9292/image/264682304?terms=walker,war,civil,george,united,confederate,america,army,states.
"Page 1 Civil War Service Records (CMSR) - Confederate - Georgia." n.d. Fold3. Accessed April 5, 2021. http://www.fold3.com:9292/image/52401716/?xid=1022.
"Page 1 Civil War Soldiers - Confederate - FL." n.d. Fold3. Accessed January 24, 2020. http://www.fold3.com:9292/image/109140148?terms=war,us,palmer,civil,thomas,confederate.
Pasco, Samuel. 1928. "Jefferson County, Florida, 1827-1910." *The Florida Historical Society Quarterly* 7 (2): 139-54.
Pasco, Samuel. 1990. *Private Pasco: A Civil War Diary*.
"Pensacola & Georgia Railroad, Confederacy." n.d.
"Photo Album: Nurses - US Civil War Era." n.d. Accessed March 29, 2023. https://www.wikitree.com/wiki/Space:Photo_Album:_Nurses_-_US_Civil_War_Era.
Proctor, Samuel. 1964. "State's Recruits Held Without Horses, Arms." *Florida Times Union*, March 15, 1964.
Riley, Darrell G. 1997. "Marion County History, The Civil War Years." *Star-Banner*, 1997.
"Santa Rosa Island - October 9, 1861." n.d. American Battlefield Trust. Accessed March 29, 2023. https://www.battlefields.org/learn/maps/santa-rosa-island-october-9-1861.
Sheppard, Jonathan C. 2012. *By the Noble Daring of Her Sons: The Florida Brigade of the Army of Tennessee*. University of Alabama Press.
Stallings, James E. 2008. *Georgia's Confederate Soldiers Who Died as Prisoners of War 1861-1865*. Macon, Ga.: J.E. Stallings, Sr.
"Stones River Confederate Order of Battle - Wikipedia, the Free Encyclopedia." n.d. Battle of Stones River, Confederate Units. Accessed March 8, 2015. http://en.wikipedia.org/wiki/Stones_River_Confederate_order_of_battle.
Strickland, Michael. 2014. *The Red Cotton Fields - Newly Edited Edition*. Edited by Elaine Blackburn. Mayport Publishing Company.
"The Battle of Santa Rosa Island (U.S. National Park Service)." n.d. Accessed March 29, 2023. https://www.nps.gov/articles/battle-santarosa.htm.
"The Dead Angle." n.d. American Battlefield Trust. Accessed January 23, 2022. https://www.battlefields.org/learn/primary-sources/dead-angle.
"The Town of Bailey's Mill-Lloyd." 2022. Keystone Genealogical Library, Monticello, Florida.
"Uniforms of the Confederate States Armed Forces." 2021. Wikipedia. https://en.wikipedia.org/w/index.php?title=Uniforms_of_the_Confederate_States_Ar

med_Forces&oldid=1027951688.
"United_States_Civil_War_Nurses.jpg (3600×2679)." n.d. Accessed March 29, 2023.
https://www.wikitree.com/photo.php/5/5d/United_States_Civil_War_Nurses.jpg.
"U.S., Civil War Soldier Records and Profiles, 1861-1865 - Ancestry.com." n.d. Accessed March 4, 2015.
http://search.ancestry.com/cgi-bin/sse.dll?db=civilwar_histdatasys&h=4104990&ti=0&indiv=try&gss=pt&ssrc=pt_t23894133_p1441729069_kpidz0q3d1441729069z0q26pgz0q3d32768z0q26pgplz0q3dpid.
"— — —." n.d. Accessed December 29, 2021.
https://www.ancestry.com/discoveryui-content/view/159407:1555?ssrc=pt&tid=23894133&pid=312126167172.
US National Park Service. n.d. "3rd Florida Regiment - Battle Unit Details - The Civil War (U.S. National Park Service)." Accessed July 14, 2020.
https://www.nps.gov/subjects/civilwar/search-battle-units-detail.htm.
Venet, Wendy Hamand. n.d. "A Changing Wind." *Georgia Press* (blog). Accessed January 28, 2022. https://ugapress.org/book/9780820351360/a-changing-wind.
Wikipedia. 2018. "2nd Florida Infantry." Wikipedia.
https://en.wikipedia.org/w/index.php?title=2nd_Florida_Infantry&oldid=818150009.
— — —. 2019. "3rd Florida Infantry." Wikipedia.
https://en.wikipedia.org/w/index.php?title=3rd_Florida_Infantry&oldid=921630509.
Wright, Mike. 1998. *What They Didn't Teach You about the Civil War*. Novato, Calif.: Presidio Press: Presidio Press.

* * *

www.ingramcontent.com/pod-product-compliance
Lightning Source LLC
Chambersburg PA
CBHW061928220426
43662CB00012B/1834